Organisational Transformation for Sustainability

Routledge Studies in Business Ethics

Organisational Transformation for Sustainability

An Integral Metatheory

Mark G. Edwards

Routledge
Taylor & Francis Group
New York   London

First published 2010
by Routledge
270 Madison Avenue, New York, NY 10016

Simultaneously published in the UK
by Routledge
2 Park Square, Milton Park, Abingdon, Oxon OX14 4RN

Routledge is an imprint of the Taylor & Francis Group, an informa business

© 2010 Taylor & Francis

Transferred to digital printing 2010

Typeset in Sabon by IBT Global.

Library of Congress Cataloging-in-Publication Data
Edwards, Mark G.
  Organisational transformation for sustainability : an integral metatheory / Mark G. Edwards.
    p. cm.—(Routledge studies in business ethics ; 2)
    Includes bibliographical references and index.
  1. Organisational change.   2. Theory (Philosophy)   I. Title.
    HD58.8.E348 2009
    658.4'0601—dc22
    2009030725

ISBN10: 0-415-80173-7 (hbk)
ISBN10: 0-415-88869-7 (pbk)
ISBN10: 0-203-85993-6 (ebk)
ISBN13: 978-0-415-80173-7 (hbk)
ISBN13: 978-0-415-88869-1 (pbk)
ISBN13: 978-0-203-85993-3 (ebk)

To Barbara with love and deep thanks

Contents

Figures

Tables

Foreword

William R. Torbert, Professor Emeritus,
Carroll School of Management, Boston College

Once every generation or so, a field-defining scholarly statement appears. Mark Edwards's metatheory for organisational transformation is such a book for the field of organisational change and transformation.

As demanding as it is of the reader (and it is no easy read), it ought to become a required touchstone for further theorising and research in organisational transformation. It is a comprehensive, appreciative, critical, creative revisioning of the field that helps all the members of that field locate themselves anew within it, helps them see the issues their own work has neglected, helps them reassess the scale of the field's challenges and helps them locate aspects of their field's literature that they may have heretofore altogether missed.

The fact that this book presents a metatheory of organisational transformation—in tandem with the fact that metatheorising has been out of fashion in the organisation sciences generally (and particularly within the field of organisation change)—is one source of this book's power and significance. It throws a different kind of light on the field from a different kind of angle. Metatheorising is an unaccustomed mental discipline for most of us. Fortunately, Edwards guides us with patience and clarity through the issues at stake.

A second source of this book's power and significance derives from the author's extraordinary systematic care and impartiality in discovering and presenting the variety of issues, lenses and perspectives that have been touched upon by prior researchers in the field. In particular, the detailed and imaginative series of tables and figures throughout the book should become a cherished reference for current and future researchers.

A third important contribution of this book is that it begins to knit together the significant contributions of developmental theorists, such as philosopher Ken Wilber and psychologist Robert Kegan, with mainstream research in organisational change. This is an important step for two reasons. First, what constitutes an individual or an organisational transformation has been notoriously undefined and poorly documented by most organisational research that uses the term "transformation". Developmental theory is one theory that offers descriptions of, and instruments to measure, a number of distinctive transformations. Second, the path-breaking work of Wilber, in particular, has been undertaken and then taken up largely outside the domain of scholarly social science. Edwards's dispassionate review, appreciation and critique of Wilber's All Quadrants, All Levels (AQAL) theory rescues it from "true believers", compares it to another developmental approach, and thus makes it more available for future scholarly use.

A fourth important contribution of this book is its application of Edwards's metatheory to the particular issue of sustainability. As the global history of terrorism, unilateral war and financially generated economic crisis during the first decade of the twenty-first century already unmistakably demonstrate, economic, political and ecological sustainability can be generated only by a profound transformation in the assumptions we make about money, power and our relationship to our host planet (including the other living species that share it with us and make our lives possible). Therefore, any activist or scholar seriously concerned with the issue of sustainability must work at sharpening his or her understanding of what constitutes an individual, familial, organisational or societal transformation . . . and of what kinds of power generate the kinds of transformations that lead to the widespread adoption of sustainable practices.

Finally, just in case any reader imagines that this introductory paean of praise is evidence of a total lack of critical perspective, let me add that, although Edwards mentions the possibility of transforming social science itself, this writer wishes more attention had been given to the imperative that our notions of power, of social science and of the relationship between theory and action must transform if organisations are to transform toward sustainability. Nevertheless, Edwards has provided references for others to follow into this domain too.

Bravo for this challenging masterwork!

Introduction
An Integrative Pluralism

> A man with one theory is lost. He needs several of them, or lots! He should stuff them in his pockets like newspapers hot from the press always, you can live well surrounded by them, there are comfortable lodgings to be found between the theories. If you are to get on you need to know that there are lots of theories. (Bertolt Brecht cited in Fuegi, 1987, p. 174)

I

Knowing one theory or one conceptual perspective inside out might make us erudite specialists within certain fields but it won't help us to find our way in a world awash with theories. The accumulation of an ever-growing number of theories and research paradigms has been the cause for considerable alarm and even despondency for many social scientists. I take a different view. Rather than taking it as evidence of an immature science, I see the diversity of social theories as a genuine outcome of the multifaceted nature of social realities and therefore an opportunity for appreciating and learning rather than as a problem to be overcome. More than this, theoretical pluralism also gives us the chance to develop integrative overviews by which we can discover connections within that variety.

This book is about building those integrative connections, in other words, building metatheory. It describes the research journey of constructing an integrative and pluralistic conceptual framework for more sustaining forms of organisation. The motivation for this book comes from the idea that every theory embodies some insight and that systematically bringing theories together makes possible the emergence of more humane and efficacious ways of understanding the world we live in. This rather simple idea, however, immediately raises several complex issues. The intention here is not to bring theories together in order to create the biggest and the brightest super-theory that subsumes other explanations and understandings. Every theoretical position that has some valid research basis or authentic tradition of cultural knowledge behind it has something to offer and we need to find ways of integrating those insights while also respecting their characteristic and often conflicting differences. What I am suggesting here is not just another call for eclecticism or more interdisciplinary research. These responses to theoretical pluralism do not possess the necessary capacities for systematically linking multiple perspectives into an integrative framework. What is required is a balance between an integrative synthesis and a respect for the pluralism of perspectives. The creation of a more inclusive vision of organisational life will need a nuanced approach, one that values the synthesising instincts of modernity as well as the pluralising intuitions of the postmodern.

II

Bringing theories and constructs together can be done at several levels of sophistication. A basic level of review involves cataloguing what is there in the literature, assessing the scope of extant theories, identifying strengths and weaknesses and perhaps drawing out some common themes and patterns of connection. A more sophisticated approach builds on this review task to also engage in the active synthesis and integration of ideas and to add to the current state of understanding in a field through the development of new knowledge and innovative directions for further research. Overarching research activities such as these can result in many benefits for research and practice. First, they allow us to survey a particular landscape of ideas. Second, in so doing, we can more easily see the conceptual territory that extant theory already covers. Hence, those areas which need further exploration can subsequently be identified. Third, in locating theories within a broader landscape of ideas we can be more conscious of the theoretical assumptions we use to build the worlds we live in. Because of the reorienting involved in the process of critical review, big-picture approaches can help to challenge and deconstruct accepted truths. Fourth, we can begin to discover patterns in the way we theorise about a topic, the methods and frameworks of interpretation we adopt and the findings that have accumulated through our research journeys. Fifth, if our intentions are scientific, bringing ideas together forces us to do so methodically. We need systems of pathfinding that can reorientate us when we are lost in the detail of middle-range theorising. Finally, the integration of ideas can present us with new visions about where we are headed and which kinds of surrounds we might wish to travel through or live in. The power of metatheorising to shape our theories and research often goes unacknowledged and, perhaps more importantly, its influence on the state of broader social realities is barely even noticed.

Metatheoretical research is the systematic and deliberative study of theories and their constituent conceptual lenses. I argue here that this type of research offers all the aforementioned benefits to the scientific study of organisations and how they change. But the systematic development of overarching metatheory has not been in fashion for many years and little research of this kind has been carried out in studies of organisational change. The move towards middle-range theory in the social sciences, the postmodern distrust of the "big picture" and the contemporary concern for applied and empirical research have all meant that metatheorising has been neglected as a legitimate field of scientific inquiry. With this book I hope to take a step towards remedying this situation and suggest that there has never been a time when integrative metatheorising could be of greater importance. The systematic development of large-scale theories of transformation and change will be crucial for building and evaluating theories of organisational life that can contribute to our global and intergenerational well-being.

All of the global challenges that we currently face, whether they be environmental, socio-cultural or economic in origin, require some level of big-picture metatheoretical response. Metatheories have been extremely influential in the development of modern economies, systems of governance, health and education and yet the scientific study of metatheory has been virtually ignored as a topic for research. I hope to show the particular value of metatheoretical studies for the field of organisational transformation and how this little understood form of conceptual research might contribute to the study of sustainability. As a global network of societies, there is no more important or more difficult task before us than transformation towards truly sustaining forms of organisation. I believe that this kind of metatheoretical research will greatly enrich our capacity to develop scientific responses to the global challenges that currently beset us. During the twenty-first century organisations will undergo a level of radical and global change that has rarely been seen before. This transformation will come about as a result of the environmental, social and economic challenges that confront organisations at every level. But are our understandings and theories of change up to the task of meeting these challenges? Will we be able to develop sustaining visions of how organisations might contribute to the long-term viability of interdependent global communities? This book offers some innovative suggestions for reconceptualising organisational transformation towards sustainability and it bases these suggestions on what has been called integral or integrative metatheory (Arnold & Gasson, 1954; Sorokin, 1958; Wilber, 2005c).

Integral metatheory is a form of scholarship that draws out and connects the insights of many different paradigms and theories to create a more integrated conceptual system. The field of organisational transformation is well suited to employing such an integrative approach. Theories of change are extremely diverse and the presiding conceptual atmosphere is one of fragmentation. Yet, it seems we have overlooked the need to find links between all these theories and, whether we are educators, practitioners, researchers or students, we often have little justification for adopting one theory over another in exploring transformational phenomena. In a time of rapidly changing organisational and global environments it is urgent that we develop integrative and visionary frameworks that contribute to our understanding of transformational change towards a sustaining future. This book presents both an integrative method and a metatheoretical framework for developing this understanding.

III

During the 1960s and 1970s the explosion in the number of empirical studies being published in a large number of scientific disciplines began to reach a point where the need for more encompassing forms of data-analysis became obvious. Gene Glass was one of the pioneers of these early approaches to the integration of empirical findings and he proposed the term meta-analysis to describe the "analysis of a large collection of analysis results from individual studies for the purposes of integrating the findings" (Glass, 1976, p. 3). Glass described the emergence of meta-analysis as follows (1977, pp. 351–352):

> By the late 1960s, the research literature had swollen to gigantic proportions. Although scholars continued to integrate studies narratively, it was becoming clear that chronologically arranged verbal descriptions of research failed to portray the accumulated knowledge. Reviewers began to make crude classifications and measurements of the conditions and results of studies. Typically, studies were classified in contingency tables by type and by whether outcomes reached statistical significance. Integrating the research literature of the 1970s demands more sophisticated techniques of measurement and statistical analysis. The accumulated findings of dozens or even hundreds of studies should be regarded as complex data points, no more comprehensible without the full use of statistical analysis than hundreds of data points in a single study could be so casually understood. Contemporary research reviewing ought to be undertaken in a style more technical and statistical than narrative and rhetorical. Toward this end, I have suggested a name to make the needed approach distinctive; I referred to this approach as the meta-analysis of research.

Today, the world of organisation theory is in a similar position to that of empirical research in the 1970s. Over the last three or four decades, there has been a steady increase in the number of theoretical contributions to explaining social change. Because very few of these models and theories are ever found to be completely without merit and because they each contribute some insight into social complexities, the extant body of organisational research paradigms, theories and models is vast and it continues to expand. This is true for all social science disciplines (Abbott, 2001). Within each discipline and sub-discipline the growing body of theoretical positions is large enough to be considered now from a metalevel of analysis. Given this, it seems that a response, analogous to the development of meta-analysis within the empirical domain, is called for in the domain of theory. Some kind of integration of theories is needed in precisely the same way that the metalevel analysis of countless empirical studies is needed to establish evidence-based medical interventions. If it makes sense to draw upon the collective results of theory testing to evaluate health treatments, shouldn't there also be value in tapping into our collective theoretical knowledge to advance our understanding of organisational change, transformation and sustainability?

IV

The aim here is to see how a metatheoretical view of organisational transformation can contribute to our understanding of, and search for, organisational sustainability. In pursuing this end I will: i) demonstrate the need for integrative metatheories of organisational change, ii) address both modernist and postmodernist objections to metatheorising, iii) present a general research method for building metatheory, iv) analyse extant theories of organisational transformation and on the basis of these results, v) describe an integrative metatheory for organisational sustainability, vi) briefly evaluate the new metatheory, and vii) discuss the implications of this metatheory for organisational change and social policy regarding sustainability.

Chapter 1 provides a rationale for the main themes of the book and sets out an argument for the need for metatheory in organisational studies. A number of issues such as paradigm diversity, metatheorising and theory building will be considered. While there are numerous theories of transformation and sustainability there have been few attempts at integration and the particular problems and opportunities created by theoretical pluralism have not been adequately addressed. Metatheory is presented here as a scientific enterprise that directly serves the purpose of combining conceptual systems. There is a particular need for an integrative form of metatheory that not only analyses but also builds frameworks that stimulate new middle-range theories, new overarching models and new ways of thinking about old problems.

Chapter 2 deals with definition and domain specification. Such terms as organisational transformation, sustainability, metatheory building and integrative research are defined and their relevance to the core themes of the book outlined. The chapter provides clarifications for dealing with the semantic confusions that often characterise discussions of organisational change and transformation. The intent here is to provide basic and not final definitions. Metatheorising requires a balance between clarity and scope, between the need to use clear terminology as well as to preserve a high level of abstraction that includes very general concepts. These discussions feed into the topic of domain specification as well as considerations of the important assumptions that underlie metatheoretical research.

Metatheorising in the social sciences has been a neglected and sometimes controversial topic. Advocates of metatheoretical research need to address the arguments offered by modern and postmodern critics and in Chapter 3 I will offer a defence for conducting this type of research. Metatheorist George Ritzer has called for a greater appreciation for overarching conceptual frameworks and the contributions they can make to theory development. I point out a number of these benefits for both modernist middle-range theory and the more localised interests of postmodern research.

In Chapter 4 a brief historical overview of organisational transformation is presented which discusses the various phases in the development of theories of transformation and their application. This chapter also introduces the major theoretical resource for the metatheory building procedures to be carried out, namely, Ken Wilber's All Quadrants, All Levels (AQAL) framework and Bill Torbert's Developmental Action Inquiry (DAI). AQAL has been utilised in an extremely wide range of scientific fields, including organisational studies, and DAI is perhaps the most ambitious metalevel programme of research yet undertaken in the organisational change field. Torbert has been developing his action inquiry model of change for almost 35 years and he has constructed a formidable theoretical framework. A brief summary of these models is presented. One element of AQAL that has particular importance for this study is the holon construct. There are several fields which make substantial use of the construct for both theoretical and applied reasons. The holon plays a crucial role in the development of the integral metatheory for transformation that is proposed in later chapters.

Chapter 5 proposes a general method for metatheory building. Currently, there is only one detailed method for systematically developing metatheories in the social sciences. This is the metatriangulation method of Marianne Lewis and Andrew Grimes (1999). I build on this approach to propose a detailed qualitative research method for developing integral metatheory in organisational studies. As well as metatriangulation I draw on several other sources for developing the general method for metatheory building. These include the multiparadigm approach originally proposed by Gibson Burrell and Garreth Morgan (1979) and further developed by Dennis Gioia (Gioia, 1999; Gioia & Pitre, 1990). Although it is not a research method as such, the metatheorising system of sociologist George Ritzer (2001) also offers some guidance, as do the middle-range theory building models of more conventional empirical research methods. All these methods are compared to develop a detailed procedure for constructing metatheory. The phases of this method include: Groundwork, Domain, Design, Multiparadigm Review, Multiparadigm Analysis, Metatheory Building, Implications and Evaluation. This general method for performing metatheory building research offers the capacity for a more detailed level of analysis in constructing metatheories than has been previously available.

In Chapter 6 the results of the Multiparadigm Review and Analysis are presented. These consist primarily of the description of a number of metatheoretical lenses that were derived from the set of sampled theories. Theories were selected from many different paradigms, including systems approaches, developmental models, postmodern approaches, process models, structural approaches, cultural theories, evolutionary models, chaos and complexity theories, organisational learning, contingency theory and approaches that focus on organisational spirituality. The metatheoretical lenses derived from these theories and research paradigms are the core conceptual dimensions that transformation theorists use in understanding and explaining their subject matter. After applying some refinement techniques a final set of 24 lenses is proposed.

Concept relationships are among the most important yet under-researched areas in theory building. Chapter 7 looks at the ways metatheoretical lenses can be distorted, reduced and combined with other lenses to form models and frameworks for organisational transformation. I give many examples of how the relationships within and between lenses can influence theory development in both positive and negative ways. It is not only the relationships between lenses but also the internal relationship within lenses that is of interest here. These internal relationships refer to such things as the composition of multilevel lenses, that is, how many levels does a particular lens possess, how do those levels relate to each other, what criteria are used in building up those levels? Identifying the essential relationship between and within the elements of a theory is one of the most important steps in theory building. One way to analyse relationships between lenses is according to their conceptual shape, or as it is called here, their metamorphology. When lenses are grouped on the basis of their conceptual morphology, a number of interesting possibilities for analysing logical confusions and conceptual conflations become apparent. I suggest that the study of lens metamorphology could be an avenue for metatheoretical research that has great potential in fields like social policy analysis and political economy.

In Chapter 8, I take organisational sustainability as an exemplar topic for describing the proposed integral metatheory. Many of the lenses and lens relationships identified in Chapters 6 and 7 are applied to organisational sustainability to develop metatheoretical frameworks and their implications for developing new approaches to theorising about sustainability are discussed. This chapter also provides a detailed statement of the integral metatheory for transformation with each of the lenses and their relationships represented within intra, inter, systemic and inter-systemic orders of description.

Chapter 9 presents an evaluation of the metatheory for organisational transformation and its conceptual resources, particularly the AQAL framework, and some common ways of theorising organisational sustainability. Metatheory possesses an inherently adjudicative capacity (that is, it can be used to identify the strengths and weaknesses of its constitutive "unit-level theories"), and I will assess the theoretical use of some important lenses in transformation and sustainability theories. Some guidelines are also presented on how metatheory can itself be evaluated according to commonly used theory building criteria.

Finally, Chapter 10 discusses the broad implications of metalevel research and, drawing on a number of innovative big-picture research models, I propose a framework which I call integrative meta-studies. Integrative meta-studies is a response to the urgent need for developing scientific Big Pictures that address global issues.

V

This book is structured in a way similar to the general phases of meta/ theory building. In rough order of development, these phases consist of presenting a rationale (Introduction and Chapter 1); specifying the domain, stating definitions (Chapter 2, 3 and 4); prescribing a method (Chapter 5); identifying the core conceptual elements (Chapter 6) and the relationships within and between those conceptual elements (Chapter 7); describing the whole theoretical system (Chapter 8); evaluating the final model (Chapter 9); and considering its general implications (Chapter 10). This systematic unfurling belies the complex layering and iteration of ideas that is involved in conceptual research. However, it does give a sense of how a formal process of scientific metatheorising can be organised as is reflected in the ordering of the chapters that follow.

With a few notable exceptions it has been the norm for researchers, teachers and practitioners working in the fields of management, leadership and organisational studies to ignore or even decry the role of metatheoretical research. Empirical research, middle-range theory building and the need for practical theorising has been the preferred pathway for providing leaders and organisations with more applied and more useful conceptual tools. From the postmodern side of the academic spectrum metatheory has been regarded as a form of dissociated abstractionism that is far removed from the local realities of lived experience. In this climate of empirical research, practical application and local encounter, the formative power and the immense potential of metatheoretical research go almost unacknowledged. There is no doubt that metatheorising is abstract work, but abstraction itself is a fundamental process in social life. Some of the most powerful ideas that have shaped human history and our social and natural environments have come from metalevel abstractions of other theories. Examples from the realms of politics and economics spring to mind perhaps a little more readily but the concrete worlds of commerce and industry, management and industrial relations, and trade and finance have also been heavily shaped by metatheory. These big ideas have not only contributed to the general advancement of human freedoms and well-being but they have also encumbered us with damaging ideologies that have caused immense harm. A more conscious awareness of the role of metatheory in shaping our world and a more scientific approach to developing and criticising metatheory is sorely needed in contemporary times and this book aims to contribute to these tasks.

1 The Need for Metatheory in the Study of Organisational Transformation

> I do admit that at any moment we are prisoners caught in the framework of our theories; our expectations; our past experiences; our language. But we are prisoners in a Pickwickian sense: if we try we can break out of our frameworks at any time. Admittedly, we shall find ourselves again in a framework, but it will be a better and roomier one; and we can at any moment break out of it again. (Popper, 1970, p. 56)

"WE ARE PRISONERS"

Karl Popper understood the power of theory. Theory not only helps us to make sense of our experiences, it also actively shapes the world around us in profound and long-lasting ways. The same is true for metatheory, the big-picture approach to knowledge that attempts to integrate other theory. Big ideas and big theories have the power to transform social systems that is rarely acknowledged, much less understood. The way we describe, explain and examine the worlds we inhabit in turn creates and shapes those worlds. Theories and metatheories of organisation and management not only interpret what goes on in the world of commerce and work, they also influence the design and implementation of those systems. Anthony Giddens calls this iterative process the "double hermeneutic" (1984, p. xxxii)—the mutual co-creation of big ideas and the bricks and mortar of social realities. Theories are developed to explain and understand the practical complexities that surround us. Many theories work their way into the perspectives and actions of designers, architects, community leaders, corporate planners, engineers and builders and are taken up by policy and law makers and the general public in how we reproduce, manage and make sense of those complexities. Systems of governing, organising, educating, trading and working are created and recreated in the process. Those systems, in turn, act as sources for further theorising. Hence, the iterative cycle of the double hermeneutic.

A problematic feature of this self-reproducing cycle is that once theory and metatheory are incorporated into the social fabric of work, education, economics or politics it is extremely difficult to introduce an alternative vision or a new world of possibility. When meta/theory[1] becomes part of the institutionalised mainstream it establishes its own momentum for reproduction. It becomes an unseen lens which both frees us to create what we know and constrains us from exploring what we don't. The impact of social theory on our lives is rarely acknowledged. While we marvel at, or are dismayed by, the power of technology to influence our public and private lives, the influence of all manner of social meta/theories is hardly noticed. At its best, the widespread assumption of certain worldviews creates a stability that enables society to function in an efficient way. At its worst the unconsciousness appropriation of meta/theory institutionalises maladaptive systems of economics, education and organisation. Ideologies are reductive forms of meta/theories that are so imbedded in the exchanges of political and social life that we no longer see them, and we are unconscious of their power to resist change even when social change is desperately needed.

So it is with our conceptualisations of organisations and how they change. Change theorist Gervase Bushe (2001, p. 118) says that "theory, especially theory that is encoded in popular words or images, is a powerful force in shaping social organization because we 'see what we believe'". Theories shape possibilities and in so doing also act as constraints on what is possible. At this moment at the beginning of the twenty-first century we are, as Popper puts it, caught in the prison of our conceptual inadequacies—inadequate economic theories, inadequate organisational theories, inadequate theories of change and inadequate theories of sustainability. The economic growth models that inform so much of contemporary life have gained a powerful position in the minds and behaviours of societies, organisations and their members. Theories of economic production and consumption are driving our values and actions to the point where even the concept of "sustainability" is often framed within dominant functionalist assumptions about economic growth. In order to achieve sustainable development we are urged to work ever more furiously towards increased economic targets. As we degrade our atmospheric, biological and social environments on a global scale we are simultaneously ramping up the drive for growth as if that might leads us out of the impasse. In one moment we are calling for reductions in our reliance on carbon-based energy systems and in the next spending countless billions to fire up economic activity. We are caught in an economic vicious circle on a vast scale. One that cannot be revised without reassessing the big picture of what organisational change and organisational sustainability might mean.

A PLURALISTIC BIG PICTURE

This book takes a big-picture look at the metatheories, theories and models used for understanding and explaining organisational transformation and organisational sustainability. It endeavours to develop a more comprehensive and, as Popper puts it, "roomier" framework for metatheorising about how organisations can contribute to the intergenerational welfare of their local and global communities. This framework is grounded in a pluralistic and multiparadigm appreciation for the many contributions that organisational theorists have made to these areas. The field of organisational sustainability is characterised by a multitude of perspectives that contend for attention from researchers, teachers, students, consultants and practitioners. This diversity stems from the variety of research paradigms and schools of thought that provide general orientations for exploring organisational phenomena. Each of these research paradigms, theories and models adds their own unique insights into explaining and understanding what sustainability is and how it might be achieved. But each view is also partial and can only provide a small slice of the whole. When these partial views become imbedded within the mainstream they can also become barriers to the development of new and more comprehensive understandings.

In the quote that opens this chapter, Karl Popper describes a metaphor where he likens researchers and theorists to "prisoners caught in the framework of our theories" who need to find ways to "break out" of their conceptual prisons. The purpose of this book is to move beyond those unnecessarily restrictive forms of explaining and understanding transformational events that come from working within particular research paradigms and theoretical orientations. But in moving forward it is also important that we retain the valid contributions of our intellectual heritage. The intention here is not to replace one view with another—to substitute the "old paradigm" with a "new paradigm". In developing more inclusive frameworks it is important to recognise the contributions of extant theory and to integrate the store of knowledge that currently exists into whatever overarching framework we might end up building. I call the method used to do this integrative metatheorising. Integrative metatheory is conceptual research that responds positively to the challenges of theoretical pluralism—the diversity of theoretical perspectives (Preston, 2005). It proposes a way of connecting what might be seen as dominant mainstream views with the multitude of diverse alternatives. Thereby preserving what is of value in current ideas with the innovations of emergent perspectives. Integrative metatheorising constructs new and "roomier" conceptual frameworks that push the boundaries of our current conceptualisations. It does this while also accommodating the plurality of theoretical perspectives which characterises many fields of social research.

Integrative metatheorising is part of a tradition of scholarship and research that has a long and rather disjointed history (Molz & Hampson, in press; Sorokin, 1958). To this point very little metatheoretical work of this kind has been consciously performed within this research stream and almost none has used systematic methods that could contribute to a more rigorous scientific enterprise. In the following chapters I hope to redress some of these limitations.

AN ILLUSTRATIVE PARABLE

Although it is receiving increasing attention in the scientific study of social phenomena (see, for example, Carr & Zanetti, 1999; Tsoukas & Knudsen, 2003a), metatheorising is largely neglected as a form of conceptual research in organisational and management studies. There are several reasons for this neglect. Applied research has focused on gathering empirical data in quest of testing middle-range theory. Postmodern research has focused on deconstructing theory to identify the underlying assumptions that characterise objectivist and functionalist research. When they have contributed to theory building, postmodern researchers have taken a grounded approach and constructed theory out of localised perspectives and personal narratives. For differing reasons, both have passed over the opportunities afforded by metatheoretical research.

The task ahead then is to explore the possibility of developing a flexible and integrative framework for organisational transformation through the conceptual research method of metatheorising. To do this will require identifying and describing the core conceptual elements of theories and developing a metatheory that can accommodate and connect these factors. This is more than a process of review or comparison or critique. Bringing together multiple perspectives opens up the possibility of a more comprehensive understanding of sustainability and organisational change. There is a well-known story from the Indian subcontinent that serves to illustrate this integrative goal.

The story goes that there was a king who had never come into contact with an elephant but wanted to understand what this amazing beast was and how it might be described. The king summoned six learned, blind men who set off to investigate and report back to the king of their findings. Having found an example of the curious creature, the first blind wise man approached the elephant, felt its sturdy side and concluded the elephant to be "very like a wall", the second felt a tusk and said, "an elephant is like a spear", the third happened to touch the trunk and decided that elephants were "like snakes", the fourth wrapped his arms around one leg and concluded, "the elephant is very like a tree", the fifth chanced upon the ear and said, "this marvel of an elephant is very like a fan", and finally, the sixth seized upon the swinging tail and said, "the elephant is very like a rope". And the story goes that these six learned men compared their findings and each argued that he had the most astute understanding of this elephant creature (Saxe, 1873, p. 78):

> And so these men of Indostan
> Disputed loud and long,
> Each in his own opinion
> Exceeding stiff and strong,
> Though each was partly in the right,
> And all were in the wrong!

The moral of this story, applied to the topic of organisational transformation, is that each research paradigm and each well-researched theory contains a partial truth about the nature of organisational change, and that together, these partialities have a chance of creating a more integrative and comprehensive picture of that reality. Left to their own devices, however, partial understandings, while accurate within their own narrow fields, will always be incomplete and sometimes even misleading. The elephant in this parable is the complex, multidimensional and often baffling reality of organisational transformation; the conclusions of our "men of Indostan" are the many paradigms and theories of transformation that have been proposed over the last four decades; the quality of blindness in this parable represents our collective inability to see the assumptions that our individual theories are often based on; and the attempt to bring together the partial truths that each wise man offers is the proposed integral metatheory for organisational transformation that this book contributes.

THE NEED FOR INTEGRATIVE PLURALISM

A considerable amount of theoretical and empirical research has been devoted to the topic of organisational transformation since it first became an identifiable field of research and theory development in the late 1970s and early 1980s. Since then there has been an ever-increasing number of theories and models of transformation. Yet, apart from some notable exceptions (see, for example, Levy & Merry, 1986), little attention has been paid to the need for a general overview of these diverse theories and constructs. As Farazmand points out (2003, p. 366):

> The lack of systematic study and analysis of chaos and transformation theories in organisation theory and public management is striking.

Other transformation theorists have noted the diversity in definitions, constructs and theoretical frameworks and the lack of a coherent overview that might enable some fruitful dialogue among theorists working in this field. A systems-based study of organisational transformation points out that (Lemak, Henderson & Wenger, 2004, p. 407):

> . . . for all the attention, the field is not coherent; disagreements about basic definitions, fundamental frameworks and general values abound . . . agreement occurs primarily around very general and often vague prescriptions.

Although they point to the fragmentation and diversity of theoretical views on transformation, the authors of this study contend that "the concept of organisational transformation still has utility for those studying both organisation theory and strategy" (2004, p. 407). However, they propose that the idea of organisational transformation only has utility "if it is viewed through an appropriate theoretical lens, which we contend is systems theory" (2004, p. 407). This assumption, that there is only one appropriate "theoretical lens" for viewing transformation, is not uncommon among social theorists. Working within particular theoretical schools or research paradigms requires that there be a focus on the conceptual frameworks that define those schools. On the negative side, this dedicated focus can also become the kind of academic narrow-mindedness that gives rise to such things as the "paradigm wars" (Mingers, 2004) or even the exclusion of certain theoretical approaches (Pfeffer, 2005). Such views are not capable of dealing with the theoretical pluralism which is characteristic of all social sciences. Change theorist Marshall Poole suggests that the lack of definitional agreement and the inconsistency in conceptualising transformation derives from this theoretical pluralism (1998, p. 47):

> Perhaps the lack of definitive or widely accepted theoretical constructs dealing with the process of organisational transformation is a direct result of the variety of perspectives applied to the process.

A more generalist orientation is needed not only to respond to the multitude of vying theoretical perspectives but also to find ways of valuing the differences between mainstream and more marginal scientific discourses.

To this point the range of theoretical responses has not shown sufficient capacity for dealing positively with the issue of pluralism. The mainstream response has been simply to reassert the need for more objective, functional, economics-based theories of change. Alternative research paradigms are regarded as methodologically or conceptually inadequate. Pluralism is seen as a sign of failure of the social sciences or, at least, as a problem that will be solved through some form of "theoretical monism" (McLennan, 2002). The inter/multi/cross-disciplinary response has had some success at the practical level of project management but has provided no ongoing metatheoretical platform to stimulate metatheoretical research. Disciplinary diversity does not ensure that integrative conceptual frameworks or research methods are developed. In contrast to the modernist search for monistic unity, the postmodern response to theoretical pluralism has been one of support for further diversity. Neither the problems associated with pluralism nor the contributions of meta-perspectives are recognised. The establishment of many small research silos and the proliferation of research centres within organisation and management schools are indicative of the postmodern response. This, in itself, is a positive development but when diversity is pursued in the absence of integration, factionalisation and the compartmentalisation of knowledge are the results.

None of these responses adequately deals with the issue of diversity in theoretical positions. In their paper on exploring pluralism and paradox, Marianne Lewis and Michaela Kelemen (2002) propose the multiparadigm approach as "a provocative alternative" to the mainstream dominance of functionalism and the ongoing diversifications of postmodernism. Multi-paradigm inquiry and other types of metatheorising offer an integrative pluralism as an alternative response to theoretical monism or fragmented diversity. Integrative pluralism retains an appreciation for the multiplicity of perspectives while also developing new knowledge that connects their definitive elements to build more expansive, "roomier" metatheoretical frameworks.

Figure 1.1 depicts some of the more prominent responses to theoretical pluralism and summarises the purpose and outcome of each response. In summary, the functionalist-modernist approach of theoretical monism searches for some super-theory that supplants ("integrates") other views. The interpretivist postmodern response supports the ongoing proliferation of theories and paradigms. The inter/multidisciplinary response attempts to provide pragmatic solutions to applied problems but results in no lasting metatheoretical outcomes. Finally, I argue that integrative pluralism responds to the issue of pluralism in a positive way by retaining and also connecting the diversity of theories and thereby enabling metalevel research to be conducted. Among the very few examples of this approach to be found in the study of organisational transformation are the "integrated model of second-order change" of Amir Levy and Uri Merry (1986) and the Developmental Action Inquiry approach of Dalmar Fisher, David Rooke and Bill Torbert (2003). Levy and Merry reviewed many theories of transformation and extracted connecting themes and converging points of focus to build an integrative framework for situating various paradigms and theories. They did so, however, without any systematic method and without delving into the constitutive constructs that inform each theory. The work of Torbert and his colleagues provides an immensely rich source of integrative concepts. Their development of action inquiry as a means for scientifically exploring personal,

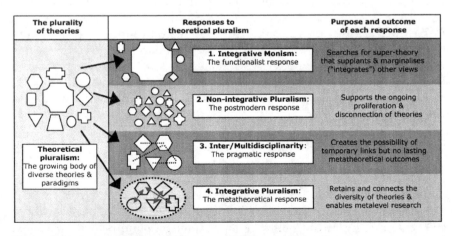

Figure 1.1   Some responses to the issue of theoretical pluralism.

relational and organisational transformation will be an important resource in the development of an integrative metatheory for transformation.

THE "BUZZING, BLOOMING, CONFUSING WORLD OF ORGANIZATION AND MANAGEMENT THEORY"

Over 20 years ago the first major review of theories of organisational transformation predicted that the capacity for an organisation to survive in the future would be directly related to its ability to "pass through dramatic changes in its purpose, culture, function, and worldview" (Levy & Merry, 1986, p. 305). The same might be said for theories of organisational transformation. Such theories will retain their relevance only to the extent that they can offer sense-making frameworks that are flexible and adaptive. Transformational forces such as globalisation, the demand for greater corporate social awareness, technological revolutions and global warming continue to stimulate the development of numerous and diverse theories of transformation. The need for integration of these views increases accordingly. Clegg, Clarke and Ibarra (2001) point out that the plethora of theoretical views has implications for more connective forms of research that shift, "from a single perspective to multiple management paradigms" (2001, p. 32). Transforming global environments are an opportunity to develop metatheoretical perspectives that are multiperspectival and conscious of the insights of different paradigms and theories.

The lack of integrative research in organisational theory means that what might otherwise be a healthy theoretical diversity is now in effect a dysfunctional fragmentation; in the words of Andrew Van de Ven (1999, p. 118), a "buzzing, blooming, confusing world of organization and management theory". In their introduction to a special issue on theory building in organisational studies, Elsbach, Sutton and Whetten state (1999, p. 627):

> The diversity of organisational theory and the range of ideas about how to develop organisational theory increased dramatically during the [past] decade. . . . There has been vigorous and unresolved debate about whether such diversity is healthy for the field.

In a recent review of the state of organisation theory Tony Watson came to the conclusion that (2006, p. 381):

> There is little sign of a willingness to seek common ground among different groupings or camps within organization theory. . . . This tendency, if anything, is worsening.

The lack of integrative metatheory building research in organisational studies has been pointed out in such fields as organisational change

(Dansereau, Yammarino & Kohles, 1999), human resource development (Swanson, 2000), leadership (Avolio, 2007) and organisational transformation (Chapman, 2002). At the same time, several authors have argued that when the theoretical basis of a particular field of organisational studies is fragmented there is a tendency to rely on empirical research methods and statistical analysis and to neglect the conceptual adequacy of theory. For example, Thomas and Pruett (1993, p. 3) comment that research into strategic management "has suffered from an inadequate theory base and sometimes mindless data mining and number crunching". Bagozzi and Yi (1991) have also drawn attention to problems that occur when little consensus exists in a particular field of organisational studies. They argue that the development of theory in highly differentiated research contexts places great emphasis on "methodology" and "experimental design and statistical techniques" but gives little attention to the "theoretical underpinnings" of those methods and techniques. The fragmented state of theory development leads to "disconnected research that does not contribute to overall understanding about how human beings operate in an organisational setting" (Hartman et al., 1998, p. 727). Grandori (2001) has spoken of the current state of conceptual fragmentation as a "balkanisation" where the plethora of theories cannot even communicate with one another. She says that while some see this situation as evidence of the essential diversity of organisational reality, others see it as resulting from the lack of integrative knowledge. Grandori (2001, p. 37) offers a middle way out of this debate:

> On an intermediate ground, we may say that, even if we acknowledge that variety enhances creativity and learning, we should add that this holds true if differentiation is accompanied by some form of integration.

Grandori argues for efforts at stimulating organisational research in theory development, which "contributes to the growth of an integrated organisation science" (2001, p. 37). These comments are particularly relevant to the organisational change and transformation literatures. There are few other topics within organisational studies that are characterised by such diversity in theoretical orientations and, hence, where there is an urgent need for the integration of knowledge as well as its differentiation. In the field of leadership studies Bruce Avolio has pointed out the narrowness of traditional theory building and called for a greater focus on integrative research (Avolio, 2007, p. 31):

> The evolution of leadership theory and practice has come to a point at which a more integrative view spanning from genetics to cultural–generational and strategic levels should be considered at the outset when building theories of leadership and leadership development.

Avolio advocates for a "fuller and more integrative focus that is multilevel, multicomponent, and interdisciplinary" (2007, p. 31).

The fragmented state of theories of transformation is not a recent phenomenon. More than 20 years ago, Dexter Dunphy and Doug Stace commented that (1988, pp. 317–318):

> A more encompassing descriptive model is needed, and also a normative model that offers broadly based assistance to organisations operating in the much more turbulent environment of post-industrial economies.

Dunphy and Stace knew that turbulent environments and theory development go hand in hand. In times of change we need to do research that develops a "more encompassing" metatheory as well as continue the task of theory testing. Good metatheory, for example, can be used to understand why one theory works in some circumstances and not in others. Karen Newman has researched the transformation of industry that occurred following the fall of Soviet communism in Eastern Europe. She points out that although there are theories that can account for incremental and radical change, there is "not much theory to explain why one occurs rather than the other" (1999, p. 9). So the lack of metatheory not only has consequences at the overarching level but can also have deleterious impact at the level of middle-range theory.

Competition, energetic debate and even conflict between theoretical alternatives can be crucial for the development of healthy scientific activity. Gibson Burrell says that "a plurality of legitimate and competing perspectives is to be expected in all sciences but especially in the social ones" (1996, p. 648). It can also be that vying positions become institutionalised into endless and non-productive conflicts as can be seen, for example, in the "paradigm wars" of the 1980s and 1990s between functionalist and interpretivist paradigms (Mingers, 2004). The integrative alternative proposed here should not be seen as a compromise for avoiding that conflict. Organisational studies include many theoretical and methodological orientations and it is this diversity, and the conflict that arises from it, that is the source of innovation and usefulness. Complementing this state of contention, there also needs to be an acknowledgement of what connects these disparate viewpoints, of what is shared by the theorists working across various research paradigms and of how those connections can be rigorously explored to advance collaborative understandings. In a discussion and review of the development of schools of organisation theory, McKinley, Mone and Moon observe that there is "a large body of literature" calling (1999, p. 634):

> attention to multiple, conflicting perspectives in organization studies, emphasizing the lack of an agreed-upon reference framework by which

logical or normative inconsistencies between the perspectives could be reconciled.

This situation of "multiple, conflicting perspectives" is particularly relevant to the study of organisational transformation and the lack of a "reference framework" is problematic for several reasons. First, there is the pedagogic issue of how students of organisational studies are to deal with the plethora of approaches to organisational change, development and transformation (the pedagogical need for metatheorising will be discussed in more detail in the following section). Second, at the level of applied use, organisational practitioners and consultants choose among many models for guiding their workplace interventions often with very little rationale for selecting one approach above another. Familiarity with, or training in, a particular approach influences the choice of theoretical framework rather than the actual organisational transformation issue that needs to be addressed. Third, academics and researchers of transformation often specialise in one particular approach to change with limited communication occurring across paradigms (Schultz & Hatch, 1996). Theoretical and methodological knowledge becomes compartmentalised and the capacity for generating interdisciplinary knowledge is reduced. In the absence of connective frameworks researchers develop their own arbitrary methods for selecting and building the theories they teach and employ in their research.

Unawareness of the conceptual state of ideas in different disciplines can also result in the reinvention of the wheel, the repeated reconstruction of similar theoretical notions. In the field of organisational change this has resulted in some theories possessing many conceptual overlaps and redundancies. Referring to the literature on the management of change, Forster (2005, p. 302) estimates that there are "at least 40 models/frameworks of change management in this literature, although many of these echo each other and/or overlap to a large extent". In later chapters we will find that this is a significant underestimation of the number of extant theories of transformational change and that integrative research is a matter of even greater priority than commentators have suggested.

THE PEDAGOGICAL NEED FOR METATHEORISING

I have mentioned that theoretical pluralism presents a major challenge not only to researchers and theorists but also to teachers and students. Andrew Van de Ven has written about the pedagogical implications of a fragmented pluralism and the lack of a coherent response from business schools and social science departments. Voicing his concern on how this plays out in the teaching of competing theories in the classroom, Van de Ven places these words in the mouth of a fictional student named Timothy. Timothy says (Van de Ven, 1999, pp. 120–121):

You exposed me to all these theories but gave me no way to sift and winnow among them. How do I know which theory is better or worse than another?

Van de Ven has his fictional director of graduate studies respond to Timothy's accusations in this way:

I'm sorry you feel that way. That's too bad. Maybe you should sleep over it. Go to bed. Rub some Vicks Vapor Rub on your chest. Put a scarf around your neck. And breathe deeply. I bet you'll feel better!

Metatheory is not about deciding which theory is "better or worse" than another, and business school professors struggle with these issues as much as students. These points aside, Van de Ven's article does tell of the perplexity felt by many students regarding theoretical pluralism and the avoidance and bafflement that this issue produces.

The development of considered and coherent responses to pluralism is a crucial issue in management education. Organisational change is complex and, to fully appreciate that complexity, students need exposure to a wide range of models and theories. However, this is no place to leave students. As well as a familiarity with the diversity of theoretical perspectives, students also benefit from some exposure to integrative views that can provide an overarching orientation. The pedagogical task here is not to avoid these issues or to search for "a single conceptual framework to unify so-called false differences between various theories and paradigms" (De Cock & Jeanes, 2006, p. 20). A metatheoretical response to the important challenges of pluralism is needed. Such a response can build on the assumptions, metaphors and explanatory concepts that distinguish between theories and which can also connect them within more integrative systems of sense-making.

There is a flip side to the pedagogy and pluralism issue. While the body of extant organisational theory continues to grow there is also a view that in the world of management education "we are indeed witnessing the increasing homogenization of management worldwide" (Clegg & Ross-Smith, 2003). Theoretical diversity abounds but this has not translated into a coherent teaching agenda that deals with that diversity. Stuart Clegg and Anne Ross-Smith (2003) are among several management educators who have commented on the dominance of U.S. focused theory and research in business and management studies. Their view is that (2003, p. 89):

Rather than reflecting a plurality of conceptual frameworks, research approaches, geographic locations, and input from the diverse cultural backgrounds and values of management scholars worldwide, this powerful U.S. construction of management knowledge has imbued it with glacierlike stability of cultural assumptions founded on the local rationalities of the U.S. world.

It seems that the conceptual plurality that is present in various literatures is not being translated into diversity within organisational and management practices. Instead of stimulating a greater awareness of the diversity of theories that have been generated within and outside of the U.S., Clegg and Ross-Smith believe, "Potential perspectives and voices that speak from the margins are eclipsed, and overall intellectual debate within the discourse of management is stilled". As suggested earlier, it appears that one of the mainstream responses to pluralism in the pedagogical domain has been a narrowing of focus onto conventional theories and the associated activities of empirical testing of those middle-range theories.

In contrast to conventional approaches to theory, critical theorists have frequently remarked on the need to include conflict and paradox in theory development (Dehler, Welsh & Lewis, 2001). They argue that this better reflects the real dilemmas that are experienced in organisational life. This is a view that values paradox and diversity as much as it does integration and connection. The conflict and contradictions that are often expressed in different theoretical perspectives create opportunities for developing deeper insights into the way organisational transformation is theorised. This is the idea of paradox as a pedagogical tool. As Gordon Dehler and his colleagues put it (2001, p. 506):

> Multiple disciplinary or paradigmatic theories may serve as lenses to deepen debates and insights (Bartenuk, 1983). Juxtaposing conflicting understandings creates a space for learning—an opportunity to recognise how differing perspectives coexist and complicate the learning milieu of organisations.

An integrative pedagogical response to this paradox is to develop students' capacities for taking multiple perspectives through a dialectical process of metatheoretical reflection, connection and accommodation. Metatheorising can be, therefore, not only a means for developing alternative solutions to old problems, but a transformational learning process for both teachers and students.

THE NEED FOR AN INTEGRAL APPROACH

There are several characteristics of an integral approach to metatheorising that make it particularly relevant for the study of organisations and change. First, integral metatheorising is applicable across many disciplinary contexts. Organisational studies is a research field that draws on the full range of social science disciplines and so any overarching approach must necessarily be adaptable to multiple scales of focus across those disciplines. In his book *Chaos of Disciplines* Andrew Abbott (2001) discusses the idea of "self-similarity" as it relates to certain conceptual patterns that appear repeatedly within and across all manner of scientific disciplines.

Self-similarity is the idea that "many social structures look the same in large scale and in small scale" (Abbott, 2001, p. xi). This is a fractal conceptualisation of knowledge where "fine detail recapitulates gross structure" (Abbott, 2001, p. xv). On the basis of very detailed observations of the way research fields develop over time, Abbott argues that the conceptual boundaries that connect one theory, paradigm or discipline with other theories, paradigms and disciplines are repeated within whatever domain a theorist chooses to work in. Consequently, the debates that occur around what distinguishes one theory or paradigm from another tend to be replicated as new fields of research emerge, establish their identity and gradually become part of the mainstream. As Abbott puts it, "intellectual life in the social sciences is organised around perennial debates that produce proliferating lineages with the peculiar properties of self-similarity" (2001, p. 121). This is why metatheoretical research can appear at virtually any scale of focus either within or between disciplines. Very similar metatheoretical constructs are used within very specific research domains all the way up to the most general inter- and transdisciplinary domains. That integrative metatheory is at all possible is due, at least in part, to this self-replicating pattern of perspectives that appear in theories from many different research paradigms. The frequent appearance of multi-phased models of transitional change in psychological models, in theories of organisational change, in philosophical writings, cultural studies and theories of leadership (see, for example, Elrod & Tippett, 2002; Nutt, 2003) is an example of the type of metatheoretical patterns that this book will explore.

A second quality that makes a metatheoretical work integrative is that it takes an appreciative stance towards the multitude of alternative theoretical positions. Rather than looking for evidence that one theory is better than another (according to some set of evaluative criteria), an integrative approach recognises the potential contributions of all theories present within, for example, some domain of published literature. I have referred to this as a process of "appreciative meta-inquiry" (Edwards, 2007). Ken Wilber (2003b) calls this the "non-exclusion principle" because integral approaches assume that different theoretical views can each contribute to the development of knowledge. In their integrative study of approaches to organisational development, Cacioppe and Edwards (2005a, p. 240) defined non-exclusion as "acknowledging, i.e. not excluding, the plurality of insights and truths that exists in all paradigms and schools of knowledge". This appreciative stance supports a research position that is open to new and diverse perspectives, that is aware of the inevitability of entrenched theoretical positions and the possible alternatives, and that carries forward the best of what has been developed in the past towards the creation of the new.

A third aspect of integral metatheorising is that the terms *integrative* and *integral* have a long history of usage within several traditions of metatheorising (Molz & Hampson, in press). Integral means "[e]ssential or necessary for completeness; constituent" (American-Heritage, 2000), and there have been many attempts within philosophy and the natural and social sciences to develop "Theories of Everything" (TOE) that aim, at some level at least, to provide complete theories within some domain. TOE metatheorising is not the approach taken here and I regard the possibility of developing complete theories in the social sciences to be highly speculative if not rather misguided. There has also been a more modest stream of integral theorising where the intent is not so much to develop complete theories as to build overarching frameworks that can integrate and accommodate several existing theories. In this vein the term *integral* has been used in a metatheorising context for many decades in such areas as cultural development, education, spirituality, and personality theory, among many other areas (Molz, in press).

Finally, the idea of integrative metatheorising is used here in a very specific and methodological sense. No metatheory or theory building endeavour starts from a conceptual blank slate (Gioia & Pitre, 1990). There are always existing resources deployed to help analyse and structure the "data" of extant theory. Conceptual resources play a crucial role in metatheory building methods and the more transparently these can be described the more assessable the research. Among the metatheoretical resources used here will be Ken Wilber's integral theory or, as it is also called, the AQAL framework (Wilber, 1999c, 2000b), Bill Torbert's DAI and George Ritzer's sociological metatheorising. Consequently, the metatheorising to be presented here is distinctly integral and integrative in the sense that it uses these other large-scale metatheories as guiding resources. The methodological role that these frameworks play in constructing integrative metatheory will become clearer in later chapters. For the moment it is enough to point out that these metatheories, particularly AQAL and DAI, have several qualities that make them well suited to the resource role in the field of organisational transformation. These metatheories: (i) have been represented in organisational transformation literature since the beginning of research in this field, (ii) have shown extensive integrative capacities in organisational contexts, (iii) can be applied on a multilevel basis and (iv) incorporate multiparadigm perspectives in building their metatheories.

For these reasons the metatheorising performed here takes a deliberately integrative orientation. Integrative metatheorising cuts across intra- and interdisciplinary boundaries, it takes an appreciative stance towards the accommodation of diverse theoretical positions, it follows in a tradition of integrative big pictures, and finally, it uses large-scale metatheories as resources in its metatheory building methods.

PUTTING THE PIECES TOGETHER

So how might it be possible to draw out the systematic connections and relationships between diverse theoretical approaches towards radical change? And what method might be followed to systematise those elements into a flexible and accommodating integral metatheory for organisational transformation?

Answering these and other related questions will mean taking an intensive journey through many paradigms and theories of organisational change and into some detailed examinations of metatheory and the methods by which metatheoretical research can be performed. This journey, as discussed earlier, will be undertaken with considerable support from the work of other researchers and thinkers who have explored the territory of metatheory. The foundational work of sociologist George Ritzer (2001) will be relied on for defining the basic types of metatheoretical research. Marianne Lewis and her colleagues (Lewis & Grimes, 1999; Lewis & Kelemen, 2002) will be important for developing a research method that can help us navigate through the terrain of multiparadigm inquiry. The writings of Ken Wilber (1999c, 2000b) will be useful for identifying important metatheoretical lenses and their relationships. Bill Torbert and his team of transformation and leadership researchers provide a rich resource of conceptual models for examining metatheoretical inquiry within the organisational change domain. Apart from these metatheoretical resources the major source of "data" to be examined in the following chapters will come from the many theories of organisational transformation that have been proposed and studied over several decades of intense scientific research.

The research method for undertaking this integrative task will be crucial for many reasons. To this point almost all metatheory has been developed using traditional methods of scholarship. These traditional methods have largely been an idiosyncratic process based on extensive reading and research across multiple disciplines and the construction of some overarching frameworks through scholarly argument and personal insight. Such approaches can result in important contributions but a much more systematic and defensible method of metatheorising is needed if metatheoretical research is to be regarded as anything other than a peculiar form of philosophical reasoning. While there have been some very isolated attempts to develop metatheory building methods, these have been developed for finding connections at the "paradigm level" (see Lewis & Grimes, 1999). No detailed method currently exists for analysing conceptual similarities and differences at the finer level of a theory's core concepts. Consequently, this integrative journey will also need to develop a more incisive qualitative research method for identifying the core conceptual elements of theories of transformation.

Once again, the aim of all this is not to replace the plurality of approaches with some super-theory of transformation but, rather, to develop a flexible metatheory for considering and situating the diversity of paradigms and theories of organisational transformation within a more encompassing and integrative conceptual landscape. This metatheory building endeavour, as the introductory quote from Popper attests, is best seen as part of an ongoing process, one that requires continuous evaluation and refinement. The purpose of such a task is essentially to "stretch the bounds of current thinking" (Jawahar & McLaughlin, 2001, p. 412) so that new understandings and explanations can be first constructed and then explored. The next step in this task is to define the domain of study in a little more detail.

2 Metatheoretical Domain and Definitions

> In the literature to date, a surprising tolerance has been shown towards the diversity of guises that 'transformation' can assume. Given the prominence of the term 'organisational transformation' in consulting practice and in both practitioner and academic literature, we might expect to find greater curiosity about its usage. (Tosey & Robinson, 2002, p. 108)

METATHEORETICAL DOMAIN AND "A TOLERANCE FOR AMBIGUITY"

Defining key terms is the most important step in setting the domain for the metatheorising process. In this chapter, terms such as *transformational* and *transitional change* and *organisation* are defined to set the boundaries of the subject matter. Other important concepts such as metatheory, metatheory building and the holon construct are also defined and considered in detail.

The theoretical diversity found within the field of organisational transformation brings with it a number of definitional and domain-setting problems. On the definitional side, there are problems which are due to the large number of idiosyncratic terms, their vagueness and abstract nature and the consequent difficulties with clarity of meaning (French, Bell & Zawacki, 2005). These definitional vagaries lead to problems in domain specification. As several researchers have pointed out, defining key terms also helps to set the domain boundaries for the theory building process (Torraco, 2002; Van de Ven, 2007). It is through defining organisational transformation that the domain boundaries for including or excluding theories will be identified.

Defining broad concepts within a metatheory building context highlights the need to retain a degree of tolerance for their level of abstractness and generalisability. Hence, this type of research requires a balance between demarcation efforts aimed at clearly defining a term and integrative intents that preserve that term's inclusiveness and capacity to encompass other concepts. Kaplan (1964) refers to this as a balance between "semantic openness", the inclusiveness of a concept, and "operational vagueness", the inherent ambiguity of a concept. In discussing this issue of balancing definitional precision and semantic openness, Van de Ven points out that the demand for exactness can prematurely close off the development of ideas in theory building. He advises that, "[t]olerance of ambiguity is important for scientific inquiry" (2007, p. 117). The strength of using broad-ranging and highly abstract concepts lies in their capacity to provide an inclusive perspective on what would otherwise be ambiguous or even mutually exclusive positions. Narrow definitions also reduce the pool of relevant theories of transformation and consequently close down the scope for sampling the diversity of theories. As with the metatheoretical research of Van de Ven and Poole, "abstract and general definitions" are adopted here to "open the field to a wide range of theories" (1995, p. 512).

The definitional tasks of this chapter are dealt with under three headings, (i) organisation and organisational transformation, (ii) metatheorising and (iii) theory building. In the course of providing these definitions, the domain and scope of the study are identified.

THE VARIETIES OF ORGANISATION

At its most elemental level, an organisation is a group of people who intentionally gather together to accomplish some shared and meaningful purpose for a significant period of time. This gathering has several implicit and explicit qualities. On the implicit side, the members of an organisation participate in a shared identity that enables the organisation to have some collective unity or organisational form. For example, members communicate in a way that allows organising to occur. They share, to lesser and greater degrees, certain behaviours and certain visions of the whole and their respective places in that whole. Stability and change, order and disorder, collaboration and conflict are the natural consequences of organisational life.

On the explicit side, organisations and their members work towards short-, middle- and long-term goals that accrue over time to build up physical, structural and communicative environments that, in turn, impact on the organisation and the lives of its members. Through these implicit and explicit processes organisations acquire characteristics, identifying qualities and specific forms. But they are also unremittingly complex and chaotic within these regularities. This paradox of chaotic complexity and ordered regularity means that the ways we think about organisations and the complexities and patterns of experience we find in them have a lot to do with the sense-making schemas and patterns of behaviour that we bring to them. This is true for the researcher as much as for anyone else. In other words, organisations are both understood from and created by our (naive and formal) theories and systems of sense-making as much as they are by the pragmatics of information technologies, buildings, markets or economic conditions. The concept of organisational form is central to discussions of how and why they change. Many theorists have developed extensive taxonomies and typologies of forms of organisation while others reject any notion of organising patterns (Romanelli, 1991). My view is that meaningful groupings of organisational forms are not only possible (as is evident from even a cursory glance at the research literature on organisational change) but that the theories and concepts of specific forms of organisation have actually been formative in the development of organisational life and that these forms are axiomatic for metatheorising about change.

The metatheory for organisational transformation that is proposed here is meant to be applicable and, hopefully, relevant to any organisation that falls within this very broad rubric, be they from the corporate world of commerce, the public world of government, the internet world of virtual organisations, the community world of NGOs or the local world of small and family businesses. All organisations change and need to change as they encounter the imperative to transform in some deep and significant way in the course of their lifespan. This is particularly true during times of great volatility and flux such as we are now experiencing.

ORGANISATIONAL TRANSFORMATION

Organisational transformation is a particular type of change that can be distinguished from incremental, translational and other forms of organisational change. Drawing out the distinguishing features of transformational change will help to establish the domain for the integrative metatheory that will be developed in later chapters.

Organisational Change and Transformation

Organisational change is an important concept that lies at the heart of much organisation theory. Change theorists Andrew Van de Ven and Marshall Poole regard organisational change as "an empirical observation of differences in form, quality, or state over time in an organisational entity" (1988, p. 36). This empirical approach to defining change has three essential aspects, (i) change is observable, (ii) change is not merely an array of differences but an alteration in the same entity over time and (iii) change affects all aspects of the organisation. While change itself may be observable, understanding and explaining change is also a matter of making inferences and of presuming relationships between organisational characteristics that may not be directly observable. To this point Van de Ven and Poole say (1988, p. 36):

> While organisational change can be directly observed empirically, it is important to emphasise that the process of change is a latent inference, that is, it is a theoretical explanation for the pattern of changes observed.

This inferential aspect of explaining change means that theories of change need to include explanations, not only of observables, but also of capacities that are deduced from those observations. This leads to the definitions of change as something that is undergone and subjectively experienced as well as objectively observed.

Another point of divergence for definitions of change has to do with the issue of substantive versus process views of change (Chia, 1999). A substantive view sees change as something that occurs to structures. According to this approach, change is a "transitory phase which is necessary for bridging the various stages of an evolutionary process" (Chia, 1999, p. 215). The process view sees structure itself as in a state of constant flux so that there is no fixed substance or inert organisational condition that undergoes change. Everything everywhere is in process and "transition is the ultimate fact" (Chia, 1999, p. 218). The dualism of process and structure is a recurring theme through the change literature. The approach taken here is that theories of change need to accommodate both objective and subjective; that is, substantive structural views as well as dynamic processual views. Structure and process are not necessarily exclusive of each other and both the "metaphysics of substance/presence" and of "change/process" must be included to develop an integrative account for change and transformation (Chia, 1999, p. 217).

Organisational transformation can be defined as a subset of the broader field of change theories in the same way that any transformative event can be regarded as a particular instance of a more general class of change. Transformation is "a very special type of change . . . All change does not constitute 'transformation'" (Flamholtz & Randle, 1998, p. 8). Although there are many different definitions of organisational transformation, a number of shared components can be identified and, together, these form a strong definitional base. These definitive components are discontinuity, adaptability, whole-system change, multidimensionality and multilevel quality. These can be briefly described as follows. Organisational transformation is discontinuous in that it involves a qualitative shift towards a more adaptive form of organising which includes all levels (micro, meso and macro[1]) and all major operational domains (dimensions) of the organisation. It is a systemic process involving both the visible, objective aspects and the invisible, subjective aspects of individuals and groups; a process that includes structures and people. These elements are succinctly captured by McNulty and Ferlie (2004, p. 1392) in their listing of the indicators of organisational transformation:

> The [organisational transformation] model consists of the following indicators of transformation: [i] multiple and interrelated changes across the system as a whole; [ii] the creation of new organisational forms at a collective level; [iii] the development of multilayered changes which impact upon the whole system, at unit and individual level; [iv] the creation of changes in the services provided and in the mode of

delivery; [v] the reconfiguration of power relationships (especially the formation of new leadership groups); [vi] the development of new culture, ideology and organisational meaning. Only when all six criteria have been fulfilled is it possible to talk of a complete organisational transformation.

Each of these criteria will be dealt with in detail in the following pages but it is worth mentioning two of these definitive elements here. The last of McNulty and Ferlie's criteria, the development of a new culture, is pivotal in conceptualising this transformative type of change. It is not only that with transformation there are significant improvements in organising but that radically new systems of identity and functioning emerge. There is a movement from one distinctive global form of organising to another. Whatever the previous form of culture and structure, it becomes integrated within a new organisational form. And this developmental and transformational movement can occur several times through an organisation's lifespan. In her review of practitioners' understandings of organisational transformation, Beverley Fletcher notes that (1990, p. 7) "the process does not end with the emergence of a new form, but that it involves a continual flow from one form to another".

Another important characteristic of transformational change approaches is the inclusion of both microlevel/individual and macrolevel/organisational transformation (McNulty and Ferlie's third criteria). Transformation at the individual level is seen in the fundamental realignment of personal attitudes, consciousness, motivation, beliefs and spirituality. The collective pole of this organisational spectrum requires all levels—the individual, the group and the whole organisation—to "reframe", to significantly alter ways of thinking, experiencing and behaving (Chapman, 2002, p. 18):

> In transformational change, every person affected by the change is a change agent to the extent that his or her personal involvement in reframing contributes to a successful outcome, supplemented by involvement in structural and other changes.

There is an important characteristic of transformation that is left out of McNulty and Ferlie's definitive criteria. This characteristic has to do with, what many theorists see as, the inherent mystery that lies at the heart of all transformational events. Several authors have pointed out that one of the most definitive aspects of deep change is, paradoxically, its inexplicable nature (Egri & Frost, 1991; Lichtenstein, 1997). The metamorphosis of a caterpillar into a butterfly is an apt analogy for that elusive aspect of transformation that escapes all attempts to understand, represent and manage radical social emergence. Biologists have a great deal of knowledge about metamorphosis from caterpillar (larvae) to chrysalis (pupa) to adult butterfly (imago), but such events are ultimately mysterious and scientific understandings of them will always be partial. So it is with social transformations. There will always be a dimension of this type of change that transcends our explanations. In an article entitled, "Grace, magic and miracles: A 'chaotic logic' of organizational transformation", Lichtenstein (1997) reports on interviews with three major theorists of organisational transformation (Peter Senge, Bill Torbert and Ellen Wingard) and they all refer to the ultimate ineffability of the transformative event. Some theorists introduce the language of spirituality to convey this aspect of transformation (see, for example, Benefiel, 2003; Cacioppe, 2000a, 2000b; Neal & Biberman, 2003; Pava, 2004) and this theme of mystery and spirituality is an important one for many approaches to defining transformation.

In summary, based on the six criteria proposed by McNulty and Ferlie (2004), organisational transformation is defined here as discontinuous change that involves subjective and objective aspects of the whole multilevel organisational system and which results in a radical multidimensional reconfiguration of culture, systems and structures. Consequently, theories that come within our domain of interest will conceptualise organisational transformation as: (i) a deep-seated process that results in a whole-of-system, qualitative shift, (ii) occurring across multiple levels of the organisation and (iii) involving all of the core domains of organisational life.

Transformation and Translation

Many other change-related terms are used synonymously with transformation. McHugh, for example, uses the term "radical change" interchangeably with transformation. For her transformation is radical, discontinuous change (2001, p. 25):

> Radical change is revolutionary—it is discontinuous, showing a decisive break with the past. Radical change is reflected in changes of strategy, organisational size, organisational systems and organisational behaviour. In other words, organisational transformation is the product or outcome of radical change.

We see here that the definitive elements of discontinuity and whole-system change are present in radical as with transformative change. Apart from radical change, other terms used synonymously with transformation are deep change, revolutionary change, qualitative change, gamma change, second-order change and paradigmatic change (Fletcher, 1990). While there are nuances between these varying terms, the common element between them is the idea of a qualitative shift, leap or dramatic emergence into a new form of organising.

These terms and their antonyms are used to distinguish transformation from other, non-transformative types of change. For example, transformation is contrasted with translational change. Where transformation is about radical shifts, translation is about the ongoing transactions that maintain an organisation's stable functioning and coherent identity. Wilber calls this type of incremental change "translational development" (2000, p. 70). This distinction has been applied to organisation theory by Ford and Backoff (1988, p. 105). They describe transformation as occurring between "vertical dimensions" of organising while "[m]ovements within hierarchical levels are horizontal movements and are termed *translations*". Figure 2.1 shows this distinction between transformation and translation, albeit in a very static form. Transformation is never a simple, progressive movement from one level to another, but always involves complex transitional tracks that are idiosyncratic to each organisation (Greenwood & Hinings, 1988).

Ford and Backoff see "horizontal or translative" change as alterations that occur within the structures and systems that pertain to a particular form of organising. Translative growth is focused on the integration, stabilisation and balancing of processes and structures that enable a particular form of organisation to function—"Translations, therefore, are concerned with morphostasis" (Ford & Backoff, 1988, p. 106). It is important to recognise that because translational change is ongoing and supports the stability and coherence of organisational forms, it plays an essential role in the transformational process. Consequently, any integrative approach to transformation will need to accommodate the insights of translational theories of change.

Transformation and Development

The transformation–translation distinction is also relevant to the differences that many theorists make between organisational transformation and organisational development. Where transformation is discontinuous and involves the whole system, organisational development is about translational improvements that can be targeted to specific areas, aspects and functions within an organisation. John Adams, who also uses Wilber's

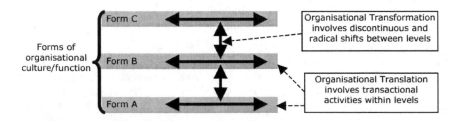

Figure 2.1   Transformational and translational change.

transform–translate distinction, argues that both types of change are necessary for the adaptive development of an organisation (1984, p. xi).

> We should avoid getting into OT [organisational transformation] versus OD [organisational development] debates, since they do not represent an either/or polarity. . . . Organisations need both. While OD develops or enhances what is, there is a sense of discontinuity and irreversibility about OT.

The relationship between organisational transformation and organisational development will be further discussed in the following chapter. For the moment, it is enough to point out that development is more concerned with the improvement of translational capacities, that is, with those changes that maintain the current values, mission, structures and systems of the organisation, and which may result in localised development but not in whole-system transformation.

Transformation and Economic Growth

Sometimes the growth associated with dramatic increase in some major organisational characteristic, such as productivity, market share or net profit, is deemed to be a type of organisational transformation. That is not the position I take and I make a strong distinction between expansive growth in economic variables and transformative change. Although it is part of the transformation story, economic growth is not specifically the goal of such change. *Transformation* refers to a process where a qualitatively different level of collective identity and functioning is achieved at the macrolevel of the organisation. This may include economic growth but, in itself, a dramatic increase in profits, market share, productivity or any other economic indicator of growth does not necessarily indicate or involve transformational change. Radical changes in organisational culture, mission, governance and structure will also need to be present for transformation to occur. As Fisher and Torbert (1991, p. 141) point out:

> Transformation involves developing commitment to a new vision along with increased trust and capacity for learning. It is a process so comprehensive—affecting values, role modelling, reward systems, selection criteria, structure and spatial arrangements—that it should be understood as culture change.

In contrast to the radical shifts involved in whole-of-system transformation, economic-based understandings of organisational transformation have more to do with product change, change in IT systems, downsizing, rebranding or some other kind of restructuring designed specifically to increase efficiency and the financial bottom line. Transformation can often take place alongside these kinds of economic growth, as shown in the dramatic development of transitional economies in Eastern Europe. However, as we have seen in the expansion of global business in the late 1990s and early 2000s, significant growth can also occur without transformative change taking place. The same corporate values, business ethos and organisational systems can remain in place even with significant growth in economic outcomes. In fact, as I will argue in a later chapter, some theorists hold that dramatic growth in the economic aspects of an organisation can actually reinforce the predominant worldviews and stultify whole-system transformation. As a certain way of organising and producing becomes successful and entrenched within an organisation's behaviour and culture, it correspondingly grows more resistant to change and inattentive to the environmental cues that signal that transformative change is required (Kets De Vries & Balazs, 1999).

Transformation and Mergers, Acquisitions and Takeovers

Transformation has also been associated with the corporate activities of mergers, acquisitions and takeovers (Daniel, David & Gregory, 1997). These forms of corporate activity often result in dramatic changes in the size of organisations, the form of organisational structures, the restructuring of labour forces and significant economic impacts on markets. Again however, these activities are more concerned with economic expansion than with new ways of thinking, doing and organising values. Substantive change does occur when organisations amalgamate but this change may have nothing whatever to do with fundamental dimensions of culture, power relationships, management systems, stakeholder relations or any core transformational dimensions. In fact, some have argued that the "mergers and acquisitions" phenomena can be, in many cases, a regressive form of organisational change rather than a progressive and transformational one (Hoffman, Frederick & Petry, 1989). Jean Bartunek, one of the first researchers of organisational transformation, argues that:

> Some [transformations] are partly the result of mergers and acquisitions . . . These types of changes end up being by definition transformations, changing organizations' understanding of themselves. . . . I think the political, economic, and social situation in the country right now is extremely conducive to that kind of situation and absolutely not at all to my ideal of a desirable transformation . . . I'm talking about a mass negative transformation happening in most organizations, with a few people getting rich from it and lots of people losing. (Bartunek cited in Fletcher, 1990, p. 105)

Mergers and acquisitions are transformations concerned with economic expansion rather than with any holistic renewal or paradigm shift in values, forms of governance, organisational identity or personal consciousness. While theorists working in the fields of organisational transformation, organisational development and organisational expansion (economic growth) may use the term *transformation*, they do so with very different points of view in mind.

Figure 2.2 depicts the relationship between organisational change, transformation, development and expansion. While there are some areas of overlap, theories of "transformation" that focus on economic expansion or corporate activities such as mergers, acquisitions and takeovers are considered here as forms of translational growth and, as such, do not meet the definitive criteria for inclusion in my meta-analysis of change theories.

Transformation and Transition

Transition refers to the dynamic, processual aspect of changing from one state to another. Both transformation and translation can be regarded as forms of transition. *Transformation* refers to the process of transitioning from one level to a qualitatively different level. *Translation* refers to the process of transition that occurs within the same level of organisational functioning. The differences between transformation, translation and transition are succinctly stated in the following quote from Ford and Backoff (1988, p. 105):

> Regardless of whether growth is translative/morphostatic (movement within horizontal level) or transformative/morphogenetic (movement between vertical levels), the movement itself is referred to as a *transition*.

While both of these transitional lenses are essential for viewing organisational change, it is the transformational "movement between vertical levels" that provides the definitive criterion for including theories in the analysis that follows. Both understandings are, however, important for an integrative metatheory of change.

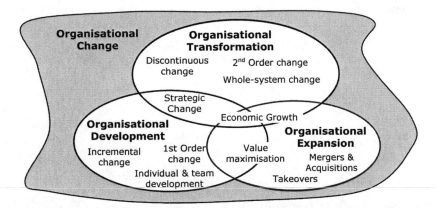

Figure 2.2   The relationship between different types of organisational change.

THEORY BUILDING AND METATHEORISING

There are many misconceptions regarding theory and metatheory building and metatheorising. Before defining these areas, I will consider a few important terms that are associated with these activities. Understanding complex constructs such as paradigm and metatheory is aided by considering the more basic elements on which these ideas are built.

Concept, Construct, Model, Framework, Theory, Paradigm

A *concept* is a "bundle of meanings or characteristics associated with events, objects or conditions" (Meredith, 1993, p. 5). Concepts are used for representing, communicating and/or understanding our experiences and the phenomena that we encounter. A *construct* is a particularly abstract concept which, together with other constructs and concepts, can form conceptual models for representing and describing complex events and situations. While models are used for descriptive explorations and for showing relationships between constructs, theories go a step further and are used for understanding, explanation and evaluation. *Theories* are "an ordered set of assertions about a generic behaviour or structure assumed to hold throughout a significantly broad range of specific instances" (Sutherland, 1975, p. 9). In other words, theories are systems of conceptual relationships that can be used to make generalised truth claims for the purposes of understanding and explanation.

Paradigm is a controversial word which has been extensively debated in many social science fields including organisation theory (Hassard & Kelemen, 2002; Schultz & Hatch, 1996). In terms of their level of abstraction, paradigms can be regarded as lying somewhere between theories and metatheories. The term is used here as a heuristic device for grouping theories based on their shared explanatory concepts and research methods. This pragmatic usage of the term is supported by Mingers (2003, p. 1303), who stresses that the idea is meant to connect as well as distinguish between groups of theories:

> Arguments about paradigm incommensurability have been overstated—there is no agreed way of defining different paradigms. . . . The paradigm concept is useful as a shorthand for a particular constellation of assumptions, theories and methods, but it is purely an heuristic device.

A paradigm is equated here with Lakatos's notion of "scientific research program" (1978). Paradigms are regarded as constellations of scientific research program involving a connected set of practices, assumptions, theories and methods. It is assumed here that theories can be grouped into paradigms based on an analysis of textual descriptions of some of these elements. Theories of organisational transformation will be grouped together and placed into paradigm categories to aid the processes of review and analysis that follow in later chapters.

Theory Building

Theory building refers to those conceptual research methods that result in the construction of theory. There are two ways to consider the theory building process. One view sees theory building as the complete cycle of theory construction and verification. Lynham (2002), for example, defines theory building as both the generation and the verification of theory through iterative cycles of "producing, confirming, applying, and adapting theory":

> Theory building is the process or recurring cycle by which coherent descriptions, explanations, and representations of observed or experienced phenomena are generated, verified, and refined. (2002, p. 222)

From this perspective, theory building includes not only the construction of new theory but also the evidential testing of a theory's explanations, hypotheses and factual claims. The second understanding, which is adopted here, distinguishes between theory building and theory testing forms of research. Although both are needed to do good science, for the past 50 years theory testing has been the predominant area of research in the social sciences. Theory building is focused on the conceptual side of the knowledge development process. It seeks to build conceptual frameworks for establishing definitions, models and explanations that help us make sense of our experiences and observations. Conceptual research and empirical research reinforce each other and both contribute to the accumulation of understanding. These two phases in the cycle of knowledge development are shown in Figure 2.3. The diagram shows the complementary nature of theory building (conceptual research) and theory testing (empirical research). Where theory testing involves operationalising, hypothesising, measuring and verifying/falsifying, the theory building task involves the definition of concepts, their domains and relations and the development of a conceptual system that brings those elements together (Wacker, 1998).

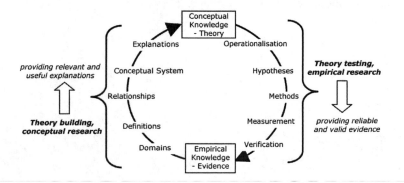

Figure 2.3 The cycle of theory building and testing.

As with all knowledge construction, theory building can be pursued within many different research paradigms (Torraco, 2002). For example, some theory building methods are more concerned with grounding theory within the immediate experiences and observations of individuals and communities. Methods such as participant observation and ethnographic research attempt to develop explanations that are based on experientially related, culturally localised and situationally contextualised "data". Other theory building approaches, such as metatheorising (Ritzer, 2001) or meta-triangulation (Lewis & Grimes, 1999) draw upon more conceptualised and abstract data that, for example, seek to establish significant patterns between concepts from different theories.

Figure 2.4 presents a spectrum of theory building approaches based on the idea of increasing abstraction in the source of the research "data". Theory can be built using data that is methodologically very close to an event or experience or it can be built from more abstract sources which include concepts, models and theories that are far removed from the empirical events they refer to. Theory building approaches that rely on empirical data include grounded theory, case study research and some methods coming from a social constructionist perspective. Moving further from the empirical event, there are quantitative approaches that are based on controlled experiments, survey research and meta-analysis. At the more abstract end of the spectrum there are metatheory building methods such as whole-systems theory building, multiparadigm approaches and metatheorising. The spectrum of conceptual research for building theory ranges from those with an empirical focus on immediate experiential, sensory and behavioural data to those that use whole theories as their object of analysis.

Metatheory building can be regarded as yet another layer of abstraction over and above middle-range theory building. Where theories are constructed from, and tested by, concepts derived from empirical data, metatheory is constructed from, and tested by, abstract second-order concepts derived from the analysis of other theories (Gioia & Pitre, 1990). The terms "framework" and "approach" are used here as general concepts for referring to any large-scale metatheoretical system.

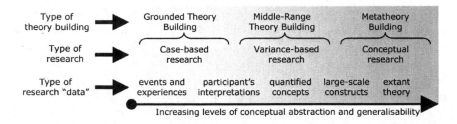

Figure 2.4   A spectrum of theory building techniques.

Metatheorising and Metatheory

Some general definitions of metatheorising regard it to be any activity that involves the study of the epistemological, ontological, methodological or axiological premises on which any theoretical statement rests. Take, for example, this definition by Tendzin Takla and Whitney Pape (1985, p. 75): "By metatheory we refer to the cluster of fundamental, but often implicit, presuppositions that underlie or embed a theory". From a less philosophical and more sociological view, metatheorising can also be defined as "the study of theories, theorists, communities of theorists, as well as the larger intellectual and social context of theories and theorists" (Ritzer, 1988, p. 188). While these definitions are adequate for many general discussions, I adopt the more refined definition offered by Barbara Paterson and her colleagues (Paterson et al., 2001, p. 91):

> Meta-theory is a critical exploration of the theoretical frameworks or lenses that have provided direction to research and to researchers, as well as the theory that has arisen from research in a particular field of study.

In this definition scientific metatheory building consciously and overtly takes other theory as its subject matter. In the words of Willis Overton (2007, p. 154): "Theories and methods refer directly to the empirical world, while metatheories refer to the theories and methods themselves".

Metatheorising of this kind is a scientific enterprise, not a philosophical one. It offers understandings and explanations based on the analysis of its "data", that is, on other theories, rather than on reasons derived from first principles. Informal varieties of metatheorising take place whenever any theoretical literature is reviewed. Ritzer (1991a) suggests that most research begins with some element of metatheorising in that scholars review the theories of other researchers in the development of their own theories and hypotheses. Metatheorising is similar to other forms of scientific sense-making in that it attempts to create understandings that derive from some body of knowledge, information, data or experience. It is different in that the body of information it draws on, its "data", is other theories (van Gigch & Le Moigne, 1989) or "unit theories", as Wagner and Berger (1985) call the middle-range theories that are the focus of study for metatheorists.

George Ritzer (2001) and Paul Colomy (1991) have identified four types of metatheorising based on the aims of the metatheoretical research involved. Metatheorising can be used: (i) for understanding and becoming familiar with the array of extant theories and paradigms across some domain (Ritzer's M_U); (ii) as a preparatory exercise to develop new middle-range theory (Ritzer's M_P); (iii) to develop overarching metatheory (Ritzer's M_O); and (iv) to evaluate and adjudicate on the conceptual adequacy and scope of other metatheories and theories (Colomy's M_A). One of the most important roles that metatheorising can perform comes from its evaluative capacity. For example, metatheories can be used to identify those orienting concepts that a particular theory utilises as well as those that it neglects or does not possess. This present study is concerned with the pursuit of M_U (metatheorising for understanding) so that a subsequent M_O (overarching metatheory) can be developed with the additional aim of performing M_A (adjudicating metatheory) forms of metatheorising.

Metatheorising can be seen as a formal activity of scientific sense-making. Figure 2.5 depicts a multilevel model of sense-making that outlines the relations between empirical, theoretical and metatheoretical levels of experience. The basis of all embodied sense-making is the primary holistic experience of empirical engagement. Meaning flows from and informs these experiences through symbols and concepts. That process is carried forward through both personal and scientific theories which use concepts as the bases for more abstract, theory-based sense-making. Finally, metatheorising develops overarching frameworks that are founded on other middle-range organisational theories. This model is intended to show that metalevel abstractions are present within any life experience and within all scientific activities.

Tsoukas and Knudsen (2003a, p. 6) present a simpler version of this holarchy of sense-making in organisational studies. Experiencing, symbolising and conceptualising provide the content for the empirical or "object level" for the study of organisations. Developing middle-range theories constitutes the "theoretical level" where theories, models and frameworks of organisational transformation are developed and tested. Metatheorising is the "metatheoretical level" where knowledge about theories of organisation are developed, validated and linked with other levels. Metatheoretical methods simply continue the process of sense-making at another order of abstraction and generalisation (Wacker, 1998). This multilevel process is dynamic and interactive in that experiences, symbols, concepts, theories and metatheories

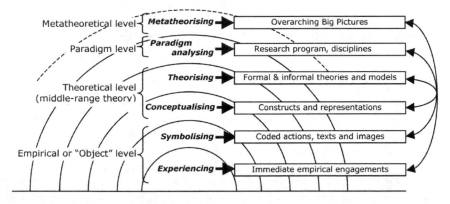

Figure 2.5   The holarchy of sense-making.

mediate and inform one another. There is an ongoing iteration of influences and mediations between experience, concepts, theories and metatheoretical perspectives (Tsoukas & Knudsen, 2003). However, each one of these layers is also a meta-layer to the one preceding it. The empirical is content to the context of the conceptual, the conceptual is content to the context of the theoretical and the theoretical is content to the context of the metatheoretical. This redoubling of content and context forms a holarchy of sense-making. The arrows in the diagram are meant to indicate the multidirectional flow of co-creation that exists between these layers. All these layers are real, all are causally efficacious and all are mutually co-creative.

Experiencing, symbolising, conceptualising, theorising and metatheorising are all types of sense-making. In other words, to make sense of something we can touch it (the empirical layer), we can name or imitate it (the symbolic layer), we can try to understand its characteristics (the conceptual layer), we can model those characteristics and describe a system of relationships between them (the theoretical layer), we can reflect on how theories relate to each other (the paradigm layer) and we can try to link and separate those theories and paradigms in a coherent overarching way (the metatheoretical layer). This holarchy is not separate from everyday sense-making. Ordinary life, whether in the home or in organisations, involves countless cycles of reflexive engagements between these sense-making strata. Science can be regarded as an institutionalised, cultural formalisation of this sense-making holarchy. Formal scientific practice is so successful at developing knowledge because it is grounded in this sense-making holarchy of building and testing theory.

The sense-making model helps us to see the relationships between theories, paradigms and metatheories and why it is that metatheorists treat other middle-range theories as the raw material, the conceptual facts from which metatheory is built. Ritzer states that "metatheory takes theory as its subject matter" (1990, p. 3) and it does not matter where these theories come from; "what counts is whether they make sense and whether they help us understand, explain, and make predictions about the social world" (Ritzer, 1990, p. 2).

Metatheoretical Lens and Orienting Generalisation

The notion of a metatheoretical lens is closely associated with the idea that we explain complex events through reducing that complexity to particular sense-making or explanatory frameworks. Explanations are accounts that convey understanding from one person to another through connecting some key factors into a communicable story. The explanatory factors of a theory are its conceptual building blocks, its "endogenous" factors (Klein, Tosi & Cannella, 1999). These conceptual building blocks are referred to here as conceptual lenses and, when they are used to build metatheory, they are called metatheoretical lenses. Together with their inter-relationships, lenses form the basic skeleton of a theory or metatheory, that is, the conceptual structure that underlies their characteristic form.

The metaphor of "lens" is frequently used in organisational and management literature as a way of representing the conceptual perspective afforded by a theory or a paradigm. The lens metaphor has been used widely within social science theory building. In organisational contexts it has been used in chaos and complexity theories of management, critical theory, technology in organisations, strategic change, systems theory and contract theory. The lens metaphor is used here to emphasise the idea that theory not only receptively interprets research findings but plays an active role in shaping what we research. In the receptive sense, theory acts as an interpretive filter that structures and makes sense of the data of its subject matter. In the active sense, theory acts in shaping the real-world of empirical realities. Giddens (1984) has referred to this dual role of theory in society as the "double hermeneutic". As Giddens says (1984, p. xxxiii): "theories help to constitute the activities and institutions that are the object of study of specialised social observers or social scientists". Theory not only creates meaning, it also concretely informs and shapes its subject matter. The metaphors of "voice" and "tool" could just as well be used to represent this more active involvement of theory in social change. From this understanding, the lenses and voices used to investigate organisational life are constitutive of that life. To paraphrase Deetz (1996, p. 192), a conceptual lens does not merely interpret organisational objects, it is core to the process of constituting those objects.

Weick has expressed the active aspect of theory as a process of disciplined imagination. He says, "When theorists build theory, they design, conduct, and interpret imaginary experiments" (1989, p. 519). For example, when adopting an individualist lens to viewing organisational transformation, a researcher not only interprets transformational events as a result of individuals' experiences and actions but that researcher also actively uses methods that disclose individualist forms of data. In this example, the conceptual lens is one of epistemological and methodological individualism and this lens both receptively interprets and actively produces certain types of data and information. That information is then fed back into the organisation and broader community and so plays a role in shaping organisational and social life. A theory may contain several of these explanatory lenses in relationship (Wacker, 2004), and a metatheory will contain many such constructs. Identifying lenses is crucial for the metatheory building goals to be pursued here because these lenses form the basic elements from which the integral metatheory for organisational transformation is constructed.

Metatheoretical lenses have been referred to in the literature by a number of different labels. Colomy (1991) uses the term "underlying theoretical code" to refer to the ideas that characterise and "animate" a particular paradigm's identity. Ritzer calls these fundamental lenses that identify a paradigm or "set of theories" their "architectonics" (1991a, p. 303). In a discussion of the relationships between some central metatheoretical lenses in sociology, Ritzer speaks of architectonics as needing to be discovered and delineated by the metatheorist:

> On a more purely metatheoretical level, the outlining of this one architectonic leads to a recognition of the likelihood that there are other such sociological architectonics lurking below the surface of other sets of substantive theories and in need of similar discovery and delineation. Furthermore, it suggests the possibility of a limited number of architectonics that lie at the base of the bewildering array of substantive sociological theories. Were we able to uncover such a limited set of architectonics, we would have a much better handle on the field of sociological theory in general. (1991a, p. 303)

Metatheorists David Wagner and Joseph Berger (1985) use the term "orienting strategies" to describe the elements from which metatheorists develop their understandings of social phenomena. They say that orienting strategies "involve the articulation of the conceptual foundations employed in the description and analysis of social phenomena" (Wagner & Berger, 1985, p. 700). All these different terms, "conceptual lens", "underlying theoretical code", "architectonic", and "orienting strategy" are used to refer to the core conceptual orientations from which metatheorists build their overarching conceptual systems. As we will see in later chapters, one of the most important forms of these lenses, and one that has particular relevance for the study of transformation, is the holon construct.

The Holon Construct

Arthur Koestler first introduced the holon neologism in his book *The Ghost in the Machine* as a means for examining any entity as both whole ("hol-") and part ("-on") at the same time (Koestler, 1967). Holons are imbedded in multilevel systems such that "sub-wholes on any level of [a] hierarchy are referred to as holons" (Koestler, 1967, p. 341). He saw the holon as the unit of analysis for a new scientific discipline that overcame the limitations of both holistic system-based and analytic atomist-based worldviews.

The holon construct has had a long and extremely varied history of use within both applied and theoretical settings in organisational studies. The notion has been applied in trans-organisational development (Boje, 2000), human resource planning (Parker & Caine, 1996), institutional modelling (Schillo, Zinnikus & Fischer, 2003), management (Sun & Venuvinod, 2001), organisational change (Mathews, 1996), continuous change manufacturing systems (Cheng, Chang & Wu, 2004) and organisational sustainability (Kay et al., 1999).

The holon has not only been used to represent objective systems of organising but also for modelling individuals' cognitive representations. According to Lane and Oliva (1998, p. 217), systems theorist Peter Checkland accorded such a prominent place to the holon construct because he saw it as "a particular type of model, one which organises thinking using systemic ideas" (Lane & Oliva, 1998, p. 217). Checkland understood the holon to be a meta-systemic lens that encourages systemic thinking about real-world issues. Checkland used the holon construct to facilitate an integrated, metaparadigm vision of the world of organisational life. His use of the holon construct is very similar to Koestler's original intent that the holon be a means for seeing how theories are connected. Checkland (1988) actually proposed that the term should be taken up by all systems theorists as a technical label for any system. He argued that (1988, p. 238):

> We could improve the clarity of systems thinking at a stroke by conceding the word system to everyday language and using holon whenever we refer to the abstract concept of a whole . . . Shall we do it? Have we got the nerve?

I agree with Checkland that the term is eminently suited to metatheoretical discussions of systems but more than this I see the use of the construct as critical for a non-reductive approach to theorising about change. For these reasons, the holon will play a crucial role in representing the integrative metatheory for organisational transformation described in later chapters.

3 "The View from Somewhere Else"
In Defence of Metatheorising

> I take it that these are the most important questions which we confront. How to deal with and fend off the simplicities implicit in a world in which: "Have theory, will travel" makes for easy intellectual and political progress. How to resist the singularities so commonly performed in the acts of naming and knowing. How to defy the overwhelming pressures on academic production to render knowing simple, transparent, singular, formulaic. How to resist the pressure to enact, yet again, the God-trick. (Law, 1999, p. 11)

> . . . may the good lord protect other political sociologists from wandering into the dead end of metatheory. (Skocpol, 1987, p. 12)

AGAINST METATHEORY

Having defined and described some key concepts relevant to metatheoretical research, it is fitting at this point to consider some of the criticisms that have been levelled against grand theorising. Indeed for several decades now, there have been substantive arguments mounted against metatheories, overarching theories and metanarratives in general (Lyotard, 1984). Mainstream empirical science has also turned away from metatheoretical research and focused instead on the testing of middle-range theory. Addressing both modern and postmodern critiques is an important task for any metatheoretical undertaking and this chapter will briefly present some of the more common arguments for and against the metatheoretical position.

THE MODERNIST CRITIQUE—THE "DEAD END OF METATHEORY"

Metatheory has been heavily criticised by both modern empiricist and postmodernist approaches to social science. From the modernist perspective, metatheory is a "dead end" (Skocpol, 1987) for several reasons. It is seen as: (i) vague and impossible to validate or test; (ii) remote from practical interests; (iii) overly concerned with categorisation; and (iv) essentially philosophical and not scientific. I will look at each of these criticisms in turn.

Metatheory currently lacks a focus on method. While there have been extensive attempts to articulate the metatheoretical method of dialecticism of Karl Marx (Paolucci, 2003), very little has emerged that actually provides even the most rudimentary methodological guidelines for performing metatheoretical research. A key reason that overarching theory in particular has always struggled to gain scientific credibility is its lack of a solid methodological basis. The history of metatheorising is, in many ways, a patchwork of sporadic waves of interest followed by decades of neglect. When metatheorising has flourished it has often been taken up with a missionary zeal that has lacked critical self-evaluation. The sad history of the use and abuse of Marxist metatheory can be viewed in this context.[1] A research method is, by definition, self-evaluating—all methods include phases where the limitations of the study, its domain specifications, its sampling problems and its interpretive limits are discussed and rectified in subsequent studies. To this point, this formal process of self-examination within a scientific community of inquiry has not been evident in the development of metatheory. And this neglect of method has not gone unnoticed within the mainstream. It is not only the rise of postmodernism that has stymied the growth of "metanarratives" and integrative frameworks of understanding. Mainstream science itself has little time for ideas based on nothing but the scholarly review of literature.

There is an interesting inconsistency here in that modernity, through its instinct for synopsis, abstraction and generalisability, has an innate appreciation for grand theorising. Modernity in the physical sciences has given birth, for example, to the "Theories of Everything" and "Grand Unified Theories" in twentieth and twenty-first century physics. In the social sciences, modernism can be seen in the grand theorising of Talcott Parsons and Max Weber. But today even modernists have largely rejected metatheory in the social sciences, concentrating instead on the task of developing middle-range theory (Merton, 1957) and statistical approaches towards social explanation (Ball, 2004). One reason for this is, I believe, the lack of method in social metatheorising. Twentieth-century science has been the age of method and for modernists there can be no science where there is no method. Any branch of scholarship that does not overtly adopt some form of rigorous method will, quite rightly, never be taken seriously by mainstream science. As the methodologists Elman and Elman put it (2002, p. 232)—"In science, Nike notwithstanding, there is no 'just doing it'".

The remedy to this is not to dismiss all metatheorising but to place more attention on the application of method in performing integrative conceptual research. The metatriangulation approach of Lewis and Grimes (1999) and Sirgy's method for developing general system theories (Sirgy, 1988) are two rare examples of methods that have been described for building overarching metatheories. The general method outlined in Chapter 5 is an attempt to redress this paucity in detailed research methods for building integrative metatheoretical frameworks.

The issue of irrelevance is another common criticism of grand theorising. It is also a common criticism of much of social science theorising in general. Such criticisms are both true and false. They are true in that much metatheory does fall on barren ground and seems to produce, at least in the short term, little of practical worth. But the same might also be argued for many other kinds of conceptual, empirical and technological research. The criticism of irrelevance is false when it is a global statement against all metatheory. As Anthony Giddens (1984) notes, the impact of social theory, and particularly of big-picture theorising, can occasionally be so deep and so ubiquitous that there could hardly be a more powerful example of the influence of ideas on concrete social practices and lived human experience. The issue here is one of awareness of the influential relationship between theory and society rather than one of practicality. Merton's notion of self-fulfilling prophecy and Giddens's idea of double hermeneutic are both attempts to describe the reflexive nature of theory and society. Giddens's double hermeneutic is the "mutual interpretive play between social science and those whose activities compose its subject matter" (Giddens, 1984, p. xxxii). Big theories about government, international relations, economics and education have their impact on society and those impacts feed into the everyday activities of the members of those societies. The question is not one of relevance of metatheory but of our awareness of the processes by which certain metatheories already influence social realities. In fact, Ritzer, Zhao and Murphy (2001) regard metatheorising as essential if we are to adequately gauge the real-world effect of social theorising:

> [The] constitutive power of theory obliges many sociologists to engage in metatheorizing in order to monitor the impact of theory on the social world and to point out the need to change theories in light of changes in that world. (2001, p. 115)

The criticism that metatheory is simply a matter of categorisation and of creating classes and types is also undeserved. First, this view underestimates the value of typologies and it misunderstands the reasons for generating frameworks that involve ideal types, categories and comparative summaries. Harold Doty and William Glick pointedly state that "typologies are complex theories that are frequently misinterpreted" (Doty & Glick, 1994, p. 231). As in Torbert's types of scientific paradigms (2000) or Burrell and Morgan's (1979) typology of organisational analyses, metatheories are often presented as typologies in which many other paradigms, theories or aspects of theories can be accommodated. These frameworks can be used to propose both grand theories and middle-range theories. Again to quote Doty and Glick (1994, pp. 234–235):

Although typologies usually have not been interpreted as theories, good typologies provide two different levels of theory, a grand theory that generalizes to all organizations and middle-range theories that are restricted to the individual types.

The categorisation of theories and conceptual elements is particularly useful in identifying the boundaries that define where theories are most appropriately applied and where they are not. Hence, "good typologies" are powerful means for identifying forms of reductionism and the colonisation of one conceptual domain by another. Often categorisation comes from the identification of core dimensions or lenses within a field and it is these dimensions which are the real products of metatheoretical research.

Metatheorising has also been rejected as being largely philosophical or, at least, that its debates are philosophical in nature and have no scientific resolution. This criticism has some value particularly when it refers to those overarching metatheories that are not based on the analysis of extant theory. Ritzer says of these *a priori* forms of grand theories that "we have no way of ascertaining the validity of the process through which the overarching perspective came into existence" (Ritzer, 2001, p. 18). Ritzer draws a strong distinction between overarching metatheorising that is drawn from an analysis of middle-range theory and the philosophical form that he describes being created "without a systematic study of theory" and which seems "to materialise out of the imaginations of the creators or to be drawn vaguely from other disciplines" (Ritzer, 1990, p. 4). This type of philosophical metatheorising may be better regarded as philosophy rather than as social science.

From the modernist perspective, metatheorising appears philosophical because its "data" is not empirical and instead concentrates on the characteristics of theories themselves. Referring to their field of sociological metatheory, Weinstein and Weinstein remark, "For those who believe that only one theory is true, metatheory will be dissolved into philosophical sociology" (1991, p. 148). The scientific nature of metatheory is only recognised when it is understood that metatheory is to theory as theory is to empirical reality. This is not a philosophical relationship.

There are two important points to be learned from the modernist critique of metatheorising. First, methodological issues need to be addressed by metatheorists. Although some important contributions have been made with the development of the metatriangulation method (Lewis & Grimes, 1999), much more needs to be done to establish formal designs and methods for performing metatheoretical research. Second, metatheorists need to better define and understand what they themselves are about. Performing metatheoretical research cannot be done satisfactorily nor recognised as a valid research without the conscious acknowledgement of its methods and goals.

The foregoing has briefly considered some of the objections to metatheory on empiricist and modernist grounds. Even harsher criticisms of metatheory have been proposed from postmodern scholars and it is to these arguments that we now turn.

THE POSTMODERN CRITIQUE OF METATHEORY IN ORGANISATIONAL STUDIES

Metatheorising has been heavily criticised for several decades by the postmodern movement in social research. The postmodern interpretive reappraisal of modern assumptions about science, culture, identity, history and language has largely had a deconstructive focus. The analytical intent has been to tease apart large-scale conceptual frameworks by exposing their underlying assumptions and unconscious commitments. Consequently, a definitive feature of postmodernism has been its highly critical stance towards metatheorising and that branch of scholarship that develops and investigates abstract theories, overarching frameworks and grand models. In fact, Lyotard famously defines postmodernism as "incredulity towards metanarratives" (1984). While a full treatment of the postmodernity and metanarratives topic is beyond the scope of this book, it is important that key aspects of the postmodern critique of metatheory are acknowledged and that a position on some of postmodernism's main criticisms be outlined.

In his critique of the multiparadigm approach of Burrell and Morgan (1979), Deetz (1996) outlines a number of arguments from the postmodern position that are highly critical of overarching models in organisational studies. These arguments are representative of criticisms raised by other writers of an interpretivist or postmodern persuasion (see, for example, Jones, 2003; Midgley, 2003). Deetz argues that metatheorising: (i) builds totalising accounts that do not appreciate the plurality of scientific and cultural perspectives; (ii) unconsciously assumes the abstract stance of objectivism—the "god-trick"; (iii) excludes marginalised theoretical voices; (iv) neglects local explanations and theories in favour of universal ones; (v) lacks a critical approach to power and the dominance of some research perspective over others; and (vi) undervalues the situational and contextualised nature of knowledge.

Metatheory as Totalising

Metatheory can be characterised as an attempt to totalise the diversity of explanatory accounts into a unified model. This attempt subsumes differences rather than integrates them. This totalising response to the fragmentation of organisational sciences is evidenced in the work of functionalist and modernist theorists (Donaldson, 1997; Pfeffer & Fong, 2005) who seek to develop theories or research paradigms that can unify a field of research. In these instances, integration is regarded as a process of developing one unified account that explains all or most of the empirical events within a certain domain. This, however, is not the goal of pluralistic metatheory building where totalising is not an outcome of the research process. The difference here is one between totalising diverse accounts into a single theoretical formulation and integrating diverse accounts into a pluralistic metatheoretical framework. Some metatheorists stipulate that pluralism is a precondition for developing metatheory (Weinstein & Weinstein, 1991, p. 148):

> Only under the condition of apparently irreducible plurality is the special move of metatheory justified, because that move embraces plurality in order to discover its underlying social and intellectual structure(s).

Defending the usefulness of pursuing integrative research depends largely on a nuanced understanding of what "integration" means. There are, ironically, different approaches even to this aim of developing integrative knowledge (Ritzer et al., 2001). Modernist approaches aim for an "integration" that unifies vying theories into a single middle-range theory that provides a single scientific language and conceptual base. In contrast to this, the metatheoretical approach seeks to accommodate diverse theories within a coherent metatheoretical framework. Such a pluralist approach is both analytical and holistic but not totalising. It is analytical in that it identifies multiple explanatory factors that can provide insights into the details of how, why and when something happens. It is holistic in that it locates those factors within an integrative conceptual system where the focus is on building connections between theories rather than unifying them (the modernist position) or deconstructing them (the postmodernist position). Totalising theories subsume other accounts within a single formulation. This is not the outcome of pluralistic forms of metatheorising. Integrative metatheory building offers a complementary role to the burgeoning diversity of theories and the theory testing research that accompanies that diversity. Like postmodernism, integrative metatheory recognises the validity of the plurality of voices that exists in any domain of inquiry (this is why metatheorists such as Ritzer[2] and Wilber see their work as a form of pluralism). The intent of integrative metatheorising is to include the contributions of different researchers and research schools rather than supplanting them. In the words of Weinstein and Weinstein (1991, p. 141), metatheory "elucidates the structure of difference, not the unity of difference".

Metatheory as "the God-trick"

The "god-trick" and "the view from nowhere" are two of many terms emanating from postmodernist writings that critically refer to the notion of a value-neutral and totalising form of objective science. "The god-trick of seeing everything from nowhere" (Haraway, 1991, p. 188) is a particularly relevant critique to the act of metatheorising because the level of abstraction and the scope of conceptualising is so noticeable. Metatheory might be simplistically regarded as a kind of objectifying idealism where Platonic constructs dominate the process of making sense of social complexity. From this angle metatheories are preconceived as abstractions into whose categories we force the inconclusiveness of everyday events. As such, meta-frameworks represent a kind of pinnacle of scientism, "for it puts one type of human understanding in charge of the universe and what can be said about it" (Nagel, 1986, p. 9).

This criticism has been extremely effective in raising awareness of some of the presumptions that modernist conceptions of science have been prone to, especially with regard to building grand theories. The modernist approach regards science as a means for discovering general truths that are abstract and law-like. One central aim in modernist social science is to search for theoretical monism, that is, "to discover general laws of human society and to put them together systematically in the form of [grand] sociological theories" (Ritzer et al., 2001, p. 116). This kind of modernist science still carries with it the Enlightenment dream of "consilience" (Wilson, 1998), which is a monistic form of integration. Richard Shweder says of this goal of modernistic science (2001, p. 218):

> I would suggest that the idea of consilience—the idea of a seamless coherency and of systematic interconnections across culture, mind, and body; across intellectual disciplines; and across units of analysis neatly arranged into decomposable levels of material organization—is far more fictional than factual.

But this objectifying kind of grand theorising is not the goal of the integrative pluralism that is pursued here. All conceptual positions, even those of a decentring postmodernism, are embodied and situated within time, place and culture. Any metatheory is only yet another perspective with its own assumptions and blind spots. But acknowledging that every overarching framework has inherent assumptions and limitations is not, in itself, an argument against metatheory building. All forms of scientific research, even localised, decentred and grounded ones, carry with them inherent assumptions. The salient issue here is not whether such assumptions exist but whether they are acknowledged through what Karl Weick refers to as "disciplined reflexivity", the balance between self-reflection and a rigorous engagement with the data. This is true for metatheory and for all other forms of formal conceptualising.

The "god-trick" of integrative monism may at times be a "false vision promising transcendence of all limits and responsibility" (Haraway, 1991, p. 189). But this is not true of a metatheorising that is based on an integrative pluralism. The "god-trick" assumes a level of objectivity and value neutrality that is not part of the philosophical baggage of integrative metatheorising. This pluralistic form of metatheorising aims for an integrative polycentricism. Additionally, the presence or absence of method should not be mistaken for particular forms of integration. The use of method does not mean that a metatheorist is seeking to stake out some falsely transcendent position. Rigorous metatheoretical research requires the standard methodological phases of domain specification, concept definition, analysis, system description and evaluation. It is true that this process can be regarded as objectifying in some form. However, it is an objectification that is "stepping back from the fray with a reflective gaze and mapping the field of play" (Weinstein & Weinstein, 1991, p. 142). This is a creative and reflexive form of objectification that expands the possibilities afforded by theoretical pluralism. To paraphrase Jeffrey Alexander (1991, p. 147), metatheory does not assume a view from nowhere, on the contrary it seeks to achieve a self-critical view from "somewhere else", somewhere less entangled in the subjectivities of personal bias and objectivities of empirical debate. And, as with all science, method can assist in finding that new view.

Metatheory as Marginalising

Postmodern epistemologies seek out a decentred position from which to make their contributions. Deetz claims that metatheory attempts to do the opposite by proposing a dominant unified central position that marginalises lesser voices and theories that have been neglected by the functionalist mainstream. Weinstein and Weinstein (1991) argue that this is a mischaracterisation of metatheory. In contrast to the postmodern depiction of metatheory as further marginalising certain theoretical views, Weinstein and Weinstein argue that (1991, pp.143–144):

> metatheory, by taking up a reflexive position toward theory, tends to level the playing field by treating less popular or less successful theoretical alternatives as elements in the field, granting them legitimacy by analysing their structure and presuppositions.

By definition, metatheory considers the broad range of extant theory that a particular domain of research entails. In so doing it brings the views from the periphery into consideration and does so consciously. One of the main findings of the metatheoretical work of Burrell and Morgan was the dominance of functionalist theories in organisational studies. This, in part, led to a greater interest in interpretive theories of organisation. Far from reinforcing dominant theoretical traditions and research methodologies, metatheorising supports a more democratic hearing of the diversity of theoretical voices.

> [Metatheorising] lends legitimacy to the socially (though not necessarily intellectually) weak in their struggle against the strong. . . . Its admission of multiplicity and its commitment to study it enhance theoretical pluralism and favour, though do not insure or presuppose, theoretical egalitarianism. (Weinstein & Weinstein, 1991, p. 144)

The criticism of metatheory as marginalising certain theories is misdirected because any systematic process of reflection across a research domain ultimately raises awareness about the range of theories and their distinctive insights. Again quoting from Weinstein and Weinstein (1991, p. 149):

> [S]imply by reviewing the entire field of theoretical discourse and by relating the ascendancy of theories to power and status structures, metatheory gives a significance to socially weaker alternatives that they would not have otherwise.

This is an inherently appreciative process (Edwards, 2007) not a marginalising one.

Metatheory as Neglecting the Local

Deetz (1996) has been particularly critical of metatheory as focusing on universalist aims and neglecting local realities. The criticism here is that the experiences of people in everyday organisational life become lost in the attempt to find universal patterns and regularities. While it is true that metatheory operates at a deep level of abstraction, it does not follow that such work always results in the dehumanisation of organisational life. Weinstein and Weinstein make a salient point here (1991, p. 144):

> Abstraction always is effected at the sacrifice of complexity, but that sacrifice can lead as well to clarity of insight as to distortion. The question here is not one of whether metatheory should be undertaken at all, but one of distinguishing between good and bad examples of metatheory.

Any scientific process that involves description, analysis or inquiry will always entail some degree of abstraction. It is not abstraction in itself that is problematic for metatheory building, it is the degree to which metatheory is solidly based on its "data" theory. As Ritzer has pointed out, some forms of metatheory are not developed from a solid familiarity with relevant research paradigms and theoretical traditions and, consequently, they lack a groundedness that compounds the level of abstraction problem that all metatheories face. Such speculative metatheories need to be distinguished from metatheory building that is developed from a close analysis of the relevant theoretical materials.

In the methodological literature on theory building, abstraction is regarded as quality that ranges from very low levels as in grounded theory building (Glaser, 2007) to moderate level as in middle-range theory (Hedstrom & Swedberg, 1996) to high levels as in metatheory (Ritzer, 2001). At none of these levels does abstraction necessarily become an unwanted characteristic of theory building. There are certainly specific challenges that abstraction sets up at various points along this spectrum, but this does not mean that any of these regions of research should be curtailed. Metatheorising can be criticised for not grounding its research in its data but then it needs to be understood that its data comes from the world of extant theories and not the world of local empirical events.

Metatheory as Uncritical

Given that metatheory is subject to the dominant theories and research paradigms of the day, postmodernism argues that overarching models simply reproduce the hegemonic relationships that exist in any contemporary social structure. In contrast to this, however, Colomy (1991) argues that one of the most important capacities of metatheory is its "adjudicative capacity", that is, the ability of metatheorists to critically analyse other theory and metatheory. This adjudicative capacity refers particularly to the criticism of dominant paradigms within a particular field of research. Weinstein and Weinstein point out that (1991, p. 144):

> Metatheory . . . critiques a dominant ideology of disciplinary positivism by naming it and giving it a place within the field of metatheoretical objects. In doing so, it deprives disciplinary positivism of the social vantage that it gained by remaining implicit.

Gioia and Pitre (1990) support this argument by pointing out that it is only by developing a "meta-paradigmatic position" that one can bring to consciousness the relationship between dominant and marginal views. Rather than simply reproducing dominant theoretical ideologies, metatheory undermines them through this reflexive raising of consciousness about the relationships between theories. And this is, in fact, why several metatheorists have argued that postmodernism is itself a metatheoretical enterprise (Zhao, 2001). It is interesting to note that, in his critical response to the Burrell and Morgan metatheory, Deetz ends up proposing a competing metatheory based on alternative generalising dimensions for distinguishing between theories. More will be said on the postmodern aspects of metatheorising in Chapter 10.

Metatheory as Decontextualising

Deetz proposes that metatheoretical analyses undervalue the situational and contextualised nature of knowledge and ignore the variety and diversity of real events. The argument goes that, in attempting to generalise beyond the particularities of time and place, metatheory loses sight of the relational, the relative and the situational context and falls back onto essentialist ontologies and foundationalist epistemologies. It is true that metatheory does attempt to find general patterns and connections that go beyond the local conditions of phenomena. However, this does not necessarily mean that it is not concerned with particulars or that it is foundationalist in the narrow sense of trying to establish some ultimate truth. On the contrary, Weinstein and Weinstein argue that because metatheory is founded on the analysis of extant theory, which is in a constant state of flux, metatheory cannot be thought of as foundationalist. Their view is that metatheory does not attempt to prematurely close off the scientific conversation or the pursuit of deeper understanding with assumptions of some final truth. They propose that (1991, p. 140):

> An alternative to closure is a hyper-reflexivity, whereby metatheory claims that no extant foundationalism has achieved general assent from sociologists or has successfully established its truth, and that unless one does either or both the way is open to pursue a wide range of inquiries into the structure(s) of extant theories.

Organisational metatheory does not investigate the particulars of empirical realities as they occur in organisational contexts. What it does is situate and contextualise theories themselves within a conceptual landscape of grounding metaphors, core assumptions and conceptual lenses. In doing this, metatheorising helps to contextualise a research field through its capacity to (Weinstein & Weinstein, 1991, pp. 142–143):

> relativise the pretension of any of the players on that field—that is, to make each of the players aware that there is a context in which they play that outruns adequate description in terms of their own particular theoretical categories.

Far from not recognising the influence of situated social factors, metatheory helps social researchers to contextualise their own work and to relate it to the broad developments that characterise their own research disciplines and theoretical orientations.

Critics of integrative approaches to social theory have argued that such endeavours result in bland overviews that are dissociated from researchers' own locales. Metatheory is characterised as a type of rationalism that is far removed from situational reality and from the pragmatic concerns of organisational life. Such views fail to understand that a situated groundedness in metatheory means being anchored in the detail of theory data *and not* empirical data. Burrell and Morgan (1979), in their seminal book on the multiparadigm approach to organisational analysis, state that it is only through the process of sifting through multiple theoretical perspectives that the researcher can fully appreciate and understand the assumptions inherent in his/her own viewpoints.

> In order to understand different points of view it is important that a theorist be fully aware of the assumptions upon which his own perspective is based. Such an appreciation involves an intellectual journey

which takes him outside the realm of his own familiar domain. It requires that he become aware of the boundaries which define his perspective. It requires that he journey into the unexplored. It requires that he become familiar with paradigms which are not his own. Only then can he look back and appreciate in full measure the precise nature of his starting point. (Burrell & Morgan, 1979, p. ix)

The real value of metatheory building lies in its capacity to link what were previously considered to be unconnected concepts and to situate them in a more integrative theoretical space. Such a process is inherently contextualised because it connects local theorising with a more encompassing network of ideas. This is what Burrell and Morgan did when they looked at the "cross linkages" between rival intellectual traditions. In so doing they developed not only their well-known grid for classifying paradigms of organisational research, but also an analytical tool that could point to new areas of investigation. While their approach has significant limitations, the rich stream of research and intellectual debate that has flowed from their ideas is testament to its value.

INTEGRATIVE METATHEORY AS INCLUDING BOTH THE MODERN AND POSTMODERN

Metatheory has been poorly characterised in both modern and postmodern critiques of overarching approaches to social research. Ritzer (1991a) has suggested that these characterisations are often based on a lack of knowledge about what metatheorising involves. Metatheorists themselves have not articulated their methods and intents clearly and, as a consequence, it is hardly surprising that there continues to be widespread misunderstanding about metatheory, its methods, goals and underlying assumptions among modernist and postmodernist traditions within the social sciences.

> The major problem is that metatheorizing has not, up to this point, been well defined and has therefore been subjected to a range of ill-conceived critiques. . . . The dialogue, such as it is, between metatheoriticians and their critics will be of little utility until critics know what they are attacking and metatheorists have a better sense of what they are defending. (Ritzer, 1990, p. 9)

Perhaps the most unfortunate of all these misunderstandings is that metatheory itself can be regarded as part of the postmodern concern for pluralism, reflexivity, consciousness raising, contextualisation and social criticism in doing social research. As Weinstein and Weinstein put it, metatheory is "a work . . . of a post-modern mind" (1991, p. 148). Consequently, this book's aim of developing a metatheory for organisational transformation can be seen as part of a contemporary, and perhaps even postmodern, approach to integrating the pluralisms of twenty-first-century organisational theory (Küpers & Edwards, 2007). This is an aim that acknowledges and supports pluralism and diversity in theory development while also seeking integrative forms of knowledge. Metatheorising also carries with it a potential for gathering together the contributions of middle-range theories from many different research paradigms. It is now beginning to develop rigorous methods that will provide a formal research base for performing metatheoretical studies. In these developments a postmodern form of metatheorising also recognises the valid goals and methods of a modernist perspective.

In the following chapters the integrative and pluralistic approach of metatheorising will be applied to the particular field of organisational transformation. It is hoped that this will provide further evidence of the immense potential that this type of research has for contemporary social science and perhaps even some inspiration to realise that potential.

4 Stories of Transformation

This is not to say the old modes of knowing are disappearing, but that in line with the shift towards meta-perspectives and many universes, we are developing multiple ways of knowing that include all of what we have created to date. (Nicoll, 1984, p. 12)

THE STATE OF PLAY

This chapter presents a review of the scientific literature on organisational transformation and the major metatheoretical resources used for developing our integrative framework. Each of these literatures tells a story of transformation that will be important for the metatheory building chapters that follow. The historical review of the development of organisational transformation gives an idea of the changing nature of this field of research and sets a social context for the range of theories to be analysed. The review of our metatheoretical resources focuses on Wilber's AQAL framework and Torbert's DAI and provides a summary of the core metatheoretical lenses that these approaches adopt. It is important that metatheory building be contextualised within a vigorous tradition of research and, consequently, that the frameworks developed here are seen building on innovative models such as AQAL metatheory and respected bodies of organisational research such as DAI.

AN HISTORICAL REVIEW OF ORGANISATIONAL TRANSFORMATION

All approaches to the study of society are located in a frame of reference of one kind or another. Different theories tend to reflect different perspectives, issues and problems worthy of study, and are generally based upon a whole set of assumptions which reflect a particular view of the nature of the subject under investigation. (Burrell & Morgan, 1979, p. 10)

In this quote, Burrell and Morgan draw attention to the interpretative influence of a particular "frame of reference" on theory. Such frames are often historical in that history, by its nature, churns out ever-changing sets of social "perspectives, issues and problems". The history of research into organisational transformation has been subject to the vagaries of social conditions and in the following sections I will describe how changing social conditions have been reflected in trends in transformation theory. But this is not the full story. There have also been a number of discernable connective threads that run through the research on radical change.

Early Uses of the Term "Organisational Transformation"

The term "organisational transformation" first appeared in the 1950s when there was a growing interest in sociological research on post-war changes to organisations. Initially, organisational transformation was used to describe the changes that were taking place as organisations moved from having a proprietary or membership-based structure to a professional management structure. Messinger (1955) used the term in reference to the process by which organisations "adapt to their changed circumstances" through "the transformation of leadership activities". Under the scientific management theory approach that was dominant at the time, change came about through directive planning. In line with this view, Messinger proposed that, when circumstances demand it, organisations had to dramatically change their *modus operandi* to survive and that when that adaptive process is completed, "the organizational character will stand transformed".

In a similar vein, Michels (1959) postulated that many community organisations are transformed through the professionalisation of their management. In these early studies organisational transformation was seen as a sociological phenomenon of change in social relations between significant groups such as members, professional groups and officers (Jenkins, 1977). Transformation referred to the changes in organisational goals that resulted from the growth in professionalism. The stages of "goal transformation" were, in effect, aligned with the movement from membership-based organisational forms to professional and bureaucratic forms of organising (Wood, 1975).

One of the first organisational theorists to refer to large-scale organisational change as transformational was Gerald Skibbins (1974). He described the process as one of radical change. Like many other writers on social change, Skibbins employed ideas from evolutionary theory to develop insights into how human organisations might develop their potential for change. Some of the elements that informed the early use of the language of transformation can still be seen in contemporary usage. The role of the organisational environment, the qualitative nature of transformative change and the critical role of the leader are all still focal points for contemporary transformational approaches. Although such ideas were in use from the 1950s and 1960s, it took several decades before a community of scholars and their distinctive set of theories and methods began to coalesce and be identified as a new field of organisational study (Adams, 1984).

Organisational Transformation and Organisational Development

Many of the formative concepts that later gave rise to the organisational transformation field first emerged during the late 1960s. It was during that decade of great social upheaval that ideas of radical social change were openly discussed within the community of organisational change researchers and practitioners. At that time, many social theorists were looking for bolder models for explaining the changes that were impacting on organisational life throughout the developed world (Fletcher, 1990). The major school of change during those years was the organisational development approach.

Organisational development (OD) included all those approaches that attempted to increase organisation effectiveness and efficiency through planned interventions and engagements with employees and teams. OD came out of a behavioural sciences approach to knowledge in that it was rational, focused on incremental change and largely drew on organisational and group psychology for its theoretical framework (Beckhard, 1969). There was also a personal development side to the OD approach that saw human resource development as an area of core concern for large organisations. The OD tradition saw change as an opportunity for "consensus, collaboration and participation" albeit within a planned and evolutionary approach to change (Ashburner, Ferlie & FitzGerald, 1996, p. 2). The approach included organisational members as participants in the process of gradually improving the culture, effectiveness and efficiency of the organisation. Chapman (2002) points out that when organisational development emerged in the 1960s it was primarily concerned with "individual and group level interventions to support gradual or incremental organisational change" (p. 16).

Other researchers note the localised impact that such change techniques had within an organisation (Glassman & Cummings, 1991). OD targeted the "unit level of organisation" rather than the organisation as a whole (Ashburner et al., 1996, p. 2). The focus of OD theory and practice was not at the inter-organisational or industry level and the intent was not to move the strategic position of organisations. In focusing on the human side of change and on the importance of quality of work life and team development, OD did not fit well with the more dramatic industry-wide upheavals that characterised forms of large-scale organisational change in the late 1980s. Consequently, for many of those working in the area of organisational change, the OD framework lacked the conceptual and practical capacity to cope with the significant demands on organisations facing radically changing environments. While organisational development models eventually went on to "encompass large-scale interventions including strategic change", their theoretical frameworks continued to "largely reflect traditional assumptions and approaches" (Chapman, 2002, p. 16). The organisational development approach has continued to be an important contributor to organisational change theory up to the present time (Golembiewski, 2004).

In the late 1970s and early 1980s ongoing cultural changes and the increasingly hectic pace of growth in national and international economies stimulated a need for theories that took a more radical stance towards organisational studies. For many organisational theorists of that time the incrementalist orientation of organisational development was not sufficient, in either its theoretical scope or practical application, to respond to the changes that were sweeping through society:

> While incrementalism has been well suited to environments producing stability in growth, increasingly since the mid to late 1970's and into the 1980's these conditions have disappeared in whole sectors of western industrial economies. The age of discontinuity, as Drucker (1969) called it, created conditions in the 1970's and 1980's which were often antithetical to an incrementalist approach. (Dunphy & Stace, 1988, p. 318)

The stable conditions that saw the rise of OD interventions were overtaken by more fundamental changes in financial, economic and social environments. Senior executive and leadership levels within organisations were under pressure to respond to the rapidly changing trade and regulatory environments, technological innovations and market-driven demands. The radical overhauling of organisations' operations through restructuring, downsizing and financial rationalisation also fed into this period of dramatic change. As a result change theorists began producing a "growing literature on large-scale organisational transitions" which involved "total structures, management processes and corporate cultures" (Dunphy & Stace, 1988, p. 319). Referring to the debate within the organisational change literature of the early 1980s, Ashburner, Ferlie and FitzGerald (1996, p. 2), note that:

> The discussion often centred on distinctions between incremental and strategic change, highlighting the fact that strategic change involved changes to the purpose of the organisation and/or several major systems, such as the technology, or core skills of employees. This clarification underlined the cosmetic nature of changes to the structure of earlier public-sector organisations, since such changes had rarely involved any alteration to the core nature or even the form of delivery of services. Extending the analysis further, writers began exploring the concept of transformatory change.

These factors, the search for more encompassing theoretical models, the accelerating social and cultural turmoil of the times and the rise of more radical forms of organisational restructuring and planning provided the conditions for the emergence of a new approach to large-scale organisational change.

The Birth of a Network

The search for a more comprehensive approach continued through the 1970s and resulted in what came to be called "organisational transformation".

Organisational transformation emerged from the organisational development field both as a response to its perceived limitations as well as the need for a more creative approach to the applied investigation of change in organisational settings (Fletcher, 1990). Organisational transformation signalled its formal beginnings in two ways. One was the publication of several books and articles overtly concerned with theories and descriptions of transformational change in organisations (Adams, 1984; Fry & Jon, 1976; Torbert, 1976). The second was the establishment of a community of practitioners through the founding of the Organisational Transformation Network (OTN) for researchers, theorists and practitioners who were working in this emerging area (Fletcher, 1990). From the very beginning of its formal study, organisational transformation was seen to be different to other types of change in that it was about a radical and comprehensive change in an organisation's identity and behaviour. During the 1980s publications on covered a great diversity of topics and used many different methodologies to research those topics (Levy & Merry, 1986). Another defining feature in the early phase of the movement was the emphasis placed on the practical side of implementing change. Many of the first contributors to publications on the topic were practitioners and consultants who were searching for a more comprehensive understanding of how organisations could meet the challenges of radical societal change (Adams, 1984).

While both theory and practice were seen as essential and complementary elements, this new field of organisational transformation was far from being a uniform discipline with well-established theoretical principles. The multiplicity of ideas and theoretical streams that fed into the newly emerging study of organisational transformation meant that it would always be a diverse discipline which embraced a great many concepts and methods. There were, however, a number of themes that characterised this new field of research and theory development.

A common feature of the work of both transformational theorists and practitioners is an emphasis on "spirituality" and "human potential" as driving forces for radical change (Banner, 1987, p. 44). Dehler and Welsh note that (1994, p. 18): "[Organisational transformation] transcends the rationality associated with the traditions of scientific management" and that it includes the intangibles of change such as "energy and flow". Transformational change frameworks at that time saw meaning, emotion, values and spirituality as central to the workplace and as complementary to objective change factors, such as behaviours, systems, technologies, structures and goals, which are more frequently associated with the study of organisational life. Some of the earliest transformation theorists and practitioners, e.g. Bill Torbert, John Adams, Harrison Owen and Jean Bartunek, came to the field through their interest in human potential and spirituality. In her analysis of the motivations of prominent leaders in transformational studies, Fletcher remarks (1990, pp. 65–66):

The idea that spirituality can figure to make an organization better seemed important for several of the participants. Many of them came from some sort of spiritual or highly conscious background which led them to an interest in Organizational Transformation.

Another commonly held assumption among the new transformational theorists was that of the evolutionary nature of change. Ideas from the biological sciences mixed with systems theory concepts to produce models of "dissipative structures", "episodic evolution", "energy exchange systems" and "punctuated development". Instances of biological transformation, as in the metamorphosis of a caterpillar into a butterfly or a tadpole into a frog, were used as metaphoric descriptors for organisational transformations (Fletcher, 1990).

Transformation theory researchers Amir Levy and Uri Merry (1986) identified three elements that characterised the emergence of organisational transformation as a separate approach to change. These were an emphasis on "spirituality and energy"; a concern for "organisational purpose, mission, and vision"; and thirdly, a focus on the cultural aspects of organisations such as values and belief systems, communication mythology and worldviews. All three emphases were set within an idea of paradigmatic, discontinuous or qualitative change. As Levy and Merry point out, these shared elements of interest were all centred on the "intangible" aspects of organisational life and, consequently, were not readily accessible to observation and objective research. This emphasis in organisational transformation theory and research on the subjective, cultural aspects of organisations was to change in later years.

During the 1970s and early 1980s parallels were being drawn between particular forms of organisational evolution and those of human development. In making these connections, organisational theorists regarded stage-based models of human development as something more than simple metaphors for organisational growth. The work of Bill Torbert is particularly noteworthy in this regard. As early as 1976, in his book *Creating a Community of Inquiry: Conflict, Collaboration, Transformation*, Torbert described organisational development as a model of "transcending stages of organisation". Essentially, Torbert performed metatheoretical research by drawing on a range of organisational and human development theorists to propose maps of qualitative stages of transformation for both individuals and organisations. On this connection between organisational transformation and the stages of human growth potentials Owen remarks (1987, p. 6):

Although the results of transformation appear with the emergence of new organizational forms, the essence of transformation lies in the odyssey or passage of the human Spirit as it moves from one formal manifestation to another. The word "transformation" says as much, for the central idea is the movement across or through forms.

Just as there are many different orders of individual development, so there are many different forms of organisational emergence. These various stages correspond to different ways of perceiving, behaving and defining identity. In transformative change, this is not a singular process but can happen repeatedly as new forms of identity emerge over an organisation's lifespan.

By the end of the 1980s organisational transformation was beginning to have a significant impact on theory and practice related to organisational change and development. However, some major global events were to change this. Through the 1990s, organisational transformation models, along with all models of change, were influenced by the fall of European communism and the opening of Eastern Europe to the political and economic systems of the West. These transition economies and their constituent organisations had to undergo radical, transformative change to accommodate the new realities of world markets and free enterprise (Newman, 1998a). There were also dramatic changes in the economic and social environments of developed nations. The excesses of the 1980s and the subsequent economic downturn that occurred in the early 1990s led to a greater appreciation for organisational efficiency and forms of productivity. As well as this, the globalisation of trade, financial markets and technological changes, especially the Internet, communications and information technology, were affecting all aspects of commercial and community life. Planning for transformational change was quickly becoming a standard part of the organisational landscape. Writing in 1997, Nutt and Backoff summarised attitudes at that time, "Transformation has become a key survival tool for organizations coping with the turbulence that characterizes today's environment" (1997a, p. 490).

The Many Paths of Transformation

In response to the socio-economic turbulence of the 1990s, transformational change theorists focused more on the behavioural aspects of organisational change in areas such as effectiveness (Mea, Sims & Veres, 2000), IT and communications systems (Allen, 2003), management performance (Newman, 1998b), structural re-engineering (Coulson-Thomas, 1993) and strategic leadership (Nutt & Backoff, 1997a). In the context of these behavioural and external aspects of change, theorists began to see transformation as a planning tool for improving the competitive position of the organisation.

At this point, a divergence appears between two major streams of research on organisational transformation and their respective understandings of that term. One stream continued along with the understanding that organisational transformation was about holistic growth and a radical change in the relationship between organisations, their stakeholders and the community. Another position was adopted by researchers who saw transformation as a strategic approach to organisational effectiveness. This stream focused on the management and economics of transformation. In their book *Breaking the Code of Change*, Beer and Nohria (2000) refer to these two streams as "Theory O" for organisational transformation and "Theory E" for economic transformation. These two very different understandings of transformation led to a subsequent increase in the number and diversity of theories of organisational transformation. The notion of organisational transformation diverged into different streams that referred not only to the qualitative change in the interior, cultural aspects of organisational life, but also to the radical change in exterior, behavioural and systems aspects.

The transformational literature subsequently broadened in scope to cover such topics as information management, organisational behaviour, strategic management and organisational effectiveness. Other theorists and researchers continued with the more traditional focus of transformational studies on the intangible, interior aspects of organisational life, i.e. its culture, values, spirituality and developmental issues. By the late 1990s, organisational transformation covered topics as disparate as the "spirituality of leadership" (Eggert, 1998), the levels of development of executives and organisational collectives (Rooke & Torbert, 1998), workforce diversity (Dreachslin, 1999b), motivation theory (Green & Butkus, 1999), worker upskilling (Leigh & Gifford, 1999) and organisational learning (Waldersee, 1996).

The increasing scope and diversity of transformational models, assumptions, research foci and theoretical frameworks meant that an identifiable school of organisational transformation was no longer practicable. In recent years, theorists and practitioners have tended to specialise in particular aspects of organisational change topics rather than under the organisational transformation banner. While the term "organisational transformation" no longer refers to any single school of organisational change or community of practitioners, it continues to be commonly used as a general label for systemic change. Seen within this context of a plurality of approaches and perspectives, organisational transformation continues to grow as a field for theory development and applied research rather than as a community of like-minded researchers and practitioners seeking a new vision of change.

Historical Phases in the Study of Organisational Transformation

Table 4.1 presents a summary of the phases that have marked the emergence of organisational transformation (OT) as an identifiable field. The six phases presented describe: (i) a preformative period (1960s and 1970s) where change theorists gradually became dissatisfied with mainstream theories of change; (ii) a birthing phase (early 1980s) where OT first emerged as an identifiable set of ideas and methods; (iii) a growth and identity phase (mid-1980s to early 1990s) where OT became a significant contributor to understandings and explanations of change and became identified as a particular approach to change research; (iv) a diversification phase (mid-1990s to present) where OT research moved into a variety of applied contexts and appeared under such guises as "strategic management"; (v) an integration phase (early 2000s to present) where attempts have been made to connect multiple paradigms and concepts; and finally (vi) a phase of renewed interest in OT spurred on by the global financial crisis and other global challenges.

The present study comes under the integration or metatheory building phase in transformational studies and also hopes to contribute to an integrative response to the global challenges that will face organisations in the next decades. The diversity of understandings of transformation has led to a fragmentation in organisational change theories and there is a need for metatheory building that can draw connections between these diverse conceptual elements. It remains to be seen whether this diversification overtakes the field's capacity to retain its own identity under the organisational transformation label or, alternatively, whether it moves into a phase of decline. It is likely, however, that transformation theories and research will continue to play an important role in the study of organisational change irrespective of the descriptive label. The radical changes we currently see in natural, social and commercial environments will continue into the foreseeable future. As a result, there will be an ongoing need for organisations to respond to those imperatives.

Although there are no distinct boundaries around any of these phases, it is reasonable to assume that the many paradigms and theories of transformation they cover will reflect the larger social dynamics of the day. Different social climates have an impact on the expression and structure of theory. Accordingly, theoretical concepts and constructs find their niche within compatible research environments. As well as this, theories within existing research paradigms are adapted and reformulated to explore emerging issues. In developing metatheories that range over diverse terrains like transformational change, which have complex research histories, it is crucial that other metatheoretical resources are called on to aid that process of review and analysis. In the following section two overarching models that are highly relevant to this field will be briefly presented.

TWO METATHEORETICAL RESOURCES

Wilber's AQAL framework (Wilber, 1999c, 2000b) and Torbert's DAI are two of the most significant metatheoretical developments that have emerged in the last 30 years. Torbert's work has been formative to the emergence of organisational transformation as a field of research. Though drawn from studies in psychology and spiritual transformation, Wilber's ideas have also been applied to organisational change and have significant relevance to organisation theory as a whole. Both contribute to the metatheory building tasks undertaken in later chapters through providing a "metaperspective" (Gioia & Pitre, 1990, p. 559). Gioia and Pitre make the point that it is not

Table 4.1 Historical Phases in the Study of Organisational Transformation

Period	Historical Phase in the development of OT	Organisational Transformation Focus	Prevailing socio-economic factors
1960s & 1970s	Preformative phase: dissatisfaction with mainstream views of change	OD is the dominant paradigm for investigating change	Widespread socio-cultural and economic change
early 1980s	Birthing phase: initial OT publications, founding of the OT network	Naming and defining OT, what is unique about the OT approach, differentiation from OD	Growing interest in organisational response to radical societal change
mid-1980s to early 1990s	Growth & Identity phase: growth in OT publications, OT is recognised as an identifiable field of research	Research focus on applied issues and particular methods of transformation are developed, e.g. "Open Space" technology	Booming economies, growing globalisation and corporate excess
mid-1990s to present	Diversification phase: OT diversifies into multiple streams of theory and research	OT focuses on strategic transformation, e.g. structure, systems & technology	Transition economies in Eastern Europe, extended period of global growth
early 2000s to present	Integration phase: sporadic attempts at finding linkages between OT models	Multilevel integration of both objective and subjective aspects of transformation	Globalisation continues, social criticism of corporate behaviour, CSR & TBL
2008–	Global phase (?): renewed interest in radical organisational transformation	The interiors of transformation, e.g. values, ethics, the psychology of change	Global financial crisis, economic recession and depression (?)

possible "to understand, to accommodate, and . . . to link" multiple views without developing or adopting some "viewpoint beyond that of an individual paradigm" (1990, p. 596). Some metalevel position must be taken. It is worth quoting their views on this issue at some length:

> Given that a uniquely correct perspective cannot exist, and given the multiplicity of organisational realities, a pluralistic, multiple-perspective view becomes a necessity for achieving any sort of comprehensive view. Such a multiple-perspectives view requires that organisational theorists consider the set of theories relevant to a given topic from some viewpoint beyond that of an individual paradigm. Comparing and contrasting diverse paradigms is difficult when confined within one paradigm; looking from a meta-level, however, can allow simultaneous consideration of multiple paradigms in their transition zones. Elevating to a metaperspective is qualitatively different from cross-boundary considerations. From this view, the intent is to understand, to accommodate, and, if possible, to link views generated from different starting assumptions. (Gioia & Pitre, 1990, pp. 595–596)

Wilber's AQAL and Torbert's DAI are helpful resources in realising a "metaperspective", a "viewpoint beyond that of an individual paradigm" from which the work of reviewing and analysing unit-level theories and paradigms can be guided. As discussed in Chapter 2, there is no sleight of hand or "god-trick" involved in adopting this posture. Like all points of view, metaperspectives involve their own assumptions, limitations and blind spots. But this is no reason to abandon the possibility for metatheorising; rather, it is reason to be more conscious and more transparent about the types of metaperspectives that we do adopt.

The development of both AQAL and DAI can be considered within the context of attempts to develop large-scale conceptual frameworks for understanding complex social phenomena. This metatheory building quest is an ancient one and its modern varieties can be traced back at least to the emergence of grand theories of macrohistory during the renaissance (Galtung & Inayatullah, 1997). In the nineteenth and twentieth centuries this quest culminated in large-scale social theory building of the kind seen in Marxist theory, Parsons's structural functionalism, von Bertalanffy's general systems theory, Wiener's cybernetics and, more recently, Gidden's structuration theory and Wilber's integral theory. This modern attempt at large-scale theory building has come partly in response to the plethora of psychological and sociological theories that have flourished during the twentieth century. It is within this context of finding connections between diverse theories of social reality that Torbert's and Wilber's work is usefully discussed.[1] In the following pages I will present a metatheoretical sketch of both these extensive bodies of ideas. The intention here is not to provide a full outline but rather to list some of the fundamental metatheoretical lenses that comprise the AQAL and DAI systems.

Wilber's AQAL Metatheory (Integral Theory)

Wilber is one thinker among many who has used the term "integral" to describe the outcomes of his big-picture conceptualisations (for other integral approaches see, Aurobindo, 1993; Gebser, 1985; Laszlo, 2003; Sorokin, 1958). The more technical term that Wilber applies to his metatheoretical framework is AQAL. AQAL is an overarching metatheory of psychosocial development that has been applied across many disciplines, including those within the environmental, psychological, social and organisational sciences. It is a large-scale conceptual system for integrating many different paradigms, theories and traditions of knowledge. AQAL has developed progressively over the last three decades, and Wilber has described the growth of his ideas as distinct phases of metatheoretical elaboration.

Phase-I saw the initial attempt by Wilber to propose a comprehensive model of human development, which brought together psychotherapeutic as well as religious models of human growth potentials. Drawing on many scientific theories and cultural sources, this early model mapped out a comprehensive set of stages of transformations for the human lifespan. This was his "spectrum of development" model and, though altered in significant ways, the spectrum metaphor has remained an important metatheoretical lens in AQAL. However, Wilber found that there were significant problems with the spectrum model. Its illustration of human development relied predominantly on Freudian and Jungian concepts. Wilber subsequently became aware of the work of developmental theorists such as Jean Piaget, Jane Loevinger, Lawrence Kohlberg, Michael Commons and Patricia Arlin, and he significantly modified his spectrum model to accommodate these more cognitive approaches. Wilber sees this incorporation of more mainstream developmental models as the hallmark of phase-II of his theorising. Where phase-I came from a "romantic" philosophical stance, phase-II was "more specifically evolutionary or developmental" (Wilber, 1999b, p. 1). However, this developmental model lacked sensitivity to the multidimensional nature of human growth and phase-III is characterised by Wilber's attempt to account for the individuality of human development, that is, to account for the idiosyncratic nature of individual differences and the variety of developmental pathways that exist for each social entity.

Phase-IV begins what might properly be considered as integral theory. This phase saw the detailed exposition of the AQAL framework. Development was now seen from both individual and collective theoretical orientations as well as from subjective and objective disciplines of inquiry. The current state of Wilber's theorising, phase-V, has seen a reconsideration of the core philosophical foundations of AQAL and is sometimes called his post-metaphysical phase (Reynolds, 2006). Wilber is now focusing on the major forms of research methodologies and their various perspectival orientations towards forms of scientific inquiry. He calls his approach "Integral Methodological Pluralism" (IMP) (Wilber, 2006). IMP is a meta-methodology that provides an overview of research methods. It is based on three principles of research—non-exclusion, enfoldment/unfoldment and enactment. The principle of non-exclusion is the acknowledgement that truth is not the province of any one scientific or cultural approach to knowledge acquisition and that valid insights come from a plurality of research and inquiry perspectives. The second principle, enfoldment/unfoldment, refers to the patterns that emerge over time when multiple truths and perspectives are considered from a metatheoretical perspective. This principle refers to the holistic and developmental nature of knowledge and methods. Wilber's third principle, the enactment principle, is about the connection between methods and data and how the types of methods we employ are influential in disclosing the types of data we find.

A useful way of seeing the progression of Wilber's theoretical "phases" is as an extended process of metatheory building. The ongoing expansion of AQAL is characterised by the regular addition of new metatheoretical lenses. Accordingly, we can say that phase-I developed the lens of deep structure development (a "romantic" spectrum of human potentials) and focused that lens on the levels of human potentiality. Phase-II saw the accommodation of the developmental lens (a developmental spectrum of levels/waves). The model expanded to include not only depth psychology and Eastern models but also Western scientific models of human development. Phase-III added the lens of multidimensionality (multimodal development of lines/streams and types), and phase-IV formally added the lenses of interior–exterior and individual–collective (the quadrants). These lenses greatly increased the sophistication of the model for explaining social complexity from both micro- and macrolevels of analysis. The current integral theory framework, phase-V, incorporates the perspectival lens (first, second, third person) into the set of explanatory tools and highlights the importance of researchers' methodological orientation towards inquiry. Phase-V also increasingly uses the states (of consciousness) lens in its analysis of development. All this results in the current AQAL framework where:

> AQAL is short for "all quadrants, all levels"—which itself is short for "all quadrants, all levels, all lines, all states, all types," which are simply five of the most basic elements that need to be included in any truly integral or comprehensive approach. (Wilber, 2005c, para. 101)

Each of the five main AQAL elements can be regarded as conceptual systems which are, in turn, made up of a number of subsystems. The qualifier "all" that prefixes the five basic elements refers to the need to include all of these subsystems when attempting a comprehensive view of some phenomenon. For example, when including developmental levels in an analysis of social transformation it is not adequate to include only some levels while leaving out others. Consequently, "all" levels need to be included for an analysis to be integral. A brief description of each of the five AQAL elements follows.

The quadrants are the central metatheoretical framework of AQAL. Integral approaches maintain that any psychosocial phenomenon requires that at least two fundamental dimensions of existence be taken into consideration—the interior–exterior dimension and the individual–collective dimension. Interior–exterior refers to the relationship between the intangible world of subjective experience and the tangible world of objective behaviour. For example, in the case of personal identity, the interior pole of this dimension is about the private world of subjective thoughts, feelings, intentions and intuitions and the exterior pole covers the public world of objective activity, observable behaviour and tangible structures. The individual–collective dimension concerns the relationship between the personal and the social. This dimension refers to the micro–macro nature of social reality. The interaction of these two dimensions produces a grid of four cells known as the four quadrants. Cacioppe and Edwards (2005a, p. 232) describe the four quadrants as follows:

> These dimensions interact to give the four domains or quadrants of consciousness (individual interiority), behaviour (individual exteriority), culture (collective interiority) and social systems (collective exteriority).

The quadrants map out the developmental domains through which all psychosocial entities change and develop. These "four quadrants of intentional, behavioral, social, and cultural unfolding" (Wilber, 1999b, p. 1) provide a minimum set of categories for an integral explanation of psychosocial development. The quadrants are often used as a foundation for applying the other elements of the AQAL framework.

The spectrum of developmental levels is another of the five AQAL elements. This lens sees change as radically transformative. The developmental lens provides a comprehensive template for considering the stages of personal and collective development. However, this developmental approach is not a sequential model of progress. Wilber's view is that development "is not a linear ladder but a fluid and flowing affair, with spirals, swirls, streams, and waves" (2000a, p. 5). Development is a mixture of idiosyncratic change complemented by deep patterns of structural regularity. This regularity shows up in general stages that unfold for both the individual and the collective in many different spheres of evolution and development. The multidimensional complexity of psychosocial development is acknowledged in the third element of AQAL—developmental lines.

Developmental lines (also called streams) are the various, "relatively independent" psychological and sociological modalities that researchers have identified as core dimensions of growth in individuals and collectives. These multiple modalities can be regarded as developing semi-independently through the various structural stages of growth. Wilber has suggested that developmental streams in the field of individual human growth include cognition, morality, affect, motivation/needs, sexuality, ego-identity, mathematical and linguistic competence, socio-emotional capacities, worldviews, values and spirituality (Wilber, 1999c, p. 460). Wilber has also speculated on the various modalities of development that might apply to groups, organisations and larger collectives. Referring to these streams of social development, Wilber says that they "can tentatively be called the various streams or lines of a societal [entity]" (Wilber, 2003c, para. 482). These might include, for example, the lines of education, leadership, politics, religion, art, economics, law, modes of entertainment, communication, medicine, technology and engineering. All of these areas of social activity are subject to developmental growth in that they can be regarded as moving through regular patterns of systematic change. The streams lens adds analytical sophistication to the AQAL approach in that it recognises the uneven and multimodal nature of development in any social entity:

> The modular streams in a society (whether paramorphic or isomorphic) can, as with all streams, develop in a relatively uneven manner, so that a society can be highly developed in some capacities, medium in others, and low in still others. (Wilber, 2003a, para. 483)

This concept has important implications for an integral approach to organisational health. While some variation in capacities is understood to be part of normative development, a balanced approach to growth would expect development to be regular across a number of key developmental lines. Elsewhere I have made the point, "As with individuals and teams, the healthy organisation will develop in a balanced way across a number of key lines" (Edwards, 2005, p. 282). For example, an organisation whose ethical line was severely out of step with its financial systems would evidence considerable problems across many important facets of its operations and culture.

When used together, the quadrants, levels and lines elements of AQAL provide a powerful tool for analysing the multidimensional nature of individual and collective development. Transformative growth is not reduced to a progressive, hard-stage model of linear or sequential growth. The quadrants framework shows that individual development and organisational development are closely intertwined and, in fact, arise together. The interior and exterior of the individual and the collective are four perspectives on each social event and so a complete understanding of how development proceeds must start with at least these four views for any particular developmental line.

One of the most distinctive characteristics of AQAL is its emphasis on states of consciousness. Rather than regarding the world of subjective experience as epiphenomenal, or at least peripheral, to the main interest of social research, integral approaches place an emphasis on topics such as values, consciousness and personal worldviews. Consequently, states of consciousness are included within the AQAL framework as yet another tool for explaining the complexity of human experience. Wilber regards the phenomenon of states as one factor among many others that can be used to understand the nature of individual experience:

> Everybody experiences various sorts of states of consciousness, and these states often provide profound motivation, meaning, and drives, in both yourself and others. In any particular situation, states of consciousness may not be a very important factor, or they may be the determining factor, but no integral approach can afford to ignore them. (Wilber, 2005c, p. 15)

The fifth element in AQAL is known as types. Types refer to the categorical elements of any typology where those elements "can be present at virtually any stage or state" (Wilber, 2005c, p. 9). Where developmental and evolutionary explanations might be said to take a vertical orientation towards change, type explanations can be represented by horizontal orientations.

Other Explanatory Elements in AQAL Metatheory

Apart from these five explicitly identified elements of the AQAL framework, there are other metatheoretical components which, while also contributing to the explanatory power of integral theory, are not formally included within the AQAL framework.[2] All of these additional elements are described in detail in Wilber's writings and they are frequently used by him and other integral researchers (see, for example, Brown, 2006; Esbjörn-Hargens, 2005a). These factors include:

- Perspectives: Perspectives are "modes of inquiry" that "disclose, highlight, bring forth, illumine, and express the various types of phenomena enacted by-and-from various perspectives" (Wilber, 2003c, para. 28). Perspectives are taken up as either first-, second- or third-person orientations when inquiring into some phenomenon.
- Agency-communion: AQAL proposes that every social entity is motivated by the drive for agency or self-expression and communion or self-adaptation. Agency is the capacity that every person or group has for expressive identity and autonomy, whereas communion is the capacity for receptive identity and relationality.
- Growth-integration (or transcendence-immanence): The AQAL concept of transformation through various levels or developmental structures necessarily entails a notion of transcendental growth and integrative immanence. Growth "beyond" is balanced by an integration of what has gone "before".
- Transformation-translation: This is the difference between radical and incremental forms of change. Wilber describes this distinction as

follows: "The movement of surface [features] we call *translation*; the movement of deep [features] we call *transformation*" (1980, p. 47).

- Relational exchange: This refers to the various systems of mutual exchange that occur between developmental structures and their environments. Wilber describes this lens as follows (1999a, p. 16):

> [The] individual and cultural are inextricably bound by patterns of relational exchange. . . . At every level, in other words, the subjective world is embedded in vast networks of intersubjective or cultural relationships, and vice versa.

- Transition process: The transition process describes the phases of change that occur between levels of development. The basic phases involve the movement from (i) a status quo state, (ii) to one of increasing chaos, (iii) to the emergence of a new identity structure and, finally, (iv) to the integration of old capacities within the new identity (Wilber, 1980).

Torbert's Developmental Action Inquiry

The other major metatheoretical resource that is used here to guide the metatheory building process is Developmental Action Inquiry (DAI). Bill Torbert and his colleagues (Fisher et al., 2003; Torbert, 1999; Torbert et al., 2004) have developed DAI as a comprehensive metatheoretical system/ practice for understanding change and activity in organisational settings. DAI is both a metatheory of organisational transformation as well as a method for implementing transformative practices within personal and collective spheres of organisational life. As an inquiry practice, DAI is a (Torbert et al., 2004, p. 1):

> way of simultaneously conducting action and inquiry as a disciplined leadership practice that increases the wider effectiveness of our actions. Such action helps individuals, teams, organizations become more capable of self-transformation and thus more creative, more aware, more just and more sustainable.

Because of its active focus on inquiry, DAI is presented less as a metatheory and more as a process for transforming self and society. However, DAI is also metatheoretical in that Torbert and his colleagues have systematically reviewed and analysed many different management, organisation and developmental theories and presented their findings in terms of large-scale conceptual frameworks.

DAI is developmental because it sees individuals as moving through various stages of growth where each stage is characterised by different interpretive frames, worldviews or action logics. These frames are expressed socio-culturally and hence are also characteristic of organisational development. DAI has been extensively applied to the study of leadership and extensive research has been carried out on the types of action logic that are consistently used by leaders in organisational settings. For example, Rooke and Torbert (2005, p. 69) have found, "Different leaders exhibit different kinds of action logic . . . when their power or safety is challenged". With the succession of action logics "one's world grows larger and more complicated at each succeeding frame" (Fisher et al., 2003, p. 42). DAI proposes that these logics or stages unfold in a consistent pattern. While this unfolding is not a linear process and individuals and organisations can develop along irregular and idiosyncratic paths, development always proceeds from formative stages to more complex and integrative structures. DAI outlines nine stages of personal development. The first two stages (Impulsive and Opportunist) are identified with pre-conventional growth, the middle three (Diplomat, Expert and Achiever) with conventional growth and the final four (Individualist, Strategist, Magician and Ironist) with postconventional development.

1. Impulsive: immediate wants govern behaviour and the expression of self
2. Opportunist: self-interests govern behaviour, self-protection and impulsivity, dominant task is to gain power
3. Diplomat: acceptance and belonging, socially expected behaviour
4. Expert: skill-governed behaviour, efficiency and improvement, rationality as a way of gaining certainty
5. Achiever: results focused, others matter when they contribute to success, focusses on translational management rather than transformation leadership
6. Individualist: process oriented, professionalism, personal standards matter in making decisions about organisational goals
7. Strategist: process and goal oriented, systems view, development over time is seen as essential in achieving goals
8. Magician: interplay of awareness, thought and action, transforming self and others and society
9. Ironist: inter-systemic development, aware of paradox as potential

DAI sees the action logics of individual transformation also expressed in the collective spheres. The micro, meso and macro expressions of transformation are regarded as analogous patterns. In describing the core similarities between both individual and collective transformation, Torbert and his colleagues (2004, p. 124) say, "As with individual persons, a given action logic [developmental stage] may characterise a given meeting or project, or a whole organisation over many years."

The collective forms of the stages of transformation are derived from both the cumulative developmental history of the organisation and the action logics of organisational leaders. The stages of organisational development correspond with individual stages in the following way:

1. Conception: initial stage of conceptualisation and discussion
2. Investment: financial, social and emotional investments
3. Incorporation: the production of valued goods and services
4. Experiments: alternative strategies tested to improve efficiency
5. Systemic Productivity: single structure/strategy institutionalised
6. Social Network: portfolio of distinctive organisational alliances
7. Collaborative Inquiry: self-amending system rules structure
8. Foundational Community: spirit sustains the organisational community
9. Liberating Disciplines: awareness links skills and incongruities at all inter- and intra-levels

The personal and organisational models of transformation parallel each other. In effect, Torbert has deployed an individual–collective lens here in describing developmental stages for both individuals and organisations. In both cases successive stages represent inclusive structures of increasing integrative power so "each transformation in organisational development represents a fundamental change and increase in the organisation's capacity" (Fisher et al., 2003, p. 144).

Another important lens in DAI is the "four territories of experience" (Fisher et al., 2003, p. 18). DAI proposes that all action takes place over four different territories of experience.

- First territory—Intentionality: attending and visioning, thoughts and passions, purposes, aims, intuitions, intentions, attention, vision
- Second territory—Planning: interpreting and meaning making, modes of reflecting on experience, strategies, schemes, ploys, game plans
- Third territory—Performing actions: "one's own behaviour", skills, patterns of activity, deeds, performance
- Fourth territory—Assessing outcomes: "the outside world" of physical environments, institutions, "governing policies", assessments and results

The first two territories, Intentionality and Planning, are interior territories. They can be "conducted entirely by mental and intuitive activities" (Fisher et al., 2003, p. 19). The third and fourth territories of Action and Outcomes are physical, visible and concerned with the behavioural and social worlds "where the strategy or plan . . . is turned into concrete behaviour" (Fisher et al., 2003, pp. 18–19). Action inquiry sees both personal and social development as holistic processes of deep engagement with these four territories of experience.

DAI places great weight on communication and speech in its understanding of transformative change—"Speaking is the primary and most influential medium of action in the human universe" (Fisher et al., 2003, p. 23). Emphasis is placed on the importance of speech and the capacity for reflective listening within the four territories of intention, behaviour, planning and social assessment. "Our claim is that speaking based on silent listening into the four territories is the secret of conscious social life" (Fisher et al., 2003, p. 23). All speech can be categorised in terms of four "parts of speech"—framing, illustrating, advocating and inquiring. Framing is related to the intentions of speakers, their feelings and cognitions. Illustrating is the concrete explication and description of what is meant. Advocating refers to the process of stating an opinion or of presenting an interpretation, value or worldview. Inquiring involves questioning in order to confirm what is real in the external and social world.

DAI also employs a learning lens in describing change. Because it has a strong appreciation for developmental processes, the DAI model proposes various levels of learning or learning loops. The first is called single-loop learning and refers to the simple feedback process where one's actions are altered on the basis of the achievement and not of specific goals. Double-loop learning is sensitive to the structure and direction of one's single-loop goal-seeking and status-maintaining system. Double-loop learning brings awareness to intentions and one's meaning-making system. This enables individuals and organisations to learn through examining alternative policies and objectives from new perspectives rather than to simply improve ways of functioning within present perspectives. Triple-loop learning is the experience of transformation itself. It is not a reflection of one action logic on another; it is the metamorphosis involved in the actual movement.

This very brief description gives a taste of the way personal transformation is intimately connected with the various forms of learning. Developing learning organisations is similarly connected to the transformational process. Single- and double-loop learning can also take place in the context of triple-loop learning, which is a type of "deeper spiritual presence" that enables individuals to experience the "actual exchange occurring among the four territories of our experience" (Torbert et al., 2004, p. 18).

Another fundamental lens in the DAI toolbox is that of inquiry perspectives as exemplified in the adoption of first-, second- and third-person perspectives (Torbert, 1999). DAI and AQAL both place great importance on this way of considering inquiry and social orientation. First-person inquiry focuses on the world of personal experience. Second-person inquiry investigates the world of interpersonal relations. Third-person inquiry examines the objective world of physical environments and concrete situations. These three perspectives also identify the basic research methods for the practice of action inquiry. Action inquiry integrates these three arenas of research and practice by always including subjective, relational and objective methods of the development and organisation of knowledge.

The core goals of action inquiry—integrity, mutuality and sustainability—are directly related to the implementation of action inquiry through first-, second- and third-person methods. When exercised in the first-person world of one's own experience and identity, action inquiry develops personal integrity; in the second-person world of relationships it develops mutuality; and in the third-person world of people and environments it supports sustainability.

Concluding Observations on AQAL and DAI

The frameworks of DAI and AQAL possess similarities in their metatheoretical lenses and in the relationships between these lenses (see Cacioppe & Edwards, 2005b). They both have a very strong developmental component and their stage-based lenses include comparable descriptions of the structures and processes by which transformation occurs. The four territories of DAI also have many parallels with the four quadrants of AQAL. Consequently, there is a similar awareness of the dimensions of interiority–exteriority and individuality–collectivity. These similarities will provide a good basis for guiding the comparing and contrasting of lenses and their relationships in the metatheory building tasks that follow. However, there are also important differences between the two approaches.

DAI is a particularly complex and extensive metatheory and inquiry practice for organisational transformation. Although Bill Torbert has been the central figure in the development of DAI, there has been extensive collaboration with many different researchers using numerous methods, including metatheoretical review and analysis, empirical research and personal reflection. AQAL, on the other hand, has been created by one thinker/philosopher through intensive metatheoretical reflection using methods of traditional scholarship. DAI has also been developed within an institutional research environment in that it has produced extensive empirical and conceptual research that has resulted not only in large-scale metatheory building but also middle-range theory and a programme of empirical testing (see, for example, Torbert, 1989). In contrast, AQAL has been developed in a more isolated context. This has disadvantages in terms of collegial interaction and collaborative research but it seems also to have allowed Wilber freedom to develop AQAL free of the usual constraints that sometimes limit the development of innovative ideas.

The two approaches differ in the general purpose of their metatheorising. DAI has presented itself as an applied method for meta-inquiry and not just a metatheoretical framework (Chandler & Torbert, 2003). The focus for DAI is on developing change practices and not merely as a map of change. But even here AQAL has its own practice-based systems (Wilber et al., 2008) and it has more recently focused on developing its own meta-methodology (Esbjörn-Hargens, 2005b). It could be argued that an important difference between the two systems, and one that has implications for the metatheoretical goals of this book, is that DAI has been developed within the domain of business and organisation studies whereas AQAL has deliberately drawn on theories and sources of cultural knowledge from many different fields and disciplines. On closer inspection though, it is clear that Torbert and his colleagues have incorporated an extremely broad range of scientific and cultural sources of knowledge in developing DAI. It is remarkable that, given their differences in scope, research method, purpose and applied focus, these two metatheoretical (and meta-methodological) systems should have so much in common. Both have been applied to the field of organisation and management theory, both share similar metatheoretical lenses, both have similar sensitivities to the importance of a full range of systems of inquiry and both share a developmental approach that outlines similar structures of growth. Such convergence augers well for the possibility of performing metatheoretical research that cuts across so many disciplines and potentially includes many different research paradigms and theoretical perspectives.

This chapter has presented an outline of the relevant literatures on organisational transformation and the metatheoretical resources that will be used to develop the integrative metatheory. In the next chapter we look at method and describe a general method that can be used in this kind of overarching research.

5 A General Method for Metatheory Building

Metadisciplinary analysis is not a method but potentially a small discipline itself. The methods used to find structures can be diverse, as can the applications of these structures. But analysis of structure requires prior understanding of content, and the more sequential nature of scientific study is inhibitory to the explorations of more generally-minded humanists. (Van Valen, 1972, p. 419)

WHERE'S THE METHOD TO OUR INTEGRATIVE MADNESS?

The above quote by evolutionary biologist Leigh Van Valen suggests a reason for the lack of interest in methods for, what he calls, "metadisciplinary analysis". He sees the mind of the generalist as not responsive to the "sequential" or, he might also have said, rule-based nature of method. If this observation has any truth in it at all, then such reservations will need to be overcome. In this chapter it is argued that generalist research must not only be open to method but be innovative and enthusiastic about its application to metatheoretical studies. Until now, most metatheory has been developed through forms of scholarship which rely on philosophical insight, idiosyncratic theory analysis and rational argument. This type of traditional scholarship might provide an excellent means for private inspiration (Billig, 2004) but it is hardly adequate for establishing a rigorous research base for what should be an important scientific field.

METHOD AND THE BIG PICTURE

All research programmes evolve and develop over time and their richness and relevance grows through the active involvement of the communities that enact the practices of those programmes. Method is crucial to this evolutionary process. Method, as Carol Becker describes in the following quote, is intimately bound up with the issue of *how* we know, *how* new socio-cultural knowledge is disclosed and *how* new disciplines and interdisciplinary activities emerge.

[I]n spite of human ambivalence to our own potential freedom, borders are crossed and disciplines merge and intertwine daily. Our job as cultural producers is to embrace these changes with the right mix of interrogation, rigor, and enthusiasm. At the same time, we must recognize that at the core of creativity is a blend of the new, the revised, the rethought, and the reimagined, all attempting to manifest the what through endless permutations of, and debates around, the how. (Becker, 2004, pp. 207–208)

Currently, metatheoretical research does not embrace the right mix of rigour and enthusiasm. "The how" of method is being badly neglected. At the collective level, method enables a community of inquiry to develop behavioural practices, techniques and organising systems that provide transparency and accountability which, in turn, support avenues for evaluation and critique. At the individual level, grappling with the demands of method is an experience that all researchers and students can identify with. This is why learning and internalising method is a core requirement of any discipline of inquiry. Method not only provides a means for learning how to uncover particular kinds of data under particular conditions, it also enables us to critically evaluate what we do to gather that data.

In metatheoretical research, the application of method provides a basis for exploring such questions as: How do we know that a metatheory has been based on a systematic analysis of theory? Has an adequate range of theories and perspectives been sampled? Have all the relevant lenses been included? How do we know if the relationships between those lenses are consistent and logical? Is it possible to evaluate metatheory according to accepted standards of reliability and validity? These questions lie at the heart of a scientific approach to building and applying metatheories frameworks. At the moment very few metatheorists can answer these questions with reference to the use of a systematic method. Ultimately, without method the quality of metatheoretical research, however insightful it may be, cannot be evaluated by a research community and so the scientific legitimisation of that research is seriously undermined.

Methodological issues are regarded here as being important irrespective of one's epistemological commitments. Attention to method is valuable for both the modernist and the postmodernist inquirer, for both qualitative and quantitative research and for both grounded empirical and overarching metatheoretical studies. The general method that will be outlined in this chapter cuts across traditional methodological boundaries and can accommodate qualitative, quantitative or mixed-method techniques. The general method is based on the assumption that there is a shared set of elements to any scientific method whose "objectives, scope, and nature of inquiry are consistent across methods and across paradigms" (Dzurec & Abraham, 1993, p. 75).

In proposing this research model I also recognise that the scientific process cannot be reduced to method. Intellectual passion, as Michael Polanyi says, is also an essential element in all this (1962, p. 143):

Theories of the scientific method which try to explain the establishment of scientific truth by any purely objective formal procedure are
doomed to failure. Any process of enquiry unguided by intellectual
passions would inevitably spread out into a desert of trivialities.

This attempt to develop a general method for metatheorising acknowledges
the greater context of insight and intellectual passion that Polanyi alludes
to. Method is a necessary but, of itself, insufficient element for the creation
of scientific insight. While the moment of creativity that gives form to those
intuitions cannot be explained methodologically, method plays a vital role
in preparing for that emergence and for grounding knowledge within a
system of critical inquiry that is based on evidence.

METATHEORY BUILDING APPROACHES
IN THE SOCIAL SCIENCES

To facilitate the development of a general method for metatheory building, a number of methods and general models of metatheoretical research
will be compared. These are traditional scholarship (Edwards, 2008c),
dialectical method (Paolucci, 2000), metatriangulation and multiparadigm
inquiry (Lewis & Grimes, 1999; Lewis & Kelemen, 2002), metatheorising
in sociology (Ritzer, 2001) and conventional middle-range theory building
(Dubin, 1978). Of these, only metatriangulation can claim to be a systematic research method for metatheory building.

Traditional Scholarship

The dominant method used in metatheorising to this point has been the traditional model of scholarship. This is an individual process (often lifelong)
involving a mixture of intensive reading, writing and creative insight (Billig,
2004). Traditional metatheorists typically read through and analyse many
writings and theories across a variety of relevant disciplines, absorb their
contents, muse upon their meanings, let their rational analyses and intuitive
inspirations guide them to produce, at some point, some large-scale framework. As Billig points out, the "quirkiness" of this traditional approach
enables the scholar "to make connections between seemingly disparate phenomena" (2004, p. 14). Sometimes these ideas are informed by dialogues
with experts in various fields or by critical reviews of previous metatheories.
Even where such approaches do include some elements of method, traditional
scholarship is usually completely non-transparent with no record being kept
of what was done, how it was done or why it was done. Metatheorists of
every persuasion have developed their ideas via some variation of this process of reviewing extant theoretical texts and making arguments.[1] There is
generally no formal process of domain specification, no sampling procedure,

no systematic techniques of analysis (either qualitative or quantitative), no setting out of results or rigorous attempt at evaluation—in other words, no transparent and repeatable research method.

Unfortunately, traditional forms of developing metatheories are still commonly used. The situation of the contemporary metatheorist is similar to that of the early scientists of pre-modernity. Those pioneers made observations and developed their theories without any real methodological system. They intuitively asked important questions, observed and analysed the world around them, proposed their theoretical systems and entered into debates with their colleagues. It was only with the institutionalisation of science in the eighteenth and nineteenth centuries that rigorous methods became an acknowledged part of doing science. Metatheorising is in a similar position to pre-modern science in that it has yet to utilise formal methods or be institutionally acknowledged by the academy as a valuable form of research in its own right (Ritzer, 2001). If integrative metatheory building is to be accepted as a scientific enterprise in the broad sense, it too will need to use rigorous methods.

Dialectical Method

Any discussion of metatheoretical methods would be remiss in not referring to the dialectical method and particularly that form of dialectics associated with the work of Karl Marx. This is a vast and complex topic and only a very brief summary of some relevant aspects can be presented here. Dialectics, as a method of questioning and rational investigation, has a long history leading back to the beginnings of both Eastern and Western philosophical traditions. The essential aim of the dialectical method is the resolution of differing perspectives through rational dialogue (von Eemeren, 2003). The potential relevance of such a process to theoretical pluralism is apparent. In this process of dialogue there is an assumption that the paradoxical and contradictory nature of change is built into the social world. Marx, in particular, used this rational method as a basis for resolving many of the tensions he saw in theories of political economy and other early forms of the social sciences of his day (Ollman, 2003). However, this method was applied by Marx within the context of traditional scholarship techniques of reading and rational argumentation rather than any more systematic process of interrogating the literature. As Engels describes in his short biography of Marx (Engels, 2008, para. 5):

> [Marx] withdrew into the British Museum and worked through the immense and as yet for the most part unexamined library there for all that it contained on political economy.

Marx used his dialectical method as a way of working in depth with immense amounts of written materials, the rich source of ideas that they contained and the varying social disciplines that they represented. Engels notes that Marx "investigated very many fields, none of them superficially" (cited in Kreis, 2008). A contemporary description of the way Marx applied his dialectical method is given by Mario Paolucci (2003). Based on this model, Marx's method consisted of the following phases:

1. inquiry (reading texts)
2. typification and conceptualisation of core elements
3. examination of commensurable cases across history and structure
4. controlled comparisons
5. deductive analysis and provisional abstractions
6. model building
7. evaluation of fit, usefulness and explanatory power of metatheory
8. presentation of findings and critique
9. continued inquiry (iteration of research cycle)

A comparison of these phases with those of other methods is given in Table 5.1.

There are other crucial aspects of Marx's dialectical method that also have relevance to methodological issues (Ollman, 2003). These include abstraction of internal and external relations (how concepts are related), level of generality (the practice of setting boundaries around particular systems) and vantage point (establishing a point from which to view a system). These aspects will be taken up in a later chapter on the implications of metatheoretical research.

Metatriangulation and Multiparadigm Inquiry

Metatriangulation was first proposed by Gioia and Pitre (1990) and subsequently developed by Lewis and Grimes (1999). The method came out of these researchers' consideration of the Burrell and Morgan multiparadigm model for organisational studies. Metatriangulation is so named because it uses multiple frames of theoretical reference to construct theory. Where standard research triangulation applies several *research methods* to the same topic of interest (Cox & Hassard, 2005), metatriangulation draws on several *research paradigms or theories* to build a metatheory for some complex social phenomenon. Saunders and her colleagues (2003, p. 244) describe this method as follows:

> Metatriangulation is a three-phase, qualitative meta-analysis process that may be used to explore variations in the assumptions of alternative paradigms, gain insights into these multiple paradigms, and address emerging themes and the resulting theories.

The three phases of metatriangulation are groundwork, data-analysis and theory building. The groundwork phase involves defining the research question, specifying the domain of inquiry and choosing data sources. Data-analysis involves scrutinising data for core insights and coding that data according to certain paradigms lenses. In the theory building phase paradigm insights and lenses are juxtaposed and assembled into a coherent theoretical framework (Lewis & Grimes, 1999). Metatriangulation has been used to develop metatheory in a variety of areas including power in organisations (Jasperson et al., 2002), communication and information technology (Adriaanse, 2005; Saunders et al., 2003), organisational geography (Del Casino et al., 2000) and organisational boundaries (Thrane & Hald, 2006). Metatriangulation acted as an important resource for developing the general method for metatheory building described later.

The multiparadigm inquiry approach of Lewis and Kelemen (2002) is not a method but a typology of metatheorising activities and as such provides some methodological clues for the comparative analysis performed here. Multiparadigm inquiry includes multiparadigm review, multiparadigm research and metaparadigm theory building. Multiparadigm reviews identify the linkages between paradigms and their associated theoretical schools. Rather than simply summarising or thematically reviewing the findings of particular theorists, multiparadigm reviews describe the underlying themes and the key conceptual factors that theorists use to explain and understand organisational phenomena. According to Lewis and Grimes (1999, p. 673) multiparadigm review involves the "recognition of divides and bridges in existing theory (e.g. characterising paradigms X and Y)". Metaparadigm inquiry goes further than simply reviewing "assumptions, key factors, linkages and differences" to actually construct explanatory frameworks which "juxtapose and link conflicting paradigm insights (X and Y) within a novel understanding (Z)". Lastly, multiparadigm research is more like traditional triangulation in that investigators run multiple empirical studies that employ very different theoretical assumptions and methods of data collection. The purpose in this type of inquiry is not integration but rather a pluralistic appreciation of the conflicting views with the aim of creating some new middle-range theoretical insights.

Metatheorising in Sociology

Although George Ritzer did not use a systematic method in his sociological metatheorising he did describe a typology based on the purposes towards which this research was aimed. This typology (along with Colomy's contribution) has already been described in detail in Chapter 2. The typology of multiparadigm inquiry shares a similar format with Ritzer's metatheorising system. Multiparadigm review corresponds closely with Ritzer's metatheorising for understanding (M_U). Both are foundational procedures for becoming familiar with the infrastructure of the relevant sample of theories. Multiparadigm research corresponds with Ritzer's metatheorising as a preparatory step for developing, not overarching models, but other middle-range theories (M_p). Metaparadigm theory building corresponds closely with Ritzer's overarching metatheorising (M_O). To Ritzer's three types of metatheorising is added here Colomy's (1991) fourth form of metatheorising—metatheorising for adjudication or M_A. Colomy builds on Ritzer's typology to argue for the inclusion of a specifically evaluative form of metatheoretical research. M_A corresponds to the evaluation and critical assessment phases of standard theory building methods. Colomy's description of adjudicative metatheorising is insightful regarding some of the methodological steps needed for more "reasoned judgements" in metatheoretical research (Colomy, 1991, pp. 279–280):

> The objective of metatheorizing as adjudication (M_A) is to render reasoned judgments about the relative analytic merits of competing traditions. With regard to generalized discourse, such judgment requires the formulation of general and highly abstract criteria to determine the significance of general problems and the viability of the solutions proposed to resolve them. With regard to research programs, such judgment requires elucidating the underlying theoretical code that animates a tradition's programs and utilizing the same generalized criteria to assess the strengths and limitations of the programs' theoretical logic. If they are to be useful, these standards must combine careful study of extant traditions and their conceptual codes along with independent metatheorizing, both aimed at generating criteria sufficiently abstract and clearly stated so that they can be readily applied to a variety of schools.

The process of "elucidating the underlying theoretical code that animates a tradition's programs" lies at the heart of the methodological problem for metatheoreticians. Finding those codes, or "orienting strategies" as David Wagner and Joseph Berger (1985) call them, is a crucial step in the metatheory building process.

Middle-range Theory Building

Middle-range theory building methods offer some important guidelines on how metatheory building might proceed. It is reasonable to assume that the middle-range theory building phases of domain specification, concept definition, clarification of relationships, system description, factual claims and evaluation (Dubin, 1978; Lynham, 2002) will also have relevance to the metatheoretical level. As Susan Lynham suggests:

> One of the challenges of theory-building research in applied disciplines is making the logic used to build the theory explicit and accessible to the user of the developed theory. Although different methods of theory building advocate different theory-building research processes, there is an inherently generic nature to theory building. (2002, p. 221)

Lynham goes on to say that researchers need to have an awareness of what she calls the "generic methodological components of theory building" (2002, p. 224). As I have pointed out previously, the point of distinction between theory and metatheory building methods is that, while middle-range theory building works with first-order concepts directly derived from empirical events and experiences, metatheory building relies on second-order concepts derived from other theory.

There are many models of middle-range theory building that provide guidelines for the metatheoretical level. Many of these are based on the seminal work of Robert Dubin. Dubin's (1978) method had several features: (i) identification of a theory's conceptual elements, (ii) patterns of interaction among these elements, (iii) description of theoretical domain, (iv) a description of the overall system, (v) a statement of the theory's main propositions, (vi) operationalisation—empirical indicators, (vii) formation of testable hypotheses and (viii) continuous refinement of the theory. This method describes a complete cycle of theory development, testing, application and refinement. The first five steps in the method concern specific aspects of theory construction and the last three relate particularly to the ongoing need for empirical testing of theory. A comparative analysis of phases of theory building and types of metatheorising will, at the least, provide a general outline of the methodological phases for metatheory building.

A CRITIQUE OF EXISTING METATHEORETICAL METHODS

Elman and Elman (2002, pp. 233–234) advocate "an open and informed debate about the comparative merits of different rationalist and sociological metrics for describing and appraising theoretical developments". Such a debate has not yet occurred in metatheoretical research. The methods outlined all suffer from significant shortcomings and this is particularly true for the method of traditional scholarship.

Problems with Traditional Approaches

Down through the centuries the traditional method of scholarship has resulted in a rich history of many important metatheoretical works. However, such a method can no longer be regarded as the foundation for performing metatheoretical research and it is undoubtedly a barrier against the mainstream scientific community's acceptance of this important branch of study. For several decades, George Ritzer (1988; 1991b) has been calling for the institutional recognition and establishment of metatheorising as a core academic activity. He says that metatheorists have been pursuing their endeavours in a "half-hidden and unarticulated way" and under increasing criticism from those who undervalue the role of integrative knowledge (Ritzer, 1991a, p. 318):

[Metatheorists] often feel as if they are out there on their own, without a tradition in which to embed themselves, and very vulnerable to outside criticism. . . . Metatheorists often feel defensive about what they are doing, because they lack a sense of the field and institutional base from which to respond to the critics. . . . Progress in meta-theorising has been hampered by these criticisms and the lack of institutionalised base to respond to the critics.

Although this situation may have improved in recent years, there is still a widespread ignorance of, and disregard for, metatheorising as a valid and useful academic activity. The lack of application of rigorous methods by metatheorists is an important reason for this lamentable situation. The development, articulation and application of systematic methods for pursuing metatheory building are all crucial steps for affirming its core scientific and cultural value. Without such activities, a specific metatheory building project can be criticised on the reliability, validity, utility and trustworthiness of its findings. It might be argued, for example, that particular metatheories have missed some branches of relevant literature and omitted the explanatory lenses used in that literature. Consequently, method provides a basis not only for organising the research process but also for defending its findings.

The development of Wilber's AQAL is an example of how metatheorising can be performed using traditional methods of scholarship. It also highlights the methodological weaknesses of that process. In developing his AQAL framework over a period of 35 years, Wilber has sifted through vast amounts of literature in order to find patterns of convergence and divergence and has employed them to develop his large-scale conceptual frameworks. Wilber has described his approach as one of "plain old-fashioned homework—you just read and read and read". He says, "I read hundreds of books during the year, and a book forms in my head—I write the book in my head" (Wilber, 2000a, p. 392). This is consistent with a traditional methodology that relies heavily on personal capacities of analysis and synthesis.

The most lengthy discussion of method in Wilber's metatheory building comes from the article by Crittenden (1997) entitled "What should we think about Wilber's method?" Crittenden sees the heart of Wilber's method as the development of "orienting generalisations". These are the core explanatory themes and definitive contributions that a particular field or tradition makes to some topic. For example, in the field of human development, stage-based explanations (however they might be conceptualised) could be regarded as an orienting generalisation. Crittenden sees three steps to Wilber's method (1997, p. 101). In step one the task is to "simply assemble all the [orienting generalisations] as if each field had incredibly important truths to tell us". The second step is to "take all of the [orienting generalisations] assembled in the first step" and incorporate them within a "coherent system" or metatheory. The third step, according to Crittenden, involves the development of a "critical theory of theories". As Colomy (1991) has argued, this critical adjudicative capacity is an important aspect of metatheorising.

The first thing to note about Crittenden's model is that it is an account of a traditional method of scholarship. The three steps amount to an intuitive and largely extemporaneous approach to metatheory building. Second, the development of orienting generalisations is not a method. They are outcomes of the metatheorising process rather than a method themselves. They do not, for example, involve issues of sampling, design, analysis and evaluation which are all essential aspects of method. Crittenden's model also, and Wilber's views have also contributed to this, gives a false impression of the nature of orienting generalisations. Orienting generalisations are not general statements upon which "everybody pretty much agrees" (Wilber, 2001, p. 4), even when those scholars might come from a particular discipline or research programme. Orienting generalisations are conceived and articulated by the metatheorist and not by those involved in researching the middle-range theories or the disciplines from which the metatheory is drawn. Disciplinary agreement among middle-range theorists is not the criteria by which to judge the adequacy of orienting generalisations. On the contrary, they need to be evaluated within a community of researchers engaged at the level of metatheoretical research. Rigorous and systematic methods of evaluation among metatheorists themselves are needed for this to occur.

Orienting generalisations, or metatheoretical lenses as they are called here, are generalities that the metatheorist develops to further his or her model building. They can be present in a highly articulated fashion at the middle-range theory level, or be implicitly assumed or present in an embryonic or partial form and await greater explication in the hands of the metatheorist. They are abstracted from theories by metatheorists through the process of review and analysis and are articulated in their complete form in the development of their overarching frameworks. Theorists and practitioners within a particular field may be completely unaware of these generalising constructs and their relevance to their specific field. Orienting generalisations have little to do with, as Crittenden contends, the points at which "various conflicting approaches actually agree with one another" (1997, p. 100). They are validated through the critical practice of performing metatheoretical research. Orienting generalisations cannot be validated at the middle-range level because they are only fully articulated at the level of metatheory.

In an article called "The significance of method", authors Jacek Szmatka and Michael Lovaglia (1996) say that "methods play a role as prominent as that of metatheory in directing social research". Theory and method are the flint and stone that light the complicated pathways of scientific activity. If either of them is deficient, the knowledge they produce will be short-lived, be misleading or be regarded suspiciously by research communities. The absence of a systematic method limits the ongoing development of integrative metatheorising. While traditional scholarship can contribute immensely to the birth of a new perspective, the ongoing contribution of scholars through systematic theory building and evaluation is essential for its continued development (Lynham, 2002). Method is needed for this to occur.

Scholars often learn to do research within their particular disciplinary matrix through learning its methods (Szmatka & Lovaglia, 1996). Without an explicit method of metatheory building, which, by definition, includes a phase of self-examination and evaluation, a research programme can become atrophied through rote application of its conceptual base. As a result, the metatheory's practitioners and adherents mechanically impose the metatheoretical edifice on whatever comes their way. The end result of such a process is a metatheory that, to quote Szmatka and Lovaglia, "resists change". They describe this process as follows (1996, pp. 407–408):

> Often, grand theorists are known for their encyclopaedic knowledge. The theory that results is often extremely comprehensive and argued at length in a book or series of books. Later researchers may publish results that support or fail to support parts of the theory. However, the theory itself resists change. Its authority is linked to the stature of the author. An attempt to alter the theory represents an attack on the author. Adherents marshal a defence. Debate continues but theory growth is limited. The relation of theory to data is simple and unidirectional in the case of [grand] theories, limiting theory growth. . . . Data informs theory construction, but thereafter the theory is resistant to change in the face of new data.

The adoption of rigorous and transparent methods in metatheory building is crucial for safeguarding it from this type of intellectual atrophy.

Problems with Metatriangulation

While metatriangulation provides an excellent base for multiparadigm research, there are a number of shortcomings that limit its flexibility and analytical capacity. Perhaps the most restrictive aspect of metatriangulation is that it is applied at the paradigm level. Lewis and Grimes state, "Metatriangulation alters the role of theoretical sensitivity dramatically, requiring theorists to focus and then employ divergent paradigm lenses" (1999, p. 678). It is at the paradigm level that metatriangulation develops its conceptual lenses and those paradigms are usually the four designated by the Burrell and Morgan model. Consequently, metatriangulation research is prone to reproduce the paradigm lenses prescribed in the four-cell multiparadigm grid. This is confirmed by noting that all four metatriangulation studies found in the literature analysed their data using the paradigm lenses framed by Burrell and Morgan. While they might be uncovering very useful insights, metatriangulation research is still simply reproducing existing theoretical and paradigmatic relationships. The only metatriangulation study to offer a thorough evaluation of its findings reports precisely this problem (Saunders et al., 2003, p. 55):

> the set of paradigm lenses we chose did not provide a thorough view of our phenomenon of interest. . . . In retrospect, this lesson suggests that the selection of lenses must be capable of providing insight about all major constructs of the phenomenon of interest. In short, we did not select the wrong lens; we failed to select all appropriate lenses.

Burrell and Morgan specified four paradigms—interpretive, functionalist, radical humanist and radical structuralist. These paradigms were derived from the two dimensions of subjective–objective and radical change–regulation. It seems highly likely that there are more paradigms and metatheoretical lenses employed in organisational studies than just these two. Saunders and her colleagues failed to select all appropriate lenses because the metatriangulation method did not enable them to dig deeper into their theoretical data to identify these alternative lenses.

Lewis and Grimes have stated that their aim is to develop a method that "transcends paradigm distinctions to reveal disparity *and* complementarity" (1999, p. 673; emphasis in the original). But their focus has been to reveal these divergences and convergences between paradigms themselves. Their method is useful for divulging distinctions at the paradigm level and not at other, more fine-grained levels of theory. Given that the identification of conceptual lenses is a central function of metatheory building, our methods must facilitate the extraction of lenses at the theory level, or even at finer levels of exploration. Several writers have noted that the paradigm notion is a very general one and that its use is not intended to distinguish between detailed theoretical features or be applied at the level of theoretical concepts (Goles & Hirschheim, 2000; Hassard & Keleman, 2002). Because metatriangulation only functions at the paradigm level it is not flexible enough to be applied at the theory or construct level. And yet, it is this finer level of analysis that is needed for metatheoretical research to discover the underlying architectonics of theories and paradigms.

Furthermore, not only does metatriangulation tend to reproduce existing paradigm boundaries in the development of its lenses, it also overlooks the need to describe the relationships between those lenses. Stanley Deetz (1996) has offered a powerful critique of the lens relationships in the Burrell and Morgan framework in terms of both their internal and external relations. For example, he has pointed out the ongoing problems with defining relationships via a subjective–objective ontology. Relationships within and between lenses are crucial for building a coherent metatheoretical system. If these relationships are partial or invalid then the metatheory will reproduce those inadequacies. And yet metatriangulation does not consider the relationships between lenses. It merely reproduces the lens structures that are described in the Burrell and Morgan framework.

John Wacker points out that "explanations of relationships are critical for 'good' theory-building" (Wacker, 1998, p. 364), and this holds for the building of good metatheory. While metatriangulation does support the sensitisation of researchers to some paradigms and their assumptions, it does not seem capable of disclosing the host of other potential candidates for "paradigm lenses" nor the relationship within or between those lenses. On these two counts metatriangulation is significantly flawed as a method for metatheory building. The general method developed described in the following attempts to incorporate the many positive elements of the metatriangulation method into a metatheoretical research method that is more flexible and capable of analysing conceptual material at a finer level of detail.

A GENERAL RESEARCH DESIGN AND METHOD FOR METATHEORY BUILDING

The comparison of the models of theory and metatheory building presented above provides a basis for developing a general design and method for metatheory building research. The general design and method for metatheory building includes the following phases (see Table 5.1):

Phase 1—Groundwork

The groundwork phase of metatheory building sets the context and the basic parameters of the study. Groundwork involves: (i) stating the topic of interest; (ii) declaring the basic aim and objectives; (iii) providing a rationale for developing metatheory on the topic of interest. Lewis and Grimes (1999), talk here of selecting a topic characterised by expansive and contested research domains with "numerous often conflicting theories" (1999, p. 678). The topic should be "multifaceted [and] characterised by expansive and contested research domains" (1999, p. 678).

Phase 2—Domain Specification

The second phase in metatheory building research sets the boundaries of the research. This involves: (i) describing the relevant domain for the study; (ii) defining key terms and concepts; (iii) describing any metatheoretical sources used in the study. Even large-scale integrative metatheorising requires the specification of a domain as there will always be viewpoints that cannot be accommodated within a particular framework. The kinds of metatheoretical resources chosen to guide the metatheory building process should also be relevant to the domain of the research.

Phase 3—Design

The design phase outlines: (i) the sampling procedures used to collect the sample of paradigms, theories, models and constructs; (ii) the ordering of conceptual data, e.g. using paradigms to group theories; (iii) the units of analysis for the study, e.g. second-order concepts, conceptual themes, etc.; (iv) the review techniques for collecting these units, e.g. text scrutinisation; (v) the techniques used to analyse the conceptual data of the research; (vi) the overall design of the study. This design phase describes how paradigms and theories chosen for the study are sampled, reviewed and analysed. As with all data-based studies, describing and justifying the sampling procedures is an important phase because it largely determines the type and number of metatheoretical lenses that can be identified. The sample of theories selected can impact significantly on the full description of a lens. Review and analysis techniques are also described here and can include whatever quantitative and qualitative techniques are involved in identifying the relevant units of analysis.

Phase 4—Multiparadigm Review

The review phase involves: (i) ordering the sampled materials; (ii) applying the review techniques for producing the data set of, for example, key themes; (iii) ensuring that multiple conceptual layers are involved in the review process, e.g. paradigms, disciplines, theories, sets of constructs. Unlike the multiparadigm review performed in metatriangulation, the review and analysis process followed here sifts below the paradigm level to delve into concepts at multiple levels. This phase involves sifting and scrutinising the primary sources and materials using the review techniques outlined in the design phase. Performing a multiparadigm review is equivalent to Ritzer's metatheorising for understanding and involves familiarisation with extant theories. Paradigm categories are used in this process as a heuristic for ordering the review and analysis (and not as the sole means for discovering lenses). The range of literature included in the multiparadigm review is a crucial aspect of the study. Wacker (1998, p. 368) points out:

> For all stages of theory-building, the role of the literature search in the research procedure is extremely important . . . Therefore, to assure that all theory-building conditions are filled, an extensive literature search of the academic as well as practitioner articles is required.

While the range of literature is governed by the domain of a study and the sampling procedure, the literature must be able to represent a wide variety of theoretical positions so that the multiparadigm analysis does not result in non-representative lenses.

Phase 5—Multiparadigm Analysis

This phase involves: (i) collating the review results; (ii) applying analytical techniques to derive metatheoretical lenses (or other second-order concepts), for example, bridging and bracketing techniques; (iii) applying comparative techniques for identifying and describing the relationships within and between these lenses; (iv) refining lenses and their relationships so that a parsimonious set of elements is available for the following metatheory building phase. Bridging and bracketing (described in more detail in the following) are used to derive the refined metatheoretical lenses from the results of the multiparadigm review. Iterations of these techniques are run to achieve a point at which metatheory building can begin. It may also be possible here to introduce quantitative methods of analysis.

Phase 6—Metatheory Building

The metatheory building phase involves: (i) a presentation of the results of the multiparadigm analysis; (ii) describing the means for guiding the metatheory building process; (iii) a description of the whole metatheoretical system; (iv) an application of the metatheory to an exemplar topic. The lenses and their relationships map out a set of possibilities that can be flexibly and creatively combined to build frameworks of understanding and explanation. Some guiding process for connecting the lenses needs to be adopted. This can be drawn from the metatheoretical resources of the study. As with the current study, exemplar topics may be chosen for the purpose of describing the new metatheory. It is a feature of the method proposed here that there may be no single combination of lenses that can be used to construct the metatheory. Consequently, imagination and the real demands of the research situation may require various ensembles of lenses to be used at different points in the research. In fact, it is proposed here that the dialectical nature of metatheory building is not compatible with a fixed representation of the metatheory. The reality of social change means that a metatheory is better regarded as a variety of evolving systems rather than as a ready-made framework awaiting application.

Phase 7—Implications

This phase focuses on: (i) stating metaconjectures concerning the implications of the metatheory; (ii) providing supporting arguments that emerge from the new metatheory; (iii) critical adjudications of other theories and metatheories; (iv) statements of other implications, e.g. further theory and metatheory development. "Metaconjectures" are the truth claims and logical propositions based on the metatheory and which relate to the specific topic of the research. These can include critical evaluations of other theories and metatheories and statements of middle-range theory that will require further empirical research to be tested.

Phase 8—Evaluation

The evaluation phase consists of: (i) an evaluation of the metatheory itself using as many relevant criteria as possible; (ii) an evaluation of the metatheoretical resources; (iii) a critical self-reflection. Both modernist and postmodern criteria are useful for formally evaluating metatheory. These include generalisability, parsimony, fecundity and abstraction level on the modernist side (Wacker, 1998) and trustworthiness, reflexivity, credibility and transferability on the postmodernist side (Guba & Lincoln, 1998; Jacques, 1992). Metatheoretical resources can be evaluated in terms of the lenses they use, the relationships between these lenses and whether the findings of the study support the ways these resources have been interpreted and applied. Critical self-reflection helps to assess the impact of researchers' own styles and preferences, cognitive dispositions and cultural assumptions.

Finally, a general method for metatheory building recognises the ongoing nature of such research both in terms of the inherent boundedness of any single expression of integrative metatheory and the need for further iterations of this cycle among members of the research community. Table 5.1 presents a summary of the phases of a general method for metatheory building and shows comparisons with other approaches to theory construction and models of metatheorising.

AN INTEGRAL METATHEORY FOR ORGANISATIONAL TRANSFORMATION

The general method for metatheory building just described was followed in the current study's investigation of organisational transformation. Table 5.1 shows the general design and method sections and how these sections correspond with other theory and metatheory building approaches. What follows is more detailed material about some technical aspects of this general method.

Sampling Procedures

Maximum variation sampling was selected as the sampling procedure in this present study of organisational transformation. This is a purposive form of sampling that is suitable for research that seeks out "important shared patterns that cut across cases and derive their significance from having emerged out of heterogeneity" (Patton, 1990, p. 172). With this type of sampling:

> Any common patterns that emerge from great variation are of particular interest and value in capturing the core experiences and central, shared aspects or impacts of a program. (Patton, 1990, p. 172)

Two means were employed for maximising the variety of theories of transformation included in the multiparadigm review. The first involved

Table 5.1   A General Method for Metatheory Building (with Comparisons Between Traditional and Alternative Methods)

General Method for Metatheory Building	Dialectical method (Paolucci, 2003)	Traditional Scholarship	Metatriangulation (Lewis & Grimes, 1999)	Theory Building (Wacker, 1998)
1: Groundwork • Aim of research • Rationale	Inquiry	Rationale based on personal interests	1. Groundwork Define area of interest Focus paradigm lenses Collect metatheoretical sample	Rationale
2: Domain • Scope & definitions • Metatheoretical resources	Conceptualisation of core elements			Domain boundaries Term definitions
3: Design • Sampling procedures • Review & analysis techniques		Extensive but haphazard literature review directed by personal insight		
4: Multiparadigm Review • Units of analysis • Systematic review	Examination of historical cases Controlled comparisons			Variable definitions
5: Multiparadigm Analysis • Perform analysis • Describe lenses & relationships	Deductive analysis and provisional abstractions	Idiosyncratic analysis	2. Data Analysis Plan paradigm itinerary Multiparadigm coding Perform analyses Accounts & insights	Variable relationships
6: Metatheory Building • Build & describe metatheory	Model building	Description of metatheory	3. Theory Building Juxtapose divergent insights Explore metaconjectures Develop metaparadigm perspective Critique metatheory Articulate critical reflection	Description of theory
7: Implications • Metaconjectures • Critical propositions	Evaluation of fit, usefulness Presentation of findings Continued inquiry	Publication & public discussion		Truth claims
8: Evaluation • Evaluate outcomes				Evaluation Phase

extensive and systematic searches of online social science databases. The search results were used to identify a comprehensive collection of articles which described theories of transformational change in organisations over the past 30 years. The second means for maximising the sample variation involved using previous reviews of organisational change.

From these two means of maximising the sample of relevant theories, approximately 600 articles and books were identified as an initial sample for consideration. These were reduced to around 300 documents by reading abstracts and contents pages to arrive at a set of documents that provided detailed descriptions of theories and models of organisational transformation as defined in this study. This set of articles and books and the theories they described formed the basic sample for the metatheoretical research described here.

Paradigm Categories

The many theories of transformation were categorised according to their theoretical paradigm. This process aided the theme analysis process and helped to organise the resulting information. Lewis and Kelemen (2002, pp. 260–261) suggest that using multiple paradigms opens up an appreciative perspective on the field of study:

> By categorising extant literature within a paradigm framework, reviewers distinguish the selection focus of different lenses. Highlighting paradigm diversity serves to open theoretical choice . . . all lenses are inherently exclusionary and parochial. By clarifying paradigm alternatives, researchers may compare their work to a wider realm of literature, recognise their theoretical predilections, and appreciate insights enabled by opposing viewpoints.

It should be noted, however, that paradigms were used here only as aids to the ordering of theories and not as the focal points for developing metatheoretical lenses. The paradigm categories were particularly useful in appreciating "insights enabled by opposing viewpoints" and in the analysis of relationships between explanatory lenses. The range of paradigms used for categorising theories was based on the paradigm categories outlined in the review literature and on other paradigm groupings that emerged from the sample of theories themselves. For example, no review had identified a learning paradigm as a particular perspective on organisational transformation and yet there were many theories that discussed transformation within a learning context.[2] The grouping of theories into paradigms orders the analysis process and aids in the tracking and collation of the results. The theme analysis itself occurs at the much finer level of detail within each theory as is described in more detail in the following sections.

Unit of Analysis and Multiparadigm Review Technique

The units of analysis for the multiparadigm review of theories of organisational transformation were the theories' core conceptual themes. The basic sample of around 300 articles and books was reviewed using a qualitative technique called "text scrutinising" (Luborsky, 1994; Ryan & Bernard, 2003). The conceptual themes identified in this process provided the basic data for the subsequent multiparadigm analysis. Scrutinising texts for core themes involves looking for textual elements that disclose fundamental patterns. These elements include (Ryan & Bernard, 2003):

- Repetitions: These are "topics that occur and reoccur" (Bogdan & Taylor, 1975, p. 83).
- Indigenous categories: These are the organising structures and schemes of a text.
- Metaphors and analogies: These are the root metaphors and guiding analogies.
- Similarities and differences: These help find convergences and divergences of themes.
- Linguistic connectors: Terms such as "because", "since", "always" and "as a result" often disclose core assumptions, causal inferences and the basic orientations of the research.
- Theory-related material: This is explicit reference to theory.
- Graphical material: This includes images, diagrams and other graphical material.
- Structural themes: These are themes evident in article titles, headings and subheadings.

The identified themes covered the entire range of different orientations towards explaining how, why, what, who and when organisational transformation occurs.

Multiparadigm Analysis Techniques

The themes derived from the multiparadigm review were analysed using bracketing and bridging techniques (Lewis & Grimes, 1999). Applying these techniques resulted in the amalgamation and refinements of themes to form more abstract conceptual lenses. These lenses were used as core elements for the metatheory building phase of the study. Bracketing is a qualitative form of abstraction used for finding underlying concepts within particular domains of ideas. Bracketing is essentially a "data reduction" process where researchers "ignore certain aspects of complex phenomena and focus on facets and issues of particular interest" (Lewis & Grimes, 1999, p. 673). Bracketing identifies "the underlying universals" (Gearing, 2004, p. 1433) that a particular theory adopts to research a phenomenon. The following is an example of the bracketing technique performed in this study.

Several theories within the learning paradigm considered transformation as a process requiring powerful subjective experience and cognitive reflection. A renewal of the interpretive frameworks and consciousness within the individual organisational member was regarded as fundamental to the capacity of an organisation to transform itself. Other theories, however, focused on behavioural forms of learning where some method, technique or practical situation had to be physically engaged in for learning to occur. Such theories emphasised the need to change structures and systems to enable individual behaviours to change. And yet other theories see the learning process of encounter between individual and collectives as the most crucial aspect of change. These theories speak of the cyclical nature of learning and employ terms such as single-, double- and triple-loop learning. Bracketing these strands of explanation together we can say that organisational learning is a cyclical process that requires interior reflection and exterior behavioural change for both individuals and collectives. Such a conception conforms with several learning cycle models (see, for example, Dixon, 1999). The learning lens will be described in greater detail in the following chapter. This example shows how bracketing together themes from various theories within the same paradigm category can form a unified and coherent conceptual lens for explaining transformational phenomena.

Bridging looks for connections and transition zones that span boundaries between theories and "across paradigms" (Lewis & Grimes, 1999, p. 675) in the development of lenses. An example of bridging can be seen in the wide use of stage-based models of transformation. Several paradigm categories saw transformation as a series of qualitative stages through which organisations transitioned in complex and idiosyncratic ways. These paradigms included spirituality, leadership, development and learning. Bridging involves a type of inter-paradigm scanning that seeks out strong thematic concordances between theories from different paradigms and brings them together to form metatheoretical lenses.

In summary, the bracketing and bridging techniques are applied to maximise parsimony, minimise conceptual redundancy and retain uniqueness of each of the explanatory lenses. Bracketing is done within some prescribed boundary (usually theories and paradigms) and bridging is performed in crossing those boundaries (between theories and paradigms).

Overall Design of Study

The overall design of this integrative metatheory building study for organisational transformation is shown in Figure 5.1. The figure shows all the major procedural phases (unboxed text) and the key outcomes of those procedures (boxed text) leading to the overall aim of the study—an

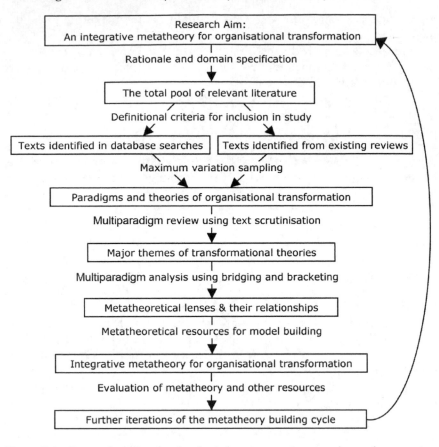

Figure 5.1 Research design for developing an integrative metatheory for organisational transformation.

integrative metatheory for organisational transformation. While the design portrays a sequence of stepwise progressions, the reality of the research process is that there are multiple iterations and excursions from prescribed pathways.

It needs to be remembered that this design is for metatheory building and not metatheory testing and that other procedures will be required to test the metatheory. In the next chapter the results from the multi-paradigm review of theories for organisational transformation will be presented.

6   A Multiparadigm Review and Analysis of Organisational Transformation Theories

Metatheory treats the multiplicity of theorizations as an opportunity for multiple operations of analysis and synthesis. (Weinstein & Weinstein, 1991, p. 140)

Given our multiparadigm perspective, we believe it would be useful for [meta]theory building to be viewed not as a search for *the* truth, but as more of a search for comprehensiveness stemming from different worldviews. This stance implies that the provincialism that comes with paradigm confinement might instead be turned toward the production of more complete views of organisational phenomena via multiparadigm consideration. (Gioia & Pitre, 1990, pp. 587–588)

AN OPPORTUNITY FOR ANALYSIS AND SYNTHESIS

This chapter presents a summary of the results of the multiparadigm review and analysis of theories of organisational transformation. A multiparadigm review differs from a standard literature review in that it specifically looks for concepts and themes that constitute the underlying architectonic of a theoretical system. It does this across multiple layers of expression, that is, at the level of basic constructs, parts of theories, complete theories, research paradigms and metatheories. In this case, the units of analysis for the review are the core explanatory themes for each of the theories of organisational transformation. These themes have been subjected to multilayered analytic procedures, to develop the final, comprehensive set of metatheoretical lenses used by theorists to conceptualise, explore and account for transformation. In subsequent chapters, these lenses are used to build an integrative metatheory for organisational transformation.

RESULTS OF THE MULTIPARADIGM REVIEW

The total number of texts included in the review sample was 335 and included books and book chapters, journal articles and a small number of online papers. These texts were chosen to maximise the range of theories included in the review. There were 107 theories of organisational transformation presented in these texts and they covered the entire range of conceptual approaches to explaining radical change. The relatively large number of theories described in the literature may have several explanations: (i) theories were counted as unique and were assumed to be the creation of the author(s) unless there was specific reference to the contrary, (ii) the sample period covered the last 30 years and, as this has been a time of extensive theory building in studies of organisation change, it is to be expected that a great many theories would be present in the extant literature, (iii) while functionalist theories have dominated the incrementalist and strategic change fields, there has been no dominant paradigm within the transformational change arena and, consequently, the proliferation of conceptual approaches has continued unabated since the early 1980s, and (iv) social science theories are difficult to falsify and it is to be expected that the total number of extant theories of radical change will continue to grow.

Using the technique of text scrutinisation (as outlined in Chapter 5), 472 explanatory themes were recorded for the 335 texts reviewed. Many theories had only one or two core themes while others had several. Perhaps the most common theme was related to leadership. There were many theories that saw transformation as the outcome of certain capacities of the CEO (see, for example, Beach, 2006; Bryman, Gillingwater & McGuinness, 1996; Leonard & Goff, 2003). However, there were also many theories whose explanatory frameworks involved the combination of multiple themes. For example, David Nadler and Michael Tushman (1999) present a model for the "organization of the future" that includes many different themes including various types of developmental stages and forms of organising, environmental factors, system dynamics and informal and formal change processes. With such a varied range and number of themes it was important that they be ordered for the purposes of performing the review and the paradigm groupings served this heuristic purpose for categorising theories and themes. Table 6.1 presents the complete set of research paradigms, some representative theories and a few of the 472 themes that were identified in the multilevel review.

There was significant redundancy, overlap and repetition among themes from both within and between different paradigm groupings. For example, within the process paradigm there were many theories which had significant similarities in the phases that made up the transitioning process (although they often differed in the precise number of transition phases). In many instances the same themes were found repeatedly across several paradigms. For example, stage-based concepts of transformation were not only described in theories from the developmental paradigm but were also present in the spirituality, leadership and learning paradigms. The many

Table 6.1 Transformational Paradigms and Representative Theories

Paradigm	Representative theories of transformation	Example themes identified in the multiparadigm review
1. Cultural	theories of cultural renewal, unwritten ground rules, individual-culture congruence	myth, ritual, ceremony, archetypes, symbols, and artefacts, shared cultural worldviews and assumptions
2. Developmental	action inquiry, spiral dynamics, corporate transformation	stages of individual and organisational transformation, transcend and include principle, deep structure
3. Evolutionary	population ecology, ecological theory of organisations	organisation–environment interaction, evolutionary selection (variation, selection, retention, reproduction)
4. Functionalist	business process re-engineering, technology and transformation, corporate transformation	behavioural norms and structural systems, impact of regulatory, economic & social environments, CIT
5. Postmodern	feminist theory, environmental models, relational leadership large group interventions	hierarchical nature of organisations, empowerment, relationality, collective meaning making, emotions, power
6. Learning	dialogical learning, knowledge levels, the learning organisation, social learning theory	learning cycles, collective learning microlevel transformation, situated change, incremental change
7. Multiparadigm	Theory E/Theory O, network organisation, discontinuous change, structuration theory	subjective–objective dimension, radical–regulatory change, collective vision, communication, team building
8. Organisational environment	holonic enterprise theory, inter-organisational theory, avalanche change, organisational ecology	inter-organisational cooperation, competition, trans-organisational drivers of change
9. Paradox	competing values framework, dialectical theories, relational theories, paradoxical change	polar relationships, internal–external, control versus flexibility, pathology & imbalance, change paradox
10. Process	Lewin's field theory, transition cycle, rhizomic model, "n" step models	unfreeze, shift, refreeze, growth and efficiency, crisis, chaos, back to basics, revitalisation, integration
11. Cognitive/ Behavioral	cognitive dissonance , reframing theory, information processing, decision-making theories, trait theory	individual learning, incentives, beliefs, schemas, cognitive dissonance, reframing, emotion, resistance

continued

Table 6.1   continued

Paradigm	Representative theories of transformation	Example themes identified in the multiparadigm review
12. Spirituality	theories of organisational spirituality and the new sciences, contemplative leadership	stages of spiritual transformation for individuals and organisations, deep meaning, organisational sustainability
13. Systems and New Sciences	soft systems theory, complex adaptive systems, dissipative structures, chaos theory	inputs, outputs, internal processes, hierarchy of organisational, dynamics transformations, holons, emergence
14. Teamwork	meso theory, group theory, team-based approach to transformation	communication, participatory, shared mental models, leadership, team development, micro-meso-macro
15. Transformational leadership	transformation leadership, transactional leadership, relational and reciprocal theories	developmental level, ethical and moral awareness, vision, empowerment, reciprocal leadership

themes extracted from the sampled texts were iteratively refined using the qualitative techniques of bridging and bracketing.

RESULTS FROM THE MULTIPARADIGM ANALYSIS

The multiparadigm analysis served to reduce the repetition and redundancy found between themes and to draw out their commonalities and differences to develop the broad conceptual lenses that theorists used to explore transformation. This process was performed iteratively at multiple layers of analysis, that is, at the levels of theoretical construct, theoretical system and paradigm. For example, some leadership-based theories of transformation only considered the importance of communication from a top-down perspective (the construct level) while other theories assumed that communication was a multilevel phenomenon (the theoretical system level) and other groups of theories shared a common focus on communication itself as the key aspect of transformation (the paradigm level). Bracketing and bridging techniques were adopted to explore themes within and across these various boundaries.

Lenses Identified Through Bracketing

Themes from within the same research paradigm were bracketed together to develop that paradigm's definitive lenses for building theories of organisational transformation. For example, under the learning paradigm three core conceptual lenses were found that many theories proposed as fundamental to explaining radical change. These three lenses were: (i) the learning process of active involvement, reflection, meaning making and evaluation, (ii) the lens of various kinds of learning loops for exploring the contexts of learning and (iii) the lens of knowledge levels which placed transformative learning within a knowledge development framework. There were other lenses that were employed by learning theorists but these three—learning process, learning loops and knowledge levels—were unique to the learning paradigm. From the 15 paradigms a total of 53 conceptual lenses were identified using the procedure of bracketing themes.

Lenses Identified Through Bridging

Bridging analysis was used to extract conceptual lenses from theories across different paradigms (Schultz & Hatch, 1996). This procedure ensures that the derived lenses do not simply reproduce existing paradigm boundaries. For example, theories from a number of paradigms emphasise the importance of having a multilevel conceptualisation of organisation in their explanations of transformation. Connecting these themes allows for the proposition of a multilevel (micro-meso-macro) lens that runs across paradigm boundaries. A total of 13 conceptual lenses were identified through the bridging of themes between research paradigms. Table 6.2 lists all lenses identified via the bracketing and bridging techniques.

This pool of 66 lenses provides an extremely rich base for developing a comprehensive metatheoretical framework for transformation. However, there is still significant room for refining these elements further into a more parsimonious set of lenses. The following section continues the process of data reduction and refinement with the aim of producing the core lenses that theorists have used to describe the transformation of organisations.

REFINING CONCEPTUAL LENSES

The refinement of lenses is a qualitative process that is guided by, among other criteria, the need for a parsimonious set of elements for building metatheory. Similarities and differences between lenses are identified to reduce the number of lenses while still retaining their conceptual scope and explanatory power. The theory building criteria of parsimony (minimal theoretical concepts variant), abstraction and internal consistency are important guiding principles in this refinement process. Several authors have highlighted the importance of these evaluation criteria in middle-range theory building (Bacharach, 1989; Torraco, 2002; Whetten, 1989; Wacker, 1998), and there is good reason to believe that these criteria are also applicable to the metatheoretical level of analysis. A theory should be parsimonious in that it use as few conceptual elements in its propositions

Table 6.2   Conceptual Lenses Identified through Bracketing and Bridging

Paradigm Category	Conceptual lenses identified through bracketing
1. Culture	i) organisational interiors, ii) archetypes, iii) organisational identity
2. Developmental	i) transformational stages, ii) sedimentation
3. Evolution	i) environmental selection, ii) evolution-revolution, iii) coevolution
4. Functionalist	i) growth, ii) technology, iii) efficiency, iv) physical design, v) time
5. Postmodern	i) gender, ii) the interpretive turn, iii) experiential approaches, iv) indigenous approaches, v) mediation & communication, vi) stakeholders, vii) diversity
6. Learning	i) learning process, ii) learning loops, iii) knowledge levels
7. Multiparadigm	i) multiparadigm thinking, ii) subjective–objective, iii) radical and regulatory change, iv) autonomy and relationality (or agency and communion)
8. Organisational Environment	i) corporate ethics, social responsibility and sustainability, ii) transformational imperatives, iii) inter-organisational networks
9. Paradox	i) paradox and dialectical change, ii) dialectical process
10. Process	i) transitional process, ii) the "dark night" theme
11. Cognitive-Behavioural	i) micro-focus, ii) reframing, iii) inclusive emergence, iv) behaviour change
12. Spirituality	i) stages of spirituality, ii) purpose and meaning, iii) spiritual process, iv) connectedness, v) spiritual leadership
13. Systems/New Science	i) deep structure, ii) system dynamics, iii) holarchy, iv) autopoiesis
14. Team work	i) the mesolevel, ii) team learning
15. Transformational Leadership	i) top-down leadership, ii) bottom-up leadership, iii) reciprocal leadership

Conceptual lenses identified through bridging

Conceptual lenses	Focus of explanation
1. Micro–macro	multilevel ecological context
2. Internal–external	intra- and extra-organisational environments
3. Interior–exterior	the subjective and objective aspects of organisations
4. Streams	the multimodal nature of organisational life
5. Perspectives	1st, 2nd and 3rd perspectives and their modes of inquiry

continued

Table 6.2 continued

6. States	transformative states of awareness
7. Emotion	the role of emotion in organisational transformation
8. Alignment	the degree of concordance between organisational entities
9. Health–pathology	personal well-being and organisational im/balance
10. Top-down/bottom-up	structural power, regulation and decision-making
11. Types	various typologies used in theorising about organisational life
12. Relational exchange	exchanges between organisational and environmental levels
13. Spirituality	profound meaning making, deep purpose & paradox

as possible. Although this is a difficult task for such a complex field as organisational transformation, it is one that needs to be attempted if data-analysis is to result in a manageable set of constructs for building metatheory.

The sorts of questions that considerations of parsimony raise include: Does a particular lens add a unique insight to our explanation that is not addressed by another lens? Is there conceptual redundancy between lenses? Can a particular lens be explained by the relationships between other lenses? How might several lenses be integrated? Abstraction is another criterion of relevance for developing metatheoretical lenses. Abstraction is important in that theory building should be able to "integrate many relationships and variables into a larger theory" (Wacker, 1998) and not be dependent on the detailed description of situational factors. The central question to be considered here is: Does a lens bring together different conceptual elements into a coherent construct? The goal of applying the criteria of parsimony and abstraction is to derive a set of conceptual lenses that are relatively independent of each other and thereby contribute unique aspects to the complex picture of transformation.

To order this refinement process, lenses can be categorised according to their research focus. This categorisation approach was adopted by Levy and Merry (1986) in their review of transformational theories and by Whetten (1989) in his discussion of approaches to theory building. Theories of organisational transformation differ as to whether they concentrate on "why" transformation occurs (causal focus[1]), "how" it occurs (process focus) and "who" (human focus) or "what" is being done (content/structure focus). There is also a metalevel category of explanation that cuts across all these areas of inquiry. These categories—how, why, who, what and meta-level inquiry—will serve as a means for ordering the refinement of lenses in the following section. These categorisations are not meant to be definitive or exclusive and other approaches could be used to order the results of the multilayered analysis.

The metatheoretical resources provided by the Wilber's AQAL and Torbert's DAI frameworks will also be called on to guide the refinement process. The resulting metatheoretical lenses are called "integral lenses" for several reasons: (i) they are informed by the use of large-scale integrative frameworks, i.e. AQAL (integral theory) and DAI; (ii) as the foregoing process of review and integrative analysis suggest, the resulting lenses themselves integrate constructs and theoretical elements from across many different perspectives and disciplines; (iii) in the later metatheory building chapters it will be suggested that these integral lenses can be generalised to fields of research beyond the transformation and sustainability domains that are the focus of this study; (iv) the generalising of lenses across multiple domains invokes comparisons with other traditions of metatheorising, several of which have also adopted the word "integral" or "integrative" in describing their conceptual frameworks.

Lenses Focusing on the "What" of Transformation

The Deep Structure Lens

Many conceptual lenses investigate the "what" of transformation, that is, the structures, systems or configurations that are transformed when an organisation undergoes radical change. A prominent group of lenses theorise that forms of organising can be seen as patterns of social interaction that persist over time and in different situations. According to this view, organisational structure is a persistent configuration that can maintain long-term arrangements of social, symbolic and material exchange. Consequently, organisations exhibit consistent traits and possess recognisable features that are definitive of the deep structures that form their cultural and social identity.

The conceptual lenses of stage-based development, institutional archetypes, deep structures and autopoiesis all hold to this structural view. The concept of "institutional archetype" (Cooper et al., 1996) also utilises the underlying interpretive scheme that provides an overall gestalt or configuration to an organisation's deep structure. Wilber has argued that "structures are always presented as holistic, transformational, and autopoietic patterns" (2003, para. 5) and it is the constellation of these qualities that enables organisational change to be studied as the unfolding of deep structure archetypes. The notion of autopoiesis also adds the quality of self-organisation to these deep structure stages of transformation (Seidl, 2005). These arguments support refinement of the archetype, stage and deep structure lenses to the one lens of deep structure.

The developmental holarchy lens

The multiparadigm review and analysis revealed many different conceptual approaches to explaining "what" was the actual content of change; that is, what were the structures, objects and elements that underwent transformation. Using AQAL and DAI as our guiding frameworks for organising these explanations, we can see that several lenses relate to developmental capacities. An important element of many developmental models is the concept of levels or stages of human development. There are many ways of presenting and describing the sequence of these stages and Wilber (2000c) and Torbert (1991) have independently described stage-based models of human development that have much in common. The following summary presents a combination of their models using my own adaption of their terms. Beginning with the fomative stages, their models include stages of physical opportunism, egocentric diplomacy, rational-technical expertise, rational-social achievement, existential strategist, world-centric transformation and cosmos-centric liberation. Most stage-models refer to the conventional levels of these developmental capacities. Many theories used lenses which focused on one or two of these stages and these lenses can be brought together to form versions of this developmental spectrum. Examples of these lenses include physical environment, affect and emotion, cognitive reframing, interpretive schemes, deep purpose and meaning, spiritual stages of transformation and stage-based development. Lenses of this kind can be accommodated within a single developmental lens that maps out this holarchy of development.

The Ecological Holarchy Lens

Research questions related to the "what" of transformation inherently involve assumptions about the micro/macro nature of what is transformed. One approach sees transformation as resulting from the microlevel of individual agency and action (Bacharach, Bamberger & Sonnenstuhl, 1996; Pettigrew, 1987). This psychological perspective is often opposed by sociological theories that frame explanations of transformation within the macrolevel context of the organisation and its environment. A critical concept in this macrolevel approach is the idea of a distinct organisational identity. Here, identity is seen not as an aggregate of individual attributes but as a holistic quality of the whole organisation and it is this collective characteristic that is presumed to undergo transformation (Hiller, Day & Vance, 2006). A non-reductionist appreciation for the causal powers of collective levels is the hallmark of macrolevel explanations of change (Giesen, 1987). Between the two poles of the individual and the collective lies the intermediate world of the mesolevel where group structures and team-based development are regarded as the driving force behind contemporary approaches to radical change. Almost all theories of organisational transformation adopted one or other of these three perspectives, but they often do so without any rationale for their particular choice. The micro-meso-macro conceptual lens is represented in AQAL as the individual–collective dimension of AQAL. This lens is also part of the DAI framework in that Torbert has described in great detail both individual and collective developmental potentials. The micro-meso-macro lens can be regarded as an ecological holarchy where the part/whole nodes are defined by a nested inclusion of many organisational levels.

The Governance Holarchy Lens

Many theories conceptualise transformation as a function of the organising power of either executive-level leaders or ordinary members of the organisation. These top-down and bottom-up approaches are frequently seen in debates over which view provides the best account of change (see, for example, Beer & Nohria, 2000). Dexter Dunphy describes this situation as follows (2000, p. 123):

> One of the most hotly debated issues in the field of organizational change has been whether change is best developed participatively with the active involvement of organizational members or lead from above by the CEO and top executive team.

However, these two orientations to organising and decision-making (and the structural systems that accompany those powers) can also be seen as complementary explanations for the "what" questions of transformation. The reciprocal leadership lens is an attempt to accommodate the top-down and bottom-up explanatory dimensions from a more multilevel perspective. The reciprocal nature of the leader–follower relationships means that leadership is a collaborative process and members of an organisation step in and out of such roles many times during their working day. It is interesting to note that the literature that addresses the spiritual nature of leadership often sees transformation as the radical reordering of the leader–follower structural relationship. *Servant leadership* is a phrase that has been coined to describe the spiritual approach to transformational leadership (Spears, 1998; Spears & Lawrence, 2001). There is a radical restructuring here which retains a hierarchy of decision-making yet turns it on its head so that the leader identifies with the "bottom" levels of the hierarchy of power and acts as their servant. The religious ritual of the leader washing the feet of the members of the congregation is a symbolic representation of this perspective (Sendjaya & Sarros, 2002).

Each of these viewpoints, the top-down/bottom-up, spiritual and reciprocal leadership and power/empowerment, offers a distinctive contribution to conceptualisations of organisational transformation as it relates to the decision-making and governance structures of organisations. They all share a concern with power and empowerment in one form or another. In each of these approaches, transformation is explained according to where in the organisational structure the source of power, decision-making and general governance resides. Such a structure exists irrespective of whether the organisation has a traditional hierarchical form, or a flattened heterarchical form or a networked team-based form. This multilevel lens is holarchical in that each organisational level possesses decision-making and organising capacities. Theorists using this lens explain transformation as a function of radical change in decision-making processes and in the forms of power and management that govern some organising function. This important lens will be called here the governance lens. This lens provides a conceptual window into multilevel issues related to an organisation's ability to govern itself and into the forms of organizing, management, power and decision-making that flow from the governance process.

Lenses Focusing on the "Why" of Transformation

The Internal–External (Environment) Lens

Theories that focus on the "why" of transformation consider all those conditions, qualities and situations which permit, enable, precipitate and trigger the transformational process (Levy & Merry, 1986). Many theories assume that the source of transformative change can be traced back to internal organisational factors, to external environments or to interactions between the two. The multiparadigm review found many themes where transformation was theorised according to the interaction of internal and external environmental factors and the interplay of these factors across organisational and inter-organisational boundaries (Diamond, Allcorn & Stein, 2004). Karen Newman (1999, 2000), for example, has developed a theory of radical change from the transformation of communist economies that, among other things, stresses the external environmental pressure on companies to be competitive and develop new internal organisational capacities. A comprehensive explanation of why transformation occurs will need to include both poles of this internal–external explanatory dimension (Carayannis, 1999).

Transformation–Translation Lens

One of the most common ways to theorise about transformation is to contrast it with theories of stability (Weick & Quinn, 1999). Theories from across many different paradigms distinguish between radical or transformative change and regulatory or translational change. Consequently, explanations can focus on stability and the status quo, on radical change and how to achieve it and on combinations of the two. An example of an approach that distinguishes between transformational and translational change is the Burrell and Morgan framework. They use the notion of "regulation" to refer to change which emphasises the "underlying unity and cohesiveness" of social entities (1979, p. 17). They use the term "radical change" to refer to explanations of change which emphasise the "radical transformations" and "deep-seated structural conflict" (1979, p. 17). These conceptions of change correspond closely to distinctions that have previously been described between, for example, first- and second-order change, evolutionary and revolutionary change, and translational or transactional and transformational change (Chapman, 2002).

An example of a hybrid approach to using the transformation–translation lens is the theory of the ambidextrous organisation (O'Reilly & Tushman, 2004). Organisations faced with dramatically changing environments need to be ambidextrous in handling both incremental and transformational change. The key idea here is that an ambidextrous organisation that balances both transformational and translational requirements can respond to the need for both stability and radical change as and when required. The transformation–translation lens incorporates all those approaches that highlight the revolution–evolution and radical–regulatory cycles that are evident in the lifespans of organisations.

The Interior–Exterior Lens

In researching the "why" of transformation theorists often formulate their explanations as subjective/objective or interpretive/functionalist dichotomies. As Burrell and Morgan (1979) pointed out 30 years ago, this divide between interpretive and functionalist understandings of change is one of the most characteristic qualities of theorising in organisational studies. Although there have been sustained criticisms of these divisions (see, for example, Law, 2000), organisation theorists continue to make use of distinctions between subjective and objective ontologies as a way of investigating change. Such approaches conceptualise change as instigated from interior intentions, conscious planning and cognitive goal-setting or as driven from the exteriors by altering organisational systems, providing behavioural incentives and objective means for measuring change.

There are many dichotomous dimensions that emphasise similar distinctions to this subjective–objective lens. These include "the view from the inside" versus "the view from the outside" (Kets de Vries & Balazs, 1998), "software" versus "hardware" (Philip & McKeown, 2004), "intangible" versus "tangible" (Barrett, 1998), nominalism–realism (Burrell & Morgan, 1979), interior–exterior (Wilber, 1995) and voluntarism–determinism (Weaver & Gioia, 1994).

Dichotomous distinctions and metaphors such as this describe the many different kinds of factors involved in transformational processes. One end of this dichotomy focuses on the different ways in which organisational behaviours and structures are manifested, expressed and communicated. These are the "hardware" aspects of the organisation. Others look at transformation as a radical change in the "software" of the organisation and see it as expressed in intangible, informal and subjective cultural forms. Both these orientations are required for developing a more comprehensive explanation of transformation. Together, they describe two poles of an explanatory lens that is called here the interior–exterior lens. Subjective, experiential and cultural approaches to transformation can be located towards the interior pole of this dimension and objective, economic growth, technology and efficiency/productivity-based theories come from the exterior pole of this bipolar lens.

The Agency–Communion lens

An agency–communion lens was used in theories that see transformation as resulting from either autonomous, agentic factors such as the decisive vision of a CEO (Rooke & Torbert, 1998) or from relational, network-based factors such peer-to-peer emergence (Arvidsson, Bauwens & Peitersen, 2008). The distinction between agency/autonomy and communion/relationality is a common ingredient in many theories of social and organisational change (Giddens, 1985; Hernes & Bakken, 2003; Lockie, 2004; Reicher, Haslam & Hopkins, 2005). This dimension is not the same as the agency–structure distinction which has more to do with the relationship between individual behaviour and collective structure. In contrast, agency–communion taps into the autonomous versus relational approaches to such things as governance, leadership, planning and decision-making.

The agency–communion lens can be applied at either end of the micro–macro scale. Consequently, with regard to the agency pole, theorists can consider transformation as personal motivation and action (Dirsmith, Heian & Covaleski, 1997; Hurley, 1998) or as collective decision-making and goal achievement (Hobson, 2000; Reicher et al., 2005). Both forms are concerned with the processes of deliberate action, self-regulation and goal-focused activity. A social entity's capacity for relationship and communion can also be seen as a characteristic of individuals and/or groups. Individuals are inherently communal and continually adjust their intentions and behaviours according to social and relational exigencies. Similarly, groups and larger collectives adapt their activities and intentions in relating to other groups so that their goals can be achieved and their identities maintained.

Theories of transformation often take preference for one side in this agency–communion dimension to the exclusion of the other and so differ strongly in their explanations for how autonomy and relationality influence change (see, for example, Bradbury & Lichtenstein, 2000; Reed, 1997). This argument appears in the literature in the debates between views of change as a function of organisational control, strategic management or transformational leadership and views that see it as a result of power relationships, communal networks and cultural identity (Beer & Nohria, 2000).

The Health–Pathology Lens

A consistent context for the theorising of transformation is that of organisational and personal health (Fineman, 1996). Wherever there are definitions of health, there are also implied definitions of pathology and illness. In identifying personal and organisational potentials of transformation, theorists are also providing ways of identifying pathological counterparts to those potentials. This has been an ongoing theme of theories of organisational transformation since the 1980s. The impetus for the early theories of transformation often came from the desire for a radically new vision for how organisations could contribute to personal and community health. How they could "enhance life" and take on the role of "nurturing servants" (McKnight, 1984, p. 152). These considerations continue to motivate theories of transformation to the present day. The health–pathology lens has been used in diagnosing the "positive zones" and "negative zones" of organisational transformation (Belasen, 2000), cooperative and non-cooperative forms of change management (Senge et al., 2007), "healthy" theorising and "sick" fads about change (Sorge & van Witteloostuijn, 2004) and "the rebalancing of polarities" to achieve "peak performance" (Quinn & Cameron, 1988, p. 306). Excessive emphasis on one side of a bipolar dimension results in many negative implications for organisations and their members. For example, the dimension of task–relationship is commonly used to investigate an individual's or team's approach to their work. Emphasising one end of this dimension over the other results in diminished levels of performance. Applying this to organisations as a whole, Forster makes the point that (2005, p. 323):

> The main disadvantages of strong task-focused organisational cultures are that they can legitimate unethical and illegal behaviour, can be highly resistant to change and can allow companies to become cut-off from the outside.

In such instances, a balance between task-focused agency and relationship-focused communion is called for. The health–pathology lens adds a crucial capacity to metatheorising frameworks for assessing the normative balance that a particular theory of transformation possesses.

Lenses Focusing on the "How" of Transformation

System dynamics lens

Questions regarding the "how" of transformation inquire into the processes and transition dynamics which produce radical change (Levy & Merry, 1986). The study of change dynamics is a strong feature of systems and new science approaches to transformation (Chiles, Meyer & Hench, 2004; Gemmill & Smith, 1985; Lemak et al., 2004; Lewis, 1996; van Eijnatten,

2001). Among the different types of dynamics that are described in systems theories, several have particular prominence in the transformation literature. These are: (i) fluctuation dynamics which refer to a system's movement between boundary states, system thresholds, bifurcation points and different orders of stability; (ii) feedback dynamics, including positive feedback which magnifies fluctuations in a system and negative feedback which weakens or shuts it down; (iii) stabilisation and dis/equilibrium dynamics which regulate and balance feedback mechanisms; (iv) self-regulation which, with enhancement and stabilisation, creates a system's capacity for autopoiesis. The systems lens contributes unique insights about organisational transformation that are based on these dynamics.

The Learning Lens

Another set of lenses that focus on the "how" of transformation comes from the organisational learning paradigm. Many learning theorists have proposed cycles of learning (Dixon, 1999) that involve interiors and exteriors (Miller, 1996) and individual and collective dimensions of learning (Casey, 2005; Fry & Griswold, 2003; Jorgensen, 2004; Mumford, 1992; Murray, 2002; Schwandt & Marquardt, 1999). A comparison between these and other learning models finds that learning phases can be associated with particular quadrants in the AQAL framework and with DAI's four territories of experience (see Appendix A). The learning process can be represented as a cycle of active physical engagement (doing and handling), conceptual reflection (thinking and experiencing), cultural interpretation (interpreting and understanding) and social validation (evaluating and expressing) that is iteratively followed to enable learning in individuals and collectives. Each learning phase utilises different learning skills that can be classified according to two dimensions: the concrete experience–abstract

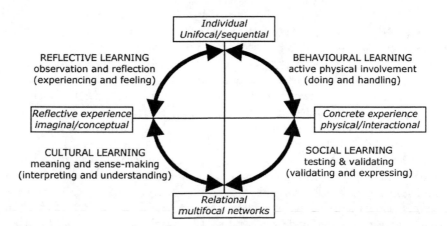

Figure 6.1 The integral cycle of learning (single-loop).

conceptualisation dimension and the individual task–interpersonal relationship dimension (Mainemelis, Boyatzis & Kolb, 2002).

Figure 6.1 shows these relationships as they relate to a single-loop learning situation. In double- and triple-loop learning, this cycle is built into a multidimensional view that describes "different hierarchical levels of learning" (Stewart, 2001, p. 143). Akbar (2003) has argued that there are clear links between knowledge levels and learning and has proposed a model for integrating "the knowledge creation view and single and double-loop learning models" (2003, p. 1997). The integration of learning process cycles, learning loops and hierarchies of knowledge (Romme & Witteloostuijn, 1999) creates a metatheoretical lens that can generate learning-based explanations of transformation.

Transition Process Lens

Theories that offer responses to the "how" research question are often called process theories (Galambos, 2005; Nutt, 2003) and are concerned with the various transitional phases of transformation. Striking similarities can be seen in the descriptions of transitional phases between process theories of transformation and other theories of social and psychological change. This similarity has been noted previously (Armenakis & Bedeian, 1999; Elrod & Tippett, 2002; Nutt, 2003; Smith, 2001) and theorists often make comparisons between change models from a wide diversity of social disciplines. In a review of models of organisational group development, Smith (2001, p. 37) concludes that:

> Many of the models, regardless of the classification scheme, exhibit similarities in terms of their form, patterns of progression, terminology, and even the nature of the phases or stages that are posited by the theorists.

These "phases" are the most apparent features of the transition process model. Collins (1998), for example, calls process models of organisational change "n-step guides for change" because they all share the notion of process phases or "steps". Collins remarks that (1998, p. 84):

> While it is true that *n-step* guides to change share a number of common and distinctive features, the recipes or schema often differ in terms of the number of steps into which they divide the change process: Some approaches outline five steps, other seven, others ten and so on.

Eighteen process theories of organisational transformation were identified in the multiparadigm review and these were compared with each other and with seven process theories from other disciplines (see Appendix B) for a summary of this comparison) to develop a process lens for transformation. A calibration of the phases of these models results in a 12-phase model which, to this date, is the most comprehensive description of the transition process lens.

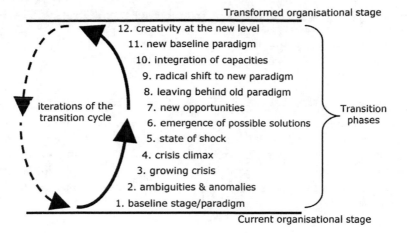

Transformed organisational stage

12. creativity at the new level
11. new baseline paradigm
10. integration of capacities
9. radical shift to new paradigm
8. leaving behind old paradigm
7. new opportunities
6. emergence of possible solutions
5. state of shock
4. crisis climax
3. growing crisis
2. ambiguities & anomalies
1. baseline stage/paradigm

iterations of the transition cycle

Transition phases

Current organisational stage

Figure 6.2   Transition process lens and its phases.

The transition process can be described as follows (see Figure 6.2): First, there is a baseline organisational system where individuals, teams or larger collectives operate from within particular patterns of organising, behaving, thinking and communicating. Out of this base condition ambiguities and anomalies arise which cannot be assimilated into this status quo system state of the organisation. These problems build into a crisis where management and staff struggle with significant problems and inefficiencies. At some point, a climax is reached which can take the form of some culminating event or series of events. This is often followed by states of shock, angry denial or moribund inactivity. From this depressed climate there slowly emerge some opportunities for investigating innovations and experimentation. Alternatives arise from these experiments which offer potential solutions to problems. Gradually, these are taken up as new forms of thinking, behaving and communicating to replace old logics and structures. A transformation occurs in which there is broad adoption of, and identification with, this new organisational system. A period of integration follows in which much of the old patterns and forms of organising are reshaped and integrated within the new order of functioning. The new transformed order of functioning and identity becomes routinised so that translational activities work to reproduce and reaffirm the new established order. As mastery of the new forms of activity and thinking increases, so levels of creativity and innovation within these new boundaries also develop. These cycles occur at multiple levels and within very different time frames within organisations.

The Inclusive Emergence Lens

Another process-based conceptualisation of change explores the relationship between stages of transformation. All the reviewed stage-based and life-cycle models regard development as a complex, non-linear process that proceeds along a variety of "tracks" (Cooper et al., 1996) and developmental pathways in navigating from one distinct form of organising to another. One aspect of this complexity comes from the "transcend-and-include" relationship between stages. More developed and complex forms of organising integrate and, to some degree, include simpler, more formative organisational stages. This process of ongoing development and integrative inclusion is called here inclusive emergence because of this non-equivalent inclusiveness of development. Examples of this inclusive emergence principle are seen in sedimentation theory (Greenwood & Hinings, 1993) and the development of action logics (Rooke & Torbert, 1998). Inclusive emergence is a dynamic cycle of transformation and integration. As organisations develop through qualitatively different forms of deep structure, they also require more integrative forms of the whole range of organisational capacities, otherwise they run the risk of becoming fragmented into a variety of subcultures with each expressing different developmental identities.

The Evolutionary Selection Lens

Evolutionary theories also concern themselves with research questions about the "how" of transformation (Burns & Dietz, 2001). Here the central concepts of variation, selection, retention and reproduction are used to explain how transformation can arise in local settings and be reproduced throughout whole systems (Jones, 2005). A major theme of evolutionary approaches deals with the dynamics of selecting new organisational forms (Tushman & O'Reilly, 1996). In this view, transformation results from the selection and retention of innovative capacities that are aligned with the demands of niche organisational and social environments. *Variation* refers to those innovative and experimental activities and flexibilities within organisations that can either succeed or fail depending on the advantages they offer to the organisation. Successful variations are selected by changing internal and external environments (Gersick, 1991; Wischnevsky & Damanpour, 2004).

Depending on the unit of analysis, selection can operate either within organisations or by dynamic environments that lie outside the organisation. Successful innovations are retained and reproduced to go on to become a major activity or dominant orientation of the organisation. This evolutionary selection lens offers powerful means for examining the impact of environmental imperatives on organisations to transform. Although neither AQAL nor DAI specifically include an evolution lens comprised of the variation, selection, retention and reproduction cycle, both metatheories do emphasise the evolving nature of individual and collective transformations.

The social mediation lens

Postmodern theories of transformation see text, language and communication as the primary site for transformational potential because they assume that it is within communicative media that forms of organisation have their source (Cooper & Burrell, 1988; Deetz, 1995; Stroeh & Jaatinen, 2001; Taylor & Every, 2000). Such approaches emphasise the role of social mediation in transformation. Social mediation occurs in the exchanges between two or more social entities, for example, in the relationships between individuals or between organisations in industry groups. Social mediation of radical change becomes particularly important when organisations are seen in the context of complex inter-organisational environments (Lee & Grover, 2000). The means of social mediation, for example, language, technologies, social norms and cultural assumptions, "provide the link or bridge between the concrete actions carried out by individuals and groups, on the one hand, and cultural, institutional, and historical settings, on the other" (Wertsch, Del Rio & Alvarez, 1995, p. 21). So, for example, the communication by media groups of community concern over climate change can be considered as mediating organisational change when it facilitates a company's intention to transform. Social mediation provides a way of envisaging large-scale change via the intermediacy of cultural artefacts such as electronic and print media (Edwards, 2008b). The mediation lens offers an alternative to those theories that conceptualise transformation as an innate, internal capacity of organisations.

The Alignment Lens

Ideas about functional fit, alignment, coevolution and congruence provide explanations which compare configurations of key transformational factors across a variety of boundaries. These comparisons are often referred to as forms of alignment between, for example, leadership style and type of change (Masood et al., 2006), organisational structure and its environment (Djelic & Ainamo, 1999), different structural levels of the organisation (Sammut-Bonnici & Wensley, 2002) or psychological traits and behaviours (Bacharach et al., 1996). For example, the theory of coevolution proposes that configurations that exist at one organisational level can initiate or support the transformation of structures at other levels and, hence, it too relies heavily on the notion of alignment in its theorising (Djelic & Ainamo, 1999).

The alignment lens develops explanations for transformation that emphasise the seeding of change across boundaries. Boundaries can refer to psychological distinctions between cognitive processes and behaviours or to the social demarcations between work teams and organisational structures. Whatever the boundary, the alignment lens seeks to find those concordances that support system stability and those dissonances that help to explain organisational change.

The Relational Exchange Lens

An important set of themes among developmental, systems and congruency theories of transformation refers to the relationships between certain organisational levels, systems and/or activities and the corresponding features of their external environments. Transformation, from this perspective, is about the flow of social and material energies and resources between these levels and systems. For example, Richard Barrett's (1998) corporate transformation model, which incorporates aspects of Maslow's needs hierarchy, describes the "motivating forces" that drive change at each of the seven levels of personal and organisational consciousness. Another example comes from the work of Dunphy, Griffiths and Benn (2003) on organisational sustainability. They propose a model of sustainability based on various organisational stages and the corresponding aspects in the natural and social environment that support and stimulate transformation through those stages. Wilber calls this relationship between developmental and environmental levels a system of "relational exchange" (Wilber, 1999b, p. 56). This lens is frequently used when change is theorised as occurring through exchanges between the structural and/or psychological levels of individuals and organisations and their environments.

Lenses Focusing on the "Who" of Transformation

The Stakeholder Lens

The "who" question of transformation investigates the experiences and characteristics of the people involved in the transformation event. This includes not only the organisational members but also other stakeholders such as customers, suppliers, shareholders, community members and so on. The stakeholders lens looks at transformation in terms of the relationships between organisations and the diversity of interests of the people involved. Depending on how one draws this boundary, the stakeholder group(s) can be regarded in a very limited way or in a very expansive way. One of the premises of change theories that use a stakeholder lens is that an organisation's capacity for large-scale innovation comes from the diversity of ideas and interests that are represented in decision-making forums (Benn & Dunphy, 2007). Adopting a limited perspective, decision-making is the prerogative of the board and/or senior executive. From a broader stakeholder perspective, the focus moves beyond shareholders, customers and suppliers to include public interest groups, local communities and natural environments. The stakeholder lens offers a fresh look at who needs to be involved in guiding the transformation process, who might be affected by the change and for whom the change process is ultimately directed.

The States of Consciousness Lens

States of consciousness is an important explanatory principle in the cognitive (Csikszentmihalyi, 2003), developmental (Cacioppe, 2000a, 2000b) and spiritual paradigms (Fry, 2005). States are the subjective aspects of consciousness and, as such, they offer a window into how change is experienced. Under the turbulent conditions of transformation, identity can be a shifting state in which consciousness is constantly moving and open to significant shifts. For example, in instances of peak experience, extraordinary performance or regressive episodes, individuals and groups can temporarily identify with forms of consciousness that are far removed from the everyday (Csikszentmihalyi, 2003). In these cases, states of consciousness can open up individuals' awareness to very different realms of experience. Pursuing transformation through altering the states of consciousness of organisational members is a feature of many intervention approaches of the 1980s (Adams, 1984; Levy & Merry, 1986) and, more recently, has been linked to organisational spirituality and its influence on organisational change (Benefiel, 2005; Dennis & Harald, 1999; Parameshwar, 2005; Shakun, 1999; Wall, 2003).

The Perspectives Lens

Other lenses that focus on the "who" issues include personal perspectives and experiential approaches. The personal perspectives lens of subjective (first-person), relational (second-person) and objective (third-person) forms of inquiry also challenges mainstream approaches to investigating change. Because it includes subjective and relational forms of inquiry, this lens discloses sources of data that open up new ways of conceptualising change beyond objective methods of inquiry (Torbert, 1999). The perspectives lens occupies a prominent position in both AQAL and DAI analyses.

Torbert, in particular, has developed a sophisticated approach to applying perspectives to the study and enactment of transformational change (Torbert, 1999). He sees first-person perspectives as (Torbert, 2000, p. 82): "Forms of research/practice that anyone of us can do by oneself by dividing and otherwise stretching one's attention to encompass all [the major] territories of experience". Second-person methods are interpersonal means for seeking understanding through dialogue. Torbert (2000, p. 82) says of the second-person that it:

> Includes all the times when we engage in supportive, self-disclosing, and confronting ways with others in shared first-person research/practice and in creating micro-communities of inquiry.

Third-person research/practice includes the familiar forms of "hard" science such as the empirical and behavioural sciences. First-, second- and third-person perspectives can, of course, be experienced and observed in both singular and plural forms, which results in six basic perspectives. I have described this lens previously in the context of a holonomic approach to organisational change and transformation (Edwards, 2005). While very few researchers overtly mention perspective as a core part of their theorising, assumptions about the perspectival nature of change, that is, whether it is subjective (first person), relational (second person) and/or objective (third person), are inherent in all theories of change.

The Postmodern or Decentring Lens

A powerful theme emerged in the multiparadigm review of feminist (Kark, 2004; Knights & Kerfoot, 2004), postmodern (Midgley, 2003), interpretive (Bartunek & Ringuest, 1989; Buchanan, 2003) and indigenous (Newhouse & Chapman, 1996; Paul & Zimbler, 1989) approaches to transformation that spoke to the underlying assumptions that privilege particular groups or forms of organising over other groups or forms. This way of examining transformation questions underlying assumptions concerning power, the control of language and the manipulation of knowledge. This lens searches out forms of meaning that are local as opposed to universal, that are relational as opposed to instrumental, that are decentring as opposed to conforming and that are community-focused as opposed to economy-focused. This postmodern lens sees change research as value-laden rather than value-neutral. Consequently, theories that employ this lens are highly critical of the basic assumptions regarding managed and planned change and, instead, emphasise an emergent and local approach that values cultural diversity over a uniform hierarchical order.

I call the lens that these postmodern theories adopt a "decentring lens" because they all theorise transformation from a critical position that assumes a non-mainstream perspective. Methodologically, the views sought come more from people and groups at the periphery, from the local, from the hidden and unheard voices of those experiencing and affected by change (Badham & Garrety, 2003). Conceptually, the explanations for transformation speak of shifts in power from the centre to the periphery and from established systems of control to decentralised systems of participation.

Meta-level Lenses

Meta-level lenses are applied by theorists across the range of research questions concerning the "what", "who", "when" and "why" of organisational transformation. Meta-level lenses derive from the cross-paradigmatic analysis of the core themes of many different theories and are, therefore, not easily reduced to other lenses.

The Spirituality Lens

Spirituality theories of transformation see change as guided by a search for deep purpose and meaning (Bell & Taylor, 2003; Fry, Vitucci & Cedillo, 2005; McKnight, 1984; Steingard, 2005). The emphasis here is not solely on the development of postconventional stages of spiritual transformation, but on the development of deeper insight into what is already and ordinarily present in people's work lives. The discovery of meaning is central to this issue. As Cacioppe puts it (2000a, p. 49), "Discovering the meaning of one's work is a central part of spiritualty". Deep fulfilment and discovery of one's true potential through work and through work relationships is regarded as a pathway to personal transformation.

Several models of spirituality (Benefiel, 2005; Elrod & Tippett, 2002) have described organisational transformation as a process of spiritual transitioning. Such models concentrate on the dynamics by which radical change and spiritual transformation occur. For example, during the change process, crises and dilemmas are encountered that initiate a phase of intense existential questioning and motivation to move to some new way of understanding or acting. The term "dark night of the soul", borrowed from the Christian mysticism literature, is used by some change theorists to describe this phase. For example, in their model of "individual, organisational and societal transformation", Neil and Lichtenstein (2000) see this phase of "dark night of the soul" as the initial phase in transformation process. This is followed by a phase of searching and questioning which in turn leads to a phase of spiritual transformation and finally to a phase of integration. The parallels here with more conventional process models of organisation transformation are obvious. The key distinction between the two is the radical nature of the transformational stages involved. Where conventional process models see transitioning as an inherent aspect of any change, models using a spirituality lens highlight those transformations that results in a complete renewal at multiple levels of organisational life (Dehler & Welsh, 1994; Howard, 2002; Pava, 2004).

Another facet found in theories that employ a spirituality lens is the notion of connectedness. Social and environmental connectedness is a common theme among theories within the spirituality paradigm. The emphasis is on the connectedness that exists between individuals, groups, organisations and communities in terms of their mutual responsibilities, ethical behaviours and care for integrity of natural and social environments. From this perspective, transformation is explained as a sense of relatedness between people, organisations and the socio-economic and environmental context in which they function (Fry, 2005). The inspiration for this approach comes from the concern for transformation in ethical conduct as well as interior consciousness. Giacalone and Jurkiewica refer to this type of connectedness when they define workplace spirituality as (2003, p. 13):

> a framework of organisational values evidenced in a culture that promotes employee's experience of transcendence through the work process, facilitating their sense of being connected in a way that provides feelings of compassion and joy.

The Streams Lens

All theories within each of the paradigm groupings regarded transformation as a whole-of-system process that involved qualitative shifts in all the main aspects of organisational life. For example, Chapman (2002) proposes that if transformation is to be successful in the long term, then radical changes need to be achieved in such things as organisational structure and culture, management systems, business processes, employee attitudes, beliefs and values. There are many such lists of different domains of transformation mentioned in theories from all paradigms. As evidenced in the following quote from Beer and Nohria (2000, p. 142), theories that use multiple lenses recognise the multimodality nature of transformation:

> One does not produce real change by relying on a single means such as reward systems or structure. Organizational designs are integrated systems consisting of structure, formal systems, informal processes, reward and measurement systems, and human resources practices. Effective change requires changing a combination of policies, or all of them, to create a new and integrated design. And all of the policies must be aligned or mutually reinforcing.

This multimodality is a focus of the research of transformation theorist Jerry Porras and his colleagues (Collins & Porras, 1997; Porras, 1987; Porras & Silvers, 1991). Porras describes a modular conceptualisation where organisations are thought of as multiple "streams" of operations or relatively independent subsystems. These streams are grouped under four main areas: (i) organising arrangements, (ii) social factors, (iii) technologies and (iv) physical settings. Organising arrangements include substreams like organisational goals and strategies, formal structure, policies and administrative systems; social streams include culture, values, norms, language, rituals and interaction processes; the technological streams consist of technical systems, tools and workflow systems; the physical settings streams consist of space configuration, physical ambience, interior design and architectural design.

Organisational streams are interconnected in "significant and powerful ways" (Porras, 1987, p. 51) and can be seen to operate at the level of individuals, groups and larger organisational units (Porras, 1987, p. 39). The streams lens enables a theorist to recognise the multidimensional nature of transformation. However, the streams lens is often applied in a unifocal fashion and a type of lens reductionism occurs when too much conceptual attention is given to one or a small number of organisational domains. We see this, for example, when transformation is theorised as a matter of leadership, or communication and information technology, or teams-based structuring or cultural renewal. Wilber calls this kind of lens reductionism "line absolutism" and more will be said on these kinds of metatheoretical errors in later chapters.

The Types Lens

Explaining transformation in terms of "types" is a common feature of theories from several paradigm groupings. Some approaches include types of transformations (Blumenthal & Haspeslagh, 1994; Tosey & Robinson, 2002), types of transformational strategies (Bamford, Rogers & Miller, 1999), organisational types (Blom & Melin, 2003; Carman & Dominguez, 2001), psychological types (de Charon, 2003) and change process types (Nutt & Backoff, 1997). These typologies are metatheoretical frameworks for classifying, describing and making factual claims about transformation (Doty & Glick, 1994). They combine many of the lenses that have already been described with moderating variables such as intensity, frequency and time.

Any lens can be used to create categories and, when combined with another metatheoretical lens or moderating variable, typologies of various kinds. Consequently, the types lens is more a way of using conceptual tools to form metatheoretical frameworks for categorising and typing than a specific theoretical perspective. Because the types lens does afford a means for developing metaconjectures and typological frameworks it will be included here as an integral lens.

SUMMARY OF INTEGRAL LENSES

The rationalisation and refinement of the large number of conceptual factors identified in the multiparadigm review and analysis has resulted in a more parsimonious set of 24 integral lenses. Even though the refinement process has greatly reduced the number of conceptual lenses derived from the multiparadigm analysis, there are still many available as basic building blocks for assembling the integrative metatheory for organisational transformation. Our final set of metatheoretical lenses for organisational transformation includes:

Lenses Addressing the "What" of Transformation

1. deep structure: the pattern of persistent features that define forms of organising, these are the core identifying features of a particular organisational form
2. developmental holarchy: transformational stages, discontinuous jumps and shift that result in radical change
3. ecological holarchy: micro-meso-macro, multiple levels of organisation
4. governance holarchy: levels of decision-making and power relations

Lenses Addressing the "Why" of Transformation

5. internal–external: the inside and outside of organisational boundaries, the distinction between organisational entities and their environments
6. transformation–translation: radical change–incremental change
7. interior–exterior: contrasting poles of, for example, subjective–objective
8. agency–communion: autonomous–relational, task–relationships
9. health–pathology: balanced–unbalanced, whole–fragmented

Lenses Addressing the "How" of Transformation

10. system dynamics: bifurcation points, feedback processes, cyclical dynamics
11. learning: single-, double-, triple-loop learning; integral cycle of learning
12. transition process: transition cycles, change processes
13. inclusive emergence: transcend-and-include cycles
14. evolutionary cycle: emergence through variation, selection, retention and reproduction cycles
15. mediation: social mediation through artefact-in-use and communication
16. alignment: concordance between two structures, processes or entities, the fit between some state and its environment
17. relational exchange: exchanges that occur between two structures or processes to facilitate growth, development and adaptive change

Lenses Addressing the "Who" of Transformation

18. stakeholder: viewpoints of employees, managers, customers, communities and all those affected by the change process
19. states of consciousness: condition of subjective awareness of stakeholders including somatic, affective and existential states
20. perspective: first-, second- and third-person perspectives—in their singular and plural forms
21. decentring: hidden and marginalised standpoints, local versus universal concerns

Meta-lenses Addressing the "What", "Why", "How" and "Who" of Transformation

22. spirituality: the transpersonal, deep purpose, connecting process
23. organisational streams: domains of organisational life, e.g. people, structures, cultures, systems
24. types: typologies of key organisational entities

This large number of lenses is an expected outcome of the multiparadigm review and analysis. There are several reason for this: (i) the complexity of social events and of transformational issues means that many forms of explanation are possible, (ii) the large number of extant paradigms and theories in the literature also means that a relatively large number of lenses should result from the theme analysis and (iii) the metatheoretical principle of non-exclusion, i.e. the inclusion of as many valid conceptual approaches as possible, inclines integrative metatheory building towards including more lenses rather than less.

In the next chapter the relationships within and between these integral lenses will be considered. Clarifying the relationships between components is an essential part of any theory or metatheory building project. These relationships determine to a large degree the shape of the metatheoretical system and consequently will be crucial for describing the framework developed in following chapters.

7   The Network of Lens Relationships

> In the relationship building step [of theory building], parsimony, fecundity, and abstraction virtues enhance the theory by using only necessary relationships, offering new areas for investigation, and integrating relationships for a higher abstraction level. Also in this stage, internal consistency is important to verify which relationships are logically compatible with each other. Generally, as more internally consistent relationships are integrated into a theory, the theory can explain more, therefore raising the theory's abstraction level. (Wacker, 1998, p. 370)

INTEGRATING LENS RELATIONSHIPS

This chapter discusses the relationships between the conceptual lenses developed from the multiparadigm review and analysis. As the quote from John Wacker testifies, identifying and describing these relationships is essential for developing any internally consistent theoretical or metatheoretical framework. Commenting further on the need to describe relationships between theoretical elements in the "relationship-building" phase of theory construction Wacker stresses that, "the literature provides the best guidelines as to which relationships are theoretically important for investigation and which relationships may be considered fundamental" (1998, p. 370). Once again, the various literatures analysed in the multiparadigm review and the metatheoretical resources of AQAL and DAI will be our guides for developing these fundamental relationships between metatheoretical lenses.

There are some metatheory building criteria that have particular relevance to the task of identifying underlying relationships between lenses. Internal consistency is one such criterion. Internal consistency means that definitions and relationships are applied across a conceptual framework in a reliable, consistent and logically coherent manner. Questions that guide this process include: Are relationships between lenses consistent and not contradictory? Do these relationships hold for all combinations of lenses? Do reductionist forms of lenses exist? High abstraction is another desirable quality for a metatheoretical system (Mowen & Voss, 2008). The abstraction level of a construct is its independence from situational and temporal particulars. When a theoretical system has a high abstraction level it has the capacity to "integrate many relationships and variables into a larger theory" (Wacker, 1998, p. 365). Metatheories are intended to do precisely this and so it is vital that overarching approaches should possess a considerable level of abstraction. Uniqueness is another criterion that is used here to judge the adequacy of a lens. Uniqueness refers to the capacity for concepts to be independent and discernably distinct from one another. Clearly, if a lens is to provide some unique insight into a social event, it must disclose very distinctive views and generate explanations that are not shared by, or at least reducible to, other lenses. These criteria of internal consistency, abstractness and uniqueness guide the following explorations of lens relationships.

LENS CATEGORIES

Both internal and external relationships need to be considered in the process of building consistent connections among integral lenses. One simple way of identifying and describing the internal relationships of lenses is to consider their basic morphology and whether they might be defined by, for example, linear, bipolar, holarchical or cyclical relationships. Mintzberg and Westley (1992) adopted this kind of morphological approach in their study of patterns of organisational change and represented those patterns as various types of cycles and spirals. The benefit of this approach is that it can draw on current research in such areas as image schemas (Hampe & Grady, 2005), mental space theory (Fauconnier & Turner, 2002) and conceptual metaphor theory (Lakoff & Johnson, 1999) to develop a better understanding of the forms of metatheoretical lenses that influence theorising and metatheorising.

Looking at the patterns that characterise the set of integral lenses identified in the multiparadigm review and analysis, it is possible to describe a number of categories based on their morphological similarites:

1. The holarchical category—these lenses take the form of multilevel holarchies, e.g. the developmental, ecological and governance lenses.
2. The bipolar category—these lenses are defined by complementary dualisms or paradoxes that form binary dimensions, e.g. agency–communion and internal–external lenses.
3. The cyclical category—these lenses are depicted as iterative or phased cycles, e.g. the transition process lens and learning lenses.
4. The relational category—these lenses share a relational form or interactive mode of representation, e.g. the mediation lens and alignment lenses.
5. The standpoint category—these lenses take the form of a web of subjective or personal perspectives, e.g. personal perspective lens and the states of consciousness lens.
6. The multiparadigm category—these lenses can appear in several categories, e.g. the spirituality lens can be expressed as a holarchy, a process and as a state of consciousness.

Table 7.1 shows the categories that result from grouping lenses according to these basic patterns of relationships. Grouping lenses into these categories assists in the investigation of how lenses inter-relate and highlights how the study of lens relationships can be linked with such emerging fields as conceptual metaphor and image schema theory.

The exploration of the relationships both within and between lenses and their categories is a branch of metatheoretical studies that has immense potential. This topic has not been considered systematically before and can only be touched on briefly in this study. This new field of metatheoretical studies can be referred to technically as epistemological metamorphology. This is the study of the shape of metatheoretical lenses and how they

Table 7.1   Categories of Integral Lenses for Organisational Transformation

Categories of Conceptual Lenses

Holarchy category: Lenses expressed as holarchical structures; the "what" of transformation
1. deep structure
2. developmental holarchy
3. ecological holarchy
4. governance/organising holarchy

Bipolar category: Lenses expressed as dualities and polarities; the "why" of transformation
5. interior–exterior
6. transformation–translation
7. internal–external
8. agency–communion
9. health–pathology

Cyclical category: Lenses expressed as cyclical processes; the "how" of transformation
10. system dynamics
11. learning
12. transition process
13. inclusive emergence
14. evolutionary selection

Relational category: Lenses expressed as relational processes; the "how" of transformation
15. mediation
16. alignment
17. relational exchange

Standpoint category: Lenses expressed as perspectival standpoints; the "who" of transformation
18. stakeholder
19. states of consciousness
20. perspectives
21. postmodern or decentring

Multimorphic category: Lenses expressed in multiple forms; the "what", "why", "how" and "who" of transformation
22. spirituality
23. organisational streams
24. types

inter-relate when used to conceptualise complex social events. Epistemological metamorphology or, more simply, lens morphology has the potential to identify and critically examine many of the basic distortions that appear in organisational theory and, more generally, in social theorising and metatheorising. There are strong links between this type of metatheoretical research and the philosophy of meta-Reality of Roy Bhaskar (2002b). Bhaskar's philosophy sees one of the major roles of any social science as adjudicating on the half-truths and false forms of ideology that reshape and greatly influence social realities or, as Bhaskar calls it "demi-reality" (2002a, p. 55):

> The task of social science is to penetrate that demi-reality through to the underlying reality and situate the conditions of possibility of the removal of illusion, of systematically false being.

In metatheoretical terms this means the identification of systematically distorted lenses and their relationships in large-scale conceptual frameworks and the study of the authentic relationships within and between metatheoretical lenses and their morphological categories. In the following pages I will touch on a few of the implications of this new field of metatheoretical research and what it means for organisational transformation and sustainability. Before that, however, I will look a little more deeply at the holarchical category of lenses.

RELATIONSHIPS BETWEEN HOLARCHICAL LENSES

The Importance of the Holon Construct

The holon construct has special importance in the description of lens relationships. There are three important reasons for highlighting the role of the holon construct in identifying the relationships between lenses. First, holons are useful in both representing complex social phenomena from a non-reductive standpoint. It is the holon's capacity to include both situational/holistic and temporal/analytical explanations which enables it to provide non-reductive explanations of social happenings. Second, theories of transformation, irrespective of the conceptual lenses they employ, will always include some construct that refers to an organisation's radical shift from one order of functioning to another. Because the holon construct was proposed by Koestler to capture precisely these kinds of multilevel change phenomena, it has been used in many theories of complex and radical change (Bell & Warwick, 2007; Edwards, 2005; Krarup, 1979; Landrum & Gardner, 2005; Mathews, 1996; McHugh, Merli & Wheeler, 1995; Terenzi, 2005; van Eijnatten, 2001). Although it might not be ostensibly stated as a central concept in the majority of transformation theories, the idea of a part/whole is inherent to many theories of discontinuous, trans-formative change. Third, the holon construct has the capacity to act as a scaffold for displaying other types of lenses. Wilber's AQAL framework and the chaordic systems thinking approaches of van Eijnatten and his col-leagues (van Eijnatten, 2001; van Eijnatten & Putnik, 2004; van Eijnat-ten & van Galen, 2002) are good examples of how holons can be used to represent multiple lenses in relationships. Wilber uses the developmental holon as a means for describing his quadrants framework and van Eijnat-ten integrates such concepts as connectivity, consciousness, emergence and complexity levels within a systems-based view of holons.

There are three different types of holonic lenses that emerged from the multiparadigm analysis and review. One is based on developmental rela-tionships between levels of transformational growth, another on spatial relationships between ecological levels of the organisation and the third on organisational relationships between levels of governance, management and decision-making. The developmental (stage-based) lens is clearly relevant to transformational concerns and its capacity to represent transformative devel-opment is fundamental for theory building in this field. However, the other two forms, while not explicitly transformational in character, are also com-monly used in theories of change. The following section describes in some detail the internal relationships of these three holarchical lenses.

Three Forms of Holarchical Relationships

Although Koestler admitted that there could be several different forms of the holon/holarchy construct (1967), he frequently emphasised the ecologi-cal form in his endeavour to represent biological, organisational and social levels in a hierarchy of spatial and functional relationships. Wilber, on the other hand, has always emphasised the developmental forms of holon and holarchy. He shows how holons can be used to represent the genealogi-cal relationships between stages of human and socio-cultural development. These are very different types of relationships and Wilber in particular has been at pains to ensure that they are not confused (Wilber, 2000b; Wilber & Zimmerman, 2005). Wilber argues that theorists who do not clearly distinguish between developmental inclusion and spatial inclusion produce confused holarchies and that the relationships between holons and holonic levels in those holarchies are invalid. This is called the "mixing problem". The literature on organisational evolutionary dynamics refers to these two different forms of structural relationships as genealogical and ecological hierarchies (Baum & Singh, 1994). Genealogical holarchies are based on time and developmental inclusion whereas ecological holarchies are based on spatial relationships and environmental inclusion. The developmental or genealogical form of holarchy (Wilber) is seen in transformational theories that focus on stage-based development. The ecological form of holarchy (Koestler) is seen in theories of transformation that focus on organisational levels, that is, on the micro-, meso- and macrolevels of organising and on transformation as it occurs within, for example, individuals, teams, organisations, industries, economies and broader socio-cultural environments.

In addition to these two, a third form of holarchy is proposed here—the governance holarchy. As explained previously, this lens is concerned with the relative organising power or decision-making capacity that exists between different individuals, levels and groups within an organisation. The governance holarchy is not built on the criteria of developmental or ecological relationships but on the relationships of organising and decision-making power. Figure 7.1 depicts the three forms of holarchical lenses and their internal relationships.

It is important to note that for each of these forms of holarchy the regulatory processes that govern interactions between sub-holons are multidirectional and relational in character. Therefore, in their ideal form, holarchies should not be equated with top-down command structures or bottom-up revolutionary structures. That is, in true governance holarchies, more encompassing levels do not determine what the less encompassing levels will do in isolation from the organising agency of those junior levels. "Higher" holarchical levels do not cause "lower" levels to behave or think. The exchange is always a two-way process. Hence, in a balanced governance holarchy, constituent holons are best seen as leader-followers. In practice, however, distorted forms of these lenses can shape and reproduce inherently unhealthy social hierarchies (as Bhaskar has noted) and it is in these instances that we see oppressive forms of top-down power hierarchies and destructive forms of bottom-up revolutionary heterarchies. Healthy holarchies are actually a balance between supportive forms of hierarchy and stabilising forms of heterarchy. Brian Robertson's (2006) work on holacracy is an example of this transformational use of the governance holarchy lens.

Each of these three holarchical lenses is present in theories of organisational transformation. The developmental lens is seen in theories that explain transformation as a function of the stage-based development. The ecological lens is most evident in systems and complexity theories that see transformation as a result of emergent processes within individuals, teams,

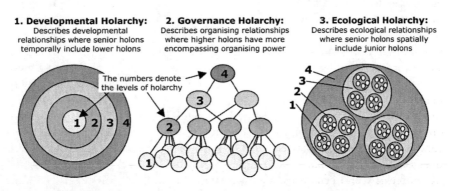

1. Developmental Holarchy: Describes developmental relationships where senior holons temporally include lower holons

2. Governance Holarchy: Describes organising relationships where higher holons have more encompassing organising power

3. Ecological Holarchy: Describes ecological relationships where senior holons spatially include junior holons

The numbers denote the levels of holarchy

Figure 7.1 Three forms of holarchical relationships.

organisations or some other ecological grouping. The governance lens is predominantly utilised by leadership theories which advocate top-down or bottom-up approaches to transformation. I will turn now to the relationships between other lens categories. Clarifying these relationships will contribute to the task of building the overall metatheory for organisational transformation.

RELATIONSHIPS BETWEEN LENS CATEGORIES

Exclusionary Relationships Between Lens Categories

In general, theorists rely on only a small number of conceptual lenses in developing their explanations of organisational transformation. This means that, for example, process theorists ignore structural lenses, such as those used by multilevel theorists, and developmental theorists make very little use of the transition process or learning lenses. Theorists who come from a standpoint or relational perspective often neglect the developmental and multilevel lenses and those lenses expressed as bipolar dualisms. In fact, the extensive list of lenses in Table 7.1 suggests that most theorists are relying on a relatively limited conceptual base in developing explanations for transformational occurrences. This exclusionism has several unfortunate implications for theories of transformation in organisational settings. One is the lack of use of the stage-based development lens.

We have seen that transformation requires a qualitative shift on the part of the whole organisational system from its current status quo to a more complex and integrative form of organising. Without a sensitivity for the existence of these transformational potentials, theorists risk proposing models of change that are inadequate for explaining real and lasting transformation. This issue will be explored in more detail in a later section. However, it is important to note at this point that whatever lenses a change theorist may work with, their approach will be very partial if the developmental holarchy lens is excluded. Their conceptualisation of transformation will be missing a definitive aspect of radically alternative forms of organising. In effect, their theories of change will reduce authentic transformation into a kind of transactional or translational change. Such models are prevalent among economic- and growth-based theories of change which focus on economic increase rather than any qualitative shift in the fundamental form of the organisation.

The exclusionary emphasis on perhaps one or two lenses from a particular research paradigm means that an incomplete picture of transformation will drive research and practice. Over time, this leads to the shaping of organisational and economic realities that do not reflect the full potentials of people or the organisations they create.

Relationships Between Holarchical and Other Lens Categories

Despite the steps taken to ensure that metatheoretical lenses are not simply reproduced according to paradigm boundaries, it appears that some lens groups are associated with particular research paradigms. Relationships between lens groupings mirror the relationships between different research paradigms. The holarchical group can be associated with a more structuralist approach to theorising, while the relational and standpoint groups of lenses can be associated with postmodern approaches. For example, theorists who rely predominantly on the developmental lens construct theories that do not capture the meditational and relational aspects of change. Such theories fall into a kind of developmentalism where theorists rely solely on the stage-based developmental lens and consequently exclude other forms of explanation (i.e. non-developmental lenses) (Howley, Spatig & Howely, 1999; Walkerdine, 1993). When cyclical, standpoint or interaction lenses are excluded, the result is forms of explanation that rely heavily on the ranking of levels of development, the grading of worldviews and the diagnosis of the relative position of social entities on particular developmental scales (as they apply to organisational members, leaders, teams or the organisation as a whole). This narrow use of the developmental lens can result in a rigid view of hierarchy where the definition of higher and lower makes no use of heterarchical and non-developmental concepts.

Theorists who adopt relational and standpoint lenses rightly criticise stage-based models and theories that make exclusive use of multilevel concepts. Postmodernist theorists, who use relational and contextual lenses in their explanations of change, are highly critical of theories that are based on notions of transformational or developmental hierarchies (Baker, 1999). Their concern is that a reliance on stage-based explanations of transformation will lead to prescriptive concepts of "progress" and to the privileging of "higher levels" of performance and functioning. Postmodernism argues forcefully that these prescriptions are part of the problem and not part of the solution and that transformation which is based on modernist (developmentalist) ideas of progress and advancement will result in injustices, environmental problems, power inequities and social dislocations of all kinds.

Although these critiques are well based, they do not address an issue that lies at the heart of all theories of transformative change. Postmodernist theorists of organisational change also call for the transformation of our organisations towards more humane and sophisticated forms. This call assumes the need for a trans-*form*-ing into some other way of organising. The concept of transformational potential necessarily means that there is some preferred state of organising. Hence, all theories must have some notion of qualitatively distinct forms of organisation. As many writers have argued (Habermas, 1995; Young, 1997), without some guiding vision of favoured social arrangements, the relativism of postmodernism is susceptible to a directionless "flatland" that merely generates deconstructive criticism with no capacity for contributing to constructive and transformative forms of change.

These two camps—the developmentalists who employ the holarchical, multilevel lens category and the relativists who employ the relational and standpoint lens categories—are in ongoing debate over many aspects of organisational change (Easley & Alvarez-Pompilius, 2004; Goles & Hirschheim, 2000; Hassard & Kelemen, 2002; Lincoln & Guba, 2000; Weaver & Gioia, 1994). Table 7.2 lists some of the debated topics and the differing positions adopted by these two metatheoretical orientations. Approaches that rely solely on the developmental lens prefer hierarchical arrangements that support top-down, transformational leadership styles. Their explanations are concerned with the presence or lack of various developmental stages and the means by which these stages can be advanced along a spectrum towards some teleological stage. Those who take a relativist position rely on the standpoint and relational lenses that support bottom-up and emergent processes that can be described in cyclical, peer-to-peer and heterarchical terms rather than structural and hierarchical ones.

Each of these viewpoints has important contributions to make towards theorising on transformational phenomena. Problems arise, however, when particular lenses are applied to the exclusion of others. This escalates into misunderstandings over the relative merits of opposing positions.

Relationships Between Cyclical and Other Lens Categories

The parochialism between developmental and postmodern theorists is only one example of the "paradigm wars" (Jackson & Carter, 1993) that can result from a reliance on certain categories of explanatory lenses to the exclusion of others. Another example is the division between theorists who employ cyclical category lenses and those who adopt the holarchical and bipolar lenses which are inherently more content-based and structural in

Table 7.2 Positional Differences between Developmentalism and Relativism

Debated topic	Developmentalist view (holarchical lens category)	Relativist view (relational & standpoint lenses)
type of transformation	stage-based or levels-based	emergent
leadership	top-down	bottom-up
management structure	hierarchical	heterarchical
aspect of change	structural	proccessual
teleology	the top of the hierarchy	cyclical
methodology	individualist	collectivist
epistemology	universalising	localising

focus. For example, process theories develop explanations that are based on the dynamics and characteristics of change as it occurs over time (Chia, 2002). In contrast, theories that use bipolar lenses emphasise the structural dimensions of different types of organisational designs and environments. The ensuing debates get polarised around the issue of change in structural types versus change as processual dynamics. One side describes typologies and categories based on the combinations of bipolar dimensions while the other eschews categorical models in favour of descriptions of process, flow, change dynamics, continuous change and learning processes (Chia, 2002). A more inclusive metatheory of transformation values both these approaches and recognises the complementary relationship between cyclical and bipolar categories of lenses.

The foregoing discussion highlights the need for a complementary approach towards using lenses from different categories. A multiparadigm and integral approach to explaining the complexities involved in transformation recognises that each of these groups of lenses can offer significant contributions. They complement each other in providing insights into the "how", "when", "why" and "who" of transformation. However, before looking at these complementary relationships, we need to look in more detail at the form of these explanatory lenses themselves. While it is important that multiple lenses be employed in our explanations it is also crucial that we use them in their most complete form. Lenses are defined by the relationships between their constitutive elements or, what might be called, facets. For example, the ecological holarchy lens requires a comprehensive multilevel model of organisation and a simple micro–macro binary distinction is not able to capture many important levels that are involved in change. The internal relationships between different facets of a lens is a crucial issue that has implications for the application of those lenses. Some theorists use reductive forms of lenses and, consequently, produce reductionist explanations of change. The following section provides a brief introduction to this issue of lens reductionism.

Reductionist Forms of Lenses

A common way of formulating conceptual lenses is as a bipolar, complementary duality where opposing qualities define a certain dimension of organisational life. We see this, for example, in the two dimensions that constitute the multiparadigm framework of Burrell and Morgan and in the AQAL framework where several of the main conceptual lenses are expressed as complementary dualities. However, many theories make use of only one pole of a bipolar dimension in researching organisational transformation. They use a reductionist form of a lens to explore change and, as a consequence, produce partial explanations and understandings.

An example of this kind of partiality is seen in the debate between theorists who see organisational culture (collective interiors) as the central explanatory concept for transformation and those who see organisational systems and structures (collective exteriors) as the main player in change. Explanations based on one end of this bipolar continuum will necessarily be partial and interventions that are designed on this reduced conceptualisation of social life often result in problematic outcomes. Researchers who come from a more integrative orientation argue strongly that culture and structure (interiors and exteriors) are two complementary sides of a continuum that exists for all social entities and that one side of this dimension cannot exist without the other (Lüscher & Lewis, 2008; Van de Ven & Poole, 1988; Wilber, 2005a). Culture and structure, the informal interior and the formal exterior aspects of organising, complement and support each other and together form two ends of an important conceptual lens for exploring transformation.

Several researchers of organisational change have commented on the very poor results of programmes that focus purely on transforming organisational culture or, alternatively, on the restructuring of organisational operations and systems (Applebaum & Wohl, 2000; Forster, 2005; Kotter, 1995). The failure of many transformational programmes may be due, in part, to the application of models that utilise reductive versions of these types of lenses. Focusing on the exterior, objective aspects of organisations can result in the dominance of outcomes over process, in measurement over meaning, products over people and in sales over service. On the other hand, a heavy focus on organisational culture can result in a lack of structure, accountability and decisiveness.

During the multiparadigm review, occasions were found where each of the bipolar lenses was used in a reductionist form. Leadership theories often emphasise agency and autonomy over the communion and relationality aspects of transformation. Discontinuous change theorists emphasise transformational leaps whereas continuous change theorists focus on translational learning and incremental change. Organisational ecology theorists see external environments as the generative factor in transformation while human relations theorists regard internal working environments and process as central. A major implication of the use of reductive forms of bipolar lenses is that they limit the types of change interventions that can be made to create more dynamic organisations.

The tendency for theorists to use truncated versions of lenses is not confined to the bipolar group of lenses. Stage-based development theorists, for example, do not always make use of the full spectrum of levels of organisational development. In the multiparadigm review many stage-based models of transformation were compared and their stages calibrated against one another (see Appendix C). Of the eight theorists included in this comparison only three specifically described the most advanced stages of transformation. Five theorists did not include the radical, postconventional levels associated with the more holistic, inquiry-based and spiritual forms of organising and three did not include stages beyond the conventional levels.

Theorists who employed truncated or reductive versions of these holarchical lenses propose restrictive models of transformation that do not consider the full range of potentials identified by other approaches.

There is another more intense form of lens truncation that drastically reduces the whole spectrum of transformational potentials to two simple levels—the current organisational "status quo" and the desired or envisioned form of the "goal state" of organising. However minimal the explicit reference to the developmental lens may be, all transformational theories assume that some form of organising is preferable to another. Even evolutionary or incremental explanations assume some degree of qualitative difference in an organisation's core functioning over time. However, reducing multiple levels of transformation potential down to the simple dichotomy of status quo versus goal state runs the risk of producing short-term, directionless change. This is "change for change's sake" and, particularly in times of environmental turmoil, any change can be appealing because it is a movement away from the status quo of uncertainty and non-action.

Reductionist forms of the ecological holarchy lens appear when ecological levels are limited to those found within the organisation and do not include levels outside the organisation. This results in the neglect of broader environmental, inter-organisational and social levels of ecology when explaining environmental imperatives and the external mechanisms that trigger or support transformation. Alternatively, some theorists, particularly those from an evolutionary dynamics perspective (Baum & Singh, 1994), develop multilevel models of organisation environments but do not consider the social ecologies within organisations themselves. In these instances the danger is to overlook the importance of individuals, dyads and teams and other organising subsystems within the organisation's own ecological levels.

Multiple ecological levels can also be restricted into a simple bipolar dimension. This occurs, for example, when a multilevel model is reduced to a bipolar micro–macro model. Multilevel models involve a distinction between the levels of the individual, dyad, triad, team, group, department, organisation, inter-organisational levels and global ecological levels. Some theorists, however, (and this is a problematic feature of Wilber's AQAL framework) reduce these multiple levels into a simple bipolar individual–collective dimension. The resulting model often ignores the crucial role of relational and team-based mesolevels of the organisation in transformational processes.

Explanatory lenses expressed as cyclical processes also suffer from forms of metamorphological reductionism. The transition process lens, in particular, is sometimes expressed in a very pared-back form. A well-known example of this reduced version is the change model of Kurt Lewin (Lewin, 1952; Rosch, 2002). Lewin's model is frequently simplified to a three-phase model of unfreeze-move-refreeze. This summary hardly does justice to the very sophisticated model that Lewin actually worked with; however, this three-phase version is widely quoted and leaves out many phases identified in other process or "N-step" models, as David Collins (1998) refers to them. A common issue with N-step models is the omission of critical steps of the transition cycle. Three examples of this type of process lens reductionism are found in models that omit: (i) the inactivity or "state of shock" phase, (ii) the experimentation phase and (iii) the integration phase. I will now look at each of these examples in more detail.

Many models of organisational transformation omit the phase dealing with the low point in the transition process. Variously described as a state of shock, depression or despair in individual transformation and as inaction, chaos or resistance in organisational transformation, this phase has been tellingly labelled, "the death valley of change" by Elrod and Tippett (2002). Models that ignore this phase present transition as a positive movement from one stage of functioning to the next and make no mention of crisis, negative affect, widespread confusion or self-doubt. These theories sometimes use neutral terms such as "adaptation" or "transitioning" phase to describe these periods of chaos. Understandably, this omission, or at least neutral labelling, is more common among functionalist approaches to transitioning where it is more likely that the experiential impacts of change are overlooked.

Another phase that is commonly omitted from the transition process lens is the "experimentation" or "emergence of possible solutions" phase (see Figure 6.2). In this phase, multiple small experiments and innovations occur in ideas, production processes, collaborative projects, conversations and technological inventions. From these local trials at novelty there emerge successful behavioural, technological and sense-making innovations that can spread through the organisation. Theories that leave this phase out of their process lens underestimate the power of local experimentation within organisations and the capacity that these smalls trials have for system-wide transformation. These models of the transition process tend to undervalue internal innovations and overestimate the value of importing new systems, technologies, personnel, structures and processes.

A third phase that is neglected in theories that utilise the transition process lens is the integration phase. Moving from one organising form to another requires not only giving up old cultural practices, structures and systems of organising but also the integration of those old capacities within the new organisational mode. New forms of organising do not merely replace old forms. They need to be retained and built on to create the new organisational design. And it is this integrated step that many transition models leave out. In these cases, the transition process becomes a one-off revolution where the old is totally replaced by the new. Such models lack the developmental insights gained from adopting the lens of inclusive emergence. Under this non-inclusive understanding of transformation, whatever is defined as old or as belonging to the previous order is seen as superfluous to the newly transformed organisational state. Consequently, "old" employees and managers, technologies, cultural and structural systems and organisational identities can all be subject to "redundancy". This view of transformation has no integrative capacity, neglects the impact of discarding its "old" human, technological and physical resources and becomes a race for whatever is new. An unintegrated neophilia, or the love of the new, is one unhealthy outcome of process models that lack an integrative phase (Bubna-Litic, 2008).

A final example of cyclical lens reductionism comes from the area of organisational learning. We have seen that the learning lens includes phases of behavioural involvement (active), cognitive involvement (reflective), sense-making (interpretive) and social validation (evaluative). Sometimes phases from these learning cycles can be omitted or neglected, resulting in dysfunctional types of learning. Where the behavioural phase is missing, learning can become overly conceptual and abstract. Here, organisational learning leading to transformation lacks a grounded process of concretising change. Where the reflective phase is missing, learning can become a simplistic and uncoordinated process of trial and error. Here, transformation attempts become chaotic processes of changing practices and structures that lack reflective planning and guided intention. Where the interpretive phase is missing, learning becomes a perfunctory and uncreative process of passive memorising. In these instances, transformational attempts suffer from inflexible programmes that are simply superimposed theoretical models without any localised sense-making or creative adaptation. Where the social validation phase is missing, learning becomes disassociated from any evaluative basis. Transformation here runs into the problems associated with a lack of monitoring and feedback, particularly from those who must implement the changes. Theories of transformation that utilise learning-based lenses need to include all four facts of learning if they are to avoid these kinds of reductionism.

The multiparadigm review also found that transformational learning theories situate these learning cycles within a vertical dimension of qualitatively different levels of analysis as seen in models of single-, double- and triple-loop learning. Learning theories that do not recognise these multiple "loops" or levels might be able to provide insight into translational learning but lack the capacity to disclose information or knowledge that is valuable for transformational learning. Translational learning, or single-loop learning, can only provide solutions to problems from within the organisation's current paradigm. Theories based on translational learning models see change as an incremental increase in knowledge, that is, as an increase in the quantity of information being processed rather than the quality of knowledge gained. As a result, what goes for transformation in single-loop models is more like an infatuation with information technologies and IT management than a real concern for deep change. Without a lens that is sensitive to qualitative change, transformational theories are reduced to focusing on horizontal increase, technological innovation and systems efficiencies rather than any qualitative change in knowledge management.

Conflated Relationships Between Lens Categories

Particular problems arise when reductionist forms of holarchical lenses are conflated with lenses from the bipolar category. When a multilevel holarchy is reduced to a bipolar form there a strong tendency to associate this false bipole with other valid bipolar lenses. An example of this is seen in transformational theories that link the poles of a reduced ecological holarchy lens (individual–collective) and other valid bipolar lenses such as agency–communion, task–relationship and masculine–feminine leadership styles. This is evidenced in the tendency to regard only individuals as having agency (Van de Ven & Poole, 1988) or leadership as an essentially agentic activity (Reicher et al., 2005).

Wilber has drawn attention to this problem in his essay "The Pre/Trans Fallacy" (PTF) where he points to the confusions that take place when multilevel developmental models are erroneously reduced to a simple two-stage bipole and then aligned with a valid bipolar structure. Referring to this conflation between multilevel and bipolar explanatory dimensions, Wilber (1990, p. 258) says: "The problem . . . is that some theorists use real or structural bipoles in order to support and carry their own versions of a PTF bipole". What he means here is that some theorists conflate truly bipolar lenses with reductionist forms of multilevel lenses, primarily from the holarchy lens category.

This confusion between developmental and binary lenses is relevant here because of its frequent occurrence in developmental theories of organisational transformation. Certain stages of organisational development, team development or personal transformation become associated with one end of a binary dimension and the logical outcome of such a model is to aim for change towards the other pole of this dimension. Transformation then becomes the movement between two ends of a complementary duality rather than a qualitative shift to a new form of organising that accommodates both poles. Without a clear conception of the range of transformational forms available to organisations, radical change runs the risk of becoming a continuous movement between two sides of the same coin. Some theorists attempt to avoid this problem by applying other bipolar models of change. The problem is, however, that these other bipolar models merely reinforce the patterns of bouncing between, for example, cultural renewal (interior transformation) and systems restructuring (exterior transformation). This kind of, what might be called, ping-pong transformation occurred on a large scale during the 1990s when the pendulum of organisational transformation swung between focusing on cultural change (the interiors) and organisational restructuring (the exteriors) and back again with limited success and substantial disruption to workforces (see Dunphy, 2000; Forster, 2005). Highly structured organisations saw transformation as a renewal of their culture, while organisations with a strong cultural base saw radical restructuring and a focusing on systems and processes as the "holy grail". Both mistakenly associated particular poles of the culture–structure dimension (interior–exterior lens) with the goal of transformation instead of integrating both culture and structure within entirely new forms of organising.

This type of lens category conflation results in destructive iterations of an unhealthy transformation where change moves endlessly between the two poles of some valid bipolar dimension of change (in this case interior culture versus exterior structure). This results in repetitive and ultimately destructive cycles of restructuring and cultural renewal. Transformation traps such as these are particularly difficult to resolve when combined with a reduced two-stage view of transformation as described earlier. The outcomes for employees of these ping-pong transformations are low morale, resistance to change programmes and the lack of positive outcome expectations. Literature on the causes and effects of excessive change (Falkenberg et al., 2005; Zajac, Kraatz & Bresser, 2000) has found that excessive change actually reduces an organisation's structural efficiencies and reduces its capacity to respond effectively to rapidly changing environments. The relevant point here is that these change traps are associated with change intervention strategies that derive from reductionist and conflated forms of conceptual lenses.

Figure 7.2 shows the steps involved in this form of lens category conflation. The first step is the reduction of the many levels of transformational potential down to the dichotomy of "the status quo" and "the goal state". The second step is identifying some valid binary lens that is used as the basic diagnostic tool for assessing problems and setting direction, e.g. interior culture–exterior structure. The third step is to associate one end of this bipole with the "status quo" and, hence, point to the other pole as "the goal". When, for example, the restructuring or cultural renewal "transformation" has been achieved, the results are generally not convincing (as we have seen from the empirical studies of transformation programmes) and so another round of ineffective transformational renewal begins, only this time in the opposite direction. The last two decades have seen several iterations of this ping-pong transformation, resulting in a

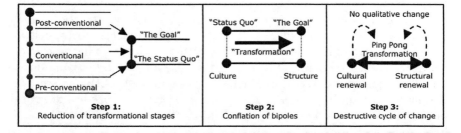

Figure 7.2 Conflated relationships between holarchical and binary lens categories.

destructive cycle of change. Badham and Garrety (2003) call the experience of working in such organisations "living in the blender of change" and they refer to the management culture that supports this endless quest for change "the carnival of control". This phenomenon has been particularly evident in the waves of reform undergone by the public service sector (Farazmand, 2003).

The example outlined here has been for the interior–exterior lens in its form as the culture–structure duality. There are several other bipolar lenses that also fall prey to this type of reductionism and lens conflation. Of particular note is the top-down or leader–follower reductionism that is associated with the hierarchical nature of decision-making in organisations (the governance holarchy lens). Applying our reduction model to this bipolar dimension we find that the "status quo" is equated with the organising style of the current CEO and "the goal" is then to find some other CEO whose organising style will provide top-down transformation of the organisation. After an average of three to four years that CEO becomes the "status quo" and the search for the new CEO ("the goal") begins again. The organisation is trapped in a bipolar cycle of current CEO and transformational CEO because it has reduced the multilevel governance holarchy into a simple top-down view of decision-making and management. The current infatuation with the notion of the transforming leader has developed to a point of unquestioned ideology when, in fact, there is little evidence that successful transformation has any correlation with the type of CEO an organisation chooses (Beer & Nohria, 2000).

Another example can be seen in the conflation between status quo–transformational goal and the agency–communion lens. Here the "ping-pong transformation" occurs between forms of organising that are based on either centralised authority or decentralised networking. Depending on the status quo condition, the transformation goal is reduced to a movement from agentic forms of organising to relational forms or vice versa. While both agency and communion are crucial aspects of organising, choosing one over the other leads to cycles of reform that merely move around on the same level of organisational development, or, using the terminology of Greenwood and Hinings, the same "design archetype". From an epistemology of change perspective, the central issue here is the lack of awareness of the multilevel nature of transformation and, in particular, the inclusive emergence of those levels. Knowing that one of the defining features of transformation is its multilevel nature should warn against the adoption of theories that explain radical change in terms of dichotomous models of transformation ("the status quo" and "the goal state"). The combination of the holarchical lens of transformational stages and the inclusive emergence lens provides a heuristic method for setting a direction for vertical development. This mitigates against the kinds of conflated associations between holarchical and bipolar lenses described here.

The preceding sections have considered some forms of reductionism that apply to the use of metatheoretical lenses in explaining transformation. The following points are offered as guidelines for minimising these problems:

- Identify and, wherever possible, utilise the full range of levels for all holarchical lenses.
- Ensure that the developmental holarchy lens is not reduced to a simple bipole and never abbreviate them to less than three levels of transformative potential (pre-conventional, conventional and postconventional stages).
- Maintain at least three intra-organisational levels of distinction for the ecological holarchy lens, e.g. micro, meso, macro.
- Include intra- and inter-organisational levels when using the ecological holarchy lens.
- Ensure holonic lenses are not associated with bipolar dualities. Don't express or reduce holonic lenses to a bipolar form and then associate its poles with those of a valid bipole.
- Include both poles of a bipolar lens by recognising its full conceptual scope (identified through a multiparadigm review of relevant paradigms and theories).
- Cyclical lenses need to retain all phases to allow for an accurate representation of change. In particular, the "death valley", experimentation and integration phases need to be included in models that utilise the transition process lens and learning models should include all four strands of the learning lens.
- Always include the inclusive emergence lens when describing or explaining deep structure transformation.
- Avoid developmentalism by including the mediation lens and, conversely, avoid relativism and environmentalism by recognising the need for the developmental holarchy lens in explanations of transformation.
- Ensure that non-reductive forms of lenses are used when combining lenses to propose metatheoretical matrices and frameworks.

These are only a few implications for the study of transformational processes that are gained from a rigorous study of lens metamorphology and the relationships that exist within and between lens categories. In later chapters some further directions for metatheoretical research into these topics will be outlined.

Metatheoretical Indexing

In most cases it would be expected that the set of lenses listed in Table 7.1 should each provide unique insights into the phenomena associated with organisational transformation. In other words, each lens opens some unique portal into conceptualising transformation that is afforded by no other lens. Each lens sees a dimension of transformation that is orthogonal to the dimensions associated with other lenses. This orthogonal relationship means that lenses can be crossed to develop matrices where each cell represents some unique aspect of transformational phenomena and provides a meta-location for accommodating theories of those phenomena. Hence, all the major explanatory themes of theories of organisational transformation can be represented as various constellations of these lenses. If, for example, we cross the lenses of interior–exterior and ecological holarchy we can develop a matrix which indexes theories of transformation according to their focus on, for instance, the relative importance of cognitive and cultural versus behavioural and structural change for each organisational level. This kind of metatheoretical indexing not only categorises theories but helps to identify their domains and relative boundaries compared to other theories of change. Metatheoretical mappings like this are essential for building integrative frameworks that establish where theories have valid application and conceptual relevance and where they might not. It also helps in identifying disciplinary blind spots and where theorists have neglected certain conceptualisations for some topic.[1]

Table 7.3 sets out this example in further detail by indexing theories of transformation according to their multilevel focus for either interior or exterior aspects of organisational life. At the microlevel of individual interiors, theories focus on cognitive changes in belief systems and states of consciousness whereas behavioural theories focus on performance, productivity and goal achievement. At the mesolevel of the team, theories concerned with the interiors focus on team culture, values and shared mental maps while exterior theories focus on performance outcomes and group incentives. At the macrolevel the organisation, cultural theorists concentrate on organisation-wide systems of meaning making and the development of collective vision whereas structural theorists look at transformations in structures, systems and technologies. Further macrolevel layers of indexing can be used to locate theories of broader cultural and societal transformation.

The point of this example is to show that any of the explanatory lenses developed to study organisational transformation can be combined to develop typologies and indexing systems to help in theorising about transformational phenomena. In the following pages, other examples will be provided where theorists have used several lenses to develop models of change. These examples show the types of relationships that are possible with different lens combinations. Wilber (2003b, para. 75) has described this indexing process of crossing the fundamental dimensions that describe his AQAL framework as follows:

AQAL indexing ("integral indexing" or "holonic conferencing") allows individual paradigms to be seated next to each other at the integrative table, in such a way that each individual paradigm is honored and acknowledged.

Table 7.3 An Example of Integral Indexing Using Interior–Exterior and Ecological Holarchy Lenses

	Interior Change	Exterior Change
Micro (individual)	Cognitive theories theories of personal transformation focusing on cognitions, beliefs systems, states of consciousness	Behavioural theories theories of personal transformation focusing on behaviours, job performance and goal achievement
Meso (team)	Team culture theories theories of team transformation focusing on team culture, shared mental maps and team values	Team performance theories theories of team transformation focusing on team performance, group incentives and outcomes
Macro (organisation)	Organisational culture theories theories of organisational transformation focusing on organisational culture, vision and meaning making	Organisational structure theories theories of organisational transformation focusing on organisational structures, systems, technologies
Macro–macro (organisational environment)	Cultural theories theories of social transformation focusing on the informal culture of industry, community and society and international environments	Socio-economic theories theories of social transformation focusing on social and economic structures, market forces and broad technological changes

Wilber emphasises here that the purpose of integral indexing is not to synthesise or unify theories and paradigms but rather to accommodate them within a metatheoretical framework that acknowledges the plurality of approaches while also showing how they might be connected in systematic ways. This type of accommodation enables metatheory building to recognise "the special and profound contribution" of different theoretical perspectives and also to identify their limitations and boundaries (Wilber, 2000a, pp. 38–39).

The large number of explanatory lenses identified in the multiparadigm review means that there are many different lens combinations available for exploring the epistemological frameworks of researchers, for accommodating their contributions and for developing new insights into explaining transformation. The following explores some of those possibilities and also points out where theorists have made mistakes in making assumptions about the relationships between lenses. What follows is further evidence that the array of conceptual lenses identified earlier can be combined in a variety of meaningful and imaginative ways. These explorations also show the theoretical fecundity that can be generated when the core insights of different theories and paradigms are allowed to converse with each other.

Relationship Between the Developmental Holarchy and Transition Process Lenses

Two of the most important and frequently used lenses for explaining transformative events are the developmental holarchy and transition process lenses. Although no theory was identified that combined these lenses in a systematic or comprehensive way, several theories provided insights into how these lenses could be amalgamated. Theories utilising the transition process lens outline change phases in moving from one form of organising to a qualitatively different one. On the other hand, developmental theories describe the structure and content of those forms of organising and say little about how the transition between them occurs. Bringing these two lenses together provides a model that describes both the spectrum of organisational forms and the transition process that occurs as organisations struggle to shift developmentally through that spectrum. Figure 7.3 gives the graphical representation of this combination of developmental holarchy and transition process lenses.

Reiteration of the transition process occurs for each stage of transformation. The change curve that describes the process of growing inconsistencies, crisis, shock, renewal, radical shift, integration and renewed stability occurs for each stage of transformation, whether that be for organisation, individuals, teams or any other organisational holon. In systematically combining both the process and stage lenses this complementary model untangles the often confused relationship between transformational stages and transitional phases. In fact, there is often no distinction made between these two explanatory lenses in the literature on organisational transformation. They are both presented as "models of change", and sometimes their phases and stages are included indiscriminately within the one model (see, for example, Nutt, 2003). However, from the metatheoretical point of view, it is clear that transformation and transition models do not refer to the same phenomena. Clarifying the relationship between these two lenses resolves several issues that are puzzling when either lens is used in isolation. This explains, for example, why transformative events are strongly

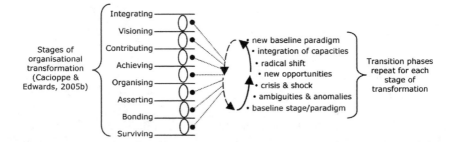

Figure 7.3 Combining developmental holarchy and transitional process lenses.

associated with confusion, negative emotion, stress and even temporarily poor performance. The complementary model provides a coherent and testable explanation for this observation. Transformation occurs through transition and transition always involves a phase that has been variously described as the "dark night" and the "death valley of change". Such a phase, as Elrod and Tippett (2002) point out, occurs whenever significant change is experienced. Authentic transformation necessarily involves such dark times and if they are not encountered at some point by an organisation then transformation has probably not occurred.

Combining the developmental and transitional lenses forms a basis for including other integral lenses, and representing these combinations holonically provides a graphical space to do this. Figure 7.4 shows a holonic framework depiction of the developmental and transition process lenses. The stages of development are aggregated into pre-conventional, conventional and postconventional stages. The transition process will take place for each shift in an organisation's journey through the spectrum of transformational stages. This process is not a linear one and unresolved process issues can stymie transformation and lead to states of rigidity and bureaucratisation and even lead to organisational regression (Kilburg, Stokes & Kuruvilla, 1998).

Bipolar Lenses and Quadrant Models

Frameworks for explaining transformation are often based on combinations of two or more bipolar lenses. These combinations create grids and simple matrices that provide a framework for outlining typologies and other explanatory models. Typologies are very important and often undervalued models for structuring knowledge and developing systems of explanation (Doty & Gluck, 1994). As transformational theorists Greenwood and Hinings (1988, p. 296) explain in the following, typologies order the structural relationships between theoretical concepts.

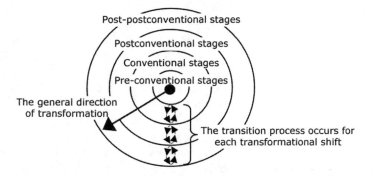

Figure 7.4 A holonic framework for development and transition.

Typologies are important, in a general sense, because they are ways of extracting and directing key theoretical ideas. They are specifically important and central to organisation theory because of the general proposition that there are different kinds of organisation and that these generic differences have consequences for performance, power, decision-making, conflict, morale, job satisfaction, etc. One of the key points about typologies is that they are holistic in nature, emphasising the totality of relationships between a set of concepts; types are based on idea of coherence between organisational elements.

An example of a quadrants typology in organisational change theory is Simpson and Cacioppe's (2001) analysis of "unwritten ground rules" and organisational culture. They crossed the individual–collective lens and the interior–exterior lens and applied this framework to informal cultural rules and norms. Because the relationship between these fundamental lenses is an orthogonal one, the authors claim that the domains that they uncover are themselves unique and definitive aspects of organisational life. If this is so, it should be the case that other organisational theorists find similar fundamental domains. Such support is found in the work of Fisher, Rooke and Torbert (2003) and their identification of four territories of experience which bear strong similarities with Wilber's four quadrants. Two of these territories, intention and planning, relate to Wilber's "interiors" and two, behaviour and assessing, relate to his "exteriors". Two other territories, intention and behaviour, are associated with individual experience and two others, planning and assessing, are associated with the social realms.

There are several other quadrants models that are derived from crossing lenses similar to those proposed in Table 7.1. In their theory of "design archetypes" Greenwood and Hinings (1996) propose a theory of transformation where organisations are represented as the confluence of four domains of human identify and activity—"ideas and beliefs", "doings and operations", "values and meanings" and "systems and processes". They derive these qualities from the interaction of two dimensions that have strong parallels with Torbert's and Wilber's quadrant dimensions. A different combination of bipolar lenses is examined by Dunphy and Stace (1988) in their review of strategic transformations. These theorists combine the individual–collective lens as it applies to strategic leadership with the transformation–translation approach to change. In so doing, they propose a typology of "change strategies" which includes dictatorial transformation (the coercive leader's approach to radical change), collaborative transformation (the collaborative leader's approach to radical change), forced evolution (the coercive leader's approach to incremental change) and participative evolution (the collaborative leader's approach to incremental change. Similarly, Nutt and Backoff (1993), in seeking to find the most important qualities of transformational leaders, investigate the interior and exterior qualities of leadership at the microlevel of interpersonal exchange and macrolevel of socio-cultural structures. In effect, they cross the interior–exterior leans with a simplified ecological holarchy lens to propose four focal points for transformational leadership: framing and language (micro-interior), interpretive meaning making (macro-interior), descriptive modelling (micro-exterior) and strategic fellowship (macro-exterior).

A great many such examples of similar binary lenses being combined to form quadrants models were discovered during the multiparadigm review. These examples are supporting evidence for the kind of relationships that exist between different bipolar lenses. For example, a notable feature of many of the quadrants models is the use of the ecological holarchy lens in its reduced form of the binary micro–macro. As explained previously, the ecological holarchy lens considers the spatial relationships between multiple levels of organising. Although this reductionism does make such frameworks more parsimonious, there are important disadvantages with reducing the ecological holarchy lens down to two levels. For example, mesolevel theories, that is, those that see teams and groups as generating transformative change, can be overlooked when relying on the micro–macro reduction. These quadrants models also support the conclusion that the bipolar lenses derived from the study of transformation theories are largely independent of one another and that they each provide unique insights into complex social phenomena.

Relationships Between Multiple Combinations of Lenses

Some theories of transformation combine several lenses to generate highly complex explanatory frameworks. One such approach will be described here in detail. Nadler and Tushman (1999) propose a diagnostic model for organisational transformation—the "contingency model"—that combines several lenses to develop an extremely rich conceptual base for exploring transformation (see Figure 7.5). Their approach includes the concept of an "organisational design" (deep structure lens) made up of quadrants of formal tasks, people issues, cultural issues and formal structures (i.e. based on interior–exterior and individual–collective lenses). This organisational design is an open system that receives inputs, manages throughputs and produces outputs (systems dynamics lens). Through the evolutionary process of variation, selection and retention (evolutionary lens) the organisational system goes through punctuated periods of revolution to appear in new transformed design (deep structure lens). For transformation to occur, the organisational design needs to adapt to both larger environmental and societal changes as well as internal needs for innovation and differentiation (hence, combining the internal–external and alignment lenses). A major weakness in the model is that there is no developmental holarchy lens and, therefore, while recognising the potential for whole-of-system transformation, the model has no capacity to identify the direction of transformative

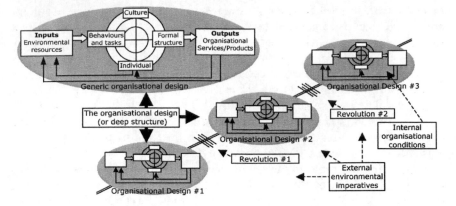

Figure 7.5   An example of a multi-lens transformational model (after Nadler & Tushman, 1999).

development. Nadler and Tushman also place an emphasis on the structural and behavioural side of the interior–exterior lens and tend to neglect the cultural, experiential and consciousness aspects of organising. However, their model does bring together many conceptual lenses and offers a fertile framework for explaining and generating new ideas about transformational events.

This example shows that very complex theories of transformation can be usefully analysed in terms of combinations of integral lenses to show their strengths and weaknesses. The Tushman and Nadler model also shows that the relationships between lenses can be regarded as orthogonal—they can be combined to generate frameworks that are generated by relatively independent factors that each provide unique perspectives on organisational transformation. Their contingency model shows that, when several lenses are combined, the complexities involved in building multiparadigm theories of transformation become strikingly apparent. However, this daunting level of complexity is the nature of organisational reality; it is complex, messy and difficult to conceptualise. Metatheory building provides a method for tackling that complexity in a systematic and rigorous way.

FLEXIBILITY OF LENS RELATIONSHIPS

In this chapter I have discussed some of the key internal and external relationships for the 24 lenses for organisational transformation developed from the multiparadigm review and analysis. One of the chief assignments for performing metatheoretical research is to develop comprehensive versions of lenses, ones that include all the known internal facets of a lens so that a more complete description can be presented. The comparative study of many different versions of the same lenses provides one technique for developing more complete forms of lenses. Without these types of comparative studies, theorists run the risk of using reduced versions of lenses and of subsequently producing very partial theories. The study of lens metamorphology is proposed here as a way of systematically examining the conceptual shape of lenses and of seeing how those distortions impact on the ways we conceptualise complex social issues such as organisational change.

Metatheoretical lenses offer unique views for theorising and so can be combined to produce a great array of frameworks and models. One of the common drawbacks seen in the theories and metatheories of transformation examined here is the inflexible way in which lenses are combined. Theorists frequently cross the same lenses to produce the same frameworks even when a great many possibilities for exploring novel combinations of lenses exist. This also applies to the two metatheoretical resources used here— Wilber's AQAL and Torbert's DAI. Although both metatheories contain several lenses, there is little experimentation in the way lenses are crossed so that new aspects of theorising and metatheorising might be explored. The many possibilities for combining lenses will become more apparent in the following chapter where I present a full description of the metatheory and apply it to the field of organisational sustainability.

8 Sustaining Visions
An Integrative Metatheory for Organisational Transformation

> Clearly, the zeitgeist is ripe for gathering divergent philosophies and competencies together in collaborative social action research and scholarship to preserve the quality of environment we now enjoy. (Geller, 1992, p. 815)

DESCRIBING THE METATHEORY

The Exemplar Topic of Organisational Sustainability

In this chapter sustainability is used as an exemplar topic for describing the integral metatheory for organisational transformation. This topic demonstrates the value of metatheorising for an applied field of organisational studies. Some foundational combinations of lenses will be presented and arguments made for how these frameworks can provide new insights into transformation within a sustainability context. It is common practice in metatheory building to apply an innovative metatheoretical framework to particular exemplar topics as a means for describing the whole conceptual system and exploring its various elements. For example, having outlined his AQAL framework in 1995, Wilber subsequently applied this approach to the fields of consciousness studies (1997), the philosophy of science (1998), psychology (2000c) and spirituality (2006). Similarly, Torbert has applied his DAI to the domains of social power (1991), social science research (1999) and personal and organisational transformation (Fisher et al., 2003). The same method will be adopted here in that, having identified and described our lenses for transformation and described some key relationships, this chapter will lay out a detailed description of the metatheory within the more focused topic of sustainability.

Why Sustainability?

There are several reasons for choosing sustainability as a platform for outlining the integral framework for organisational transformation. First, organisational sustainability is one of the major themes running through the transformational literature (see, for example, Dervitsiotis, 2003; van Marrewijk & Hardjono, 2003). This topic highlights the multitude of challenges that are currently facing organisations. These challenges include the environmental impact of organisational activities, issues of community, corporate social responsibility, leadership, human resources and questions of governance and accountability. Second, these challenges amount to a "transformation imperative" that requires the radical reassessment of organisational goals and the means by which they might be attained. While organisations need to survive to meet their primary objectives, they must also respond to the social and environmental imperatives that surround them. This, in turn, means that new ways of conceptualising change, both within organisations and the social contexts in which they function, are urgently needed. Third, organisational sustainability is a field of research that involves many viewpoints both at the level of general discourse as well as that of applied research. The variation and scope of concepts that come under the rubric of organisational sustainability require a conceptual framework that can accommodate many different paradigms and explanatory perspectives. Fourth, organisational transformation is frequently, and unreasonably, considered as relating only to organisational matters. The issue of sustainability clearly involves factors beyond the organisational boundary and includes such things as the influence of media, government regulation, macroeconomic climate and community attitudes. Organisational sustainability, as a societal goal for the beginning of the twenty-first century, needs to be considered within the context of societal transformation. And, as George Ritzer (2001) has argued, metatheorising has an important role to play in exploring such broad social issues. Fifth, the concept of a sustainable organisation is inherently concerned with transformation. Ian Lowe (2007) points out that most of the current assumptions of organisational success are based on non-sustainable economic practices. Achieving sustainability in organisational activities as well as at the macrolevel of national economies will require transformation on a very broad scale. All of these considerations strongly suggest that sustainability is not only a very suitable topic for demonstrating the utility of a metatheory for organisational transformation, but that a metatheoretical approach is also urgently needed within the field of sustainability research itself.

The Sustainability Imperative

Among the most urgent of all the transformational issues facing organisations is that of sustainability. The proliferation of terms such as "sustainable justice", "sustainability imperative" and "corporate social responsibility" is indicative of the growing pressure on organisations to consider more broadly their impact on natural systems and social communities. Organisational sustainability is "the inclusion of social and environmental concerns in business operations and interactions with stakeholders" (van Marrewijk & Werre, 2003, p. 107). These interactions can also include an intergenerational aspect and this has been linked with the expression of collective hope for the future (Brundtland, 1987; Newman & Rowe, 2003). Sustainability is an inherently transformational idea. The growing importance of international cooperation between government, non-government and commercial organisations for dealing with environmental, financial and political issues means that sustainability will be an ongoing imperative for the transformation to new, more sustainable types of organising. In the wake of the world financial and economic crises, sustainability issues appear to have taken a back seat. But they will not go away in the long term.

The traditional growth and profit-maximisation model, while still the dominant worldview of governments, markets and commercial business, has been extensively criticised by sustainability theorists (Barbier, 2006; Cogoy & Steininger, 2007). Current approaches to sustainability are focusing not only on environmental protection but also on broader societal goals such as those relating to social justice, the equitable distribution of resources and productive capacities and innovative models of economic development (Agyeman, 2005). Theories of organisational sustainability are becoming intimately involved with questions of ethics, social responsibility and the radical redesigning of organisational cultures, structures, values, goals and technologies. As such, "Sustainability cannot be a matter of tinkering around the edges, but must involve deep change" (Andrews, 2006, p. 167). In a review of types of sustainable lifestyles lived in spiritual communities across America, author John Carroll (2004, p. 2) stresses the transformational nature of sustainability:

> If therefore, we argue that sustainability of necessity is a conversion experience, if it is and must be predicated on a deep change of values themselves, and not on a half-hearted patch-it enterprise, then its expectation cannot be lodged in the prevailing system, the "dominant paradigm" as it is called. It must come from a deeper place.

The rapid environmental and economic changes that we are witness to and the increasing concern of community groups with the social impact of transnational corporations means that organisations are being called upon to reassess their fundamental responsibilities. Several theorists of organisational transformation see sustainability as the most forceful of all imperatives for change (Loren, 2005; Old, 1995; van Marrewijk, 2003; van Marrewijk & Becker, 2004; van Marrewijk & Hardjono, 2003). In their book on organisational change and corporate sustainability, the authors Dunphy, Griffiths and Benn (2003) propose a developmental model that they hope will lead corporations to make "a transformative leap to the fully sustainable and sustaining corporation". Dunphy and his colleagues argue that, (2003, pp. 3–4)

Some traditional organisational values and forms are not sustainable and, unless significantly reshaped, will continue to undermine the sustainability of society and the planet. . . . Fortunately the transformation is already underway, driven in part by the changing demands of modern society and also by the leadership of farsighted and responsible people within and outside corporations who see the need for change. However, for the transformation to be successful, many more change agents are needed.

This challenge means that organisations and the values, visions, structures and practices which form them will need to be radically redesigned. This level of radical transformation has happened before in organisational history during, for example, the industrial revolution, and a similar level of transformation is required if organisations are to meet both the sustainability and economic imperatives they now face. One implication of this for the academic world is that new ways of developing, reviewing and evaluating theory will be required for the emergence of innovative theories of sustainability.

The integral metatheory described in the following pages is one approach towards supporting the emergence of a more sustaining vision of organisational life. The integral lenses described here can be used to develop many new frameworks for exploring transformation within a sustainability context. The following selection of lens combinations is intended to exemplify some of these possibilities. To do this, lenses will be selected from each of the lens categories and be combined to form several metatheoretical frameworks for discussion. The flexibility involved in choosing lenses does not mean that they have to be arbitrarily selected. While each integral lens can provide important insights to the study of any social phenomena, some will have more immediate theoretical relevance and/or utility than others. Consequently, an integral approach to metatheory building will always be a creative one which, while grounded in a close familiarity with extant theory, will always involve the capacity for conceptual innovation and, as Karl Weick expresses it, the exercising of "disciplined imagination".

INTEGRAL LENSES FOR ORGANISATIONAL SUSTAINABILITY

Theories of transformation towards sustainability are diverse and offer multiple explanations for how organisations can move towards more sustainable philosophies and modes of practice. Every organisation is different in its purpose and mission, culture, structural design, business goals and make-up of human personalities. There are, however, patterns of similarities that exist between individuals and groups, the social structures that they create and the goals that they pursue through organised social arrangements. Theories of organisational transformation are based on patterns within those arrangements and the set of explanatory lenses that have been identified in this study can be used to probe those patterns and regularities in many different ways. The following section shows how integral lenses from each of the six lens categories (as listed in Table 7.1) can be used to explore sustainability issues.

The Developmental Holarchy Lens and Sustainability

The developmental holarchy lens focuses on the organisational design archetypes (deep structures) that are associated with qualitatively different levels of organisational sustainability. Several developmental holarchies have been proposed that describe multiple levels of organisational sustainability and a combined model of these is presented in Table 8.1. This stage-based model of sustainability development has been developed from the corporate sustainability models of van Marrewijk and his colleagues (van Marrewijk, 2003; van Marrewijk & Becker, 2004; van Marrewijk & Hardjono, 2003; van Marrewijk & Werre, 2003) and Dunphy, Griffiths and Benn (2003). The model shows the developmental holarchy of transformations that are potentially available to organisations. Each sustainability stage is associated with certain kinds of environmental factors. For example, an organisation that is at the compliance stage is focused on market-driven standards such as competitive success and the maximisation of profits for shareholders. Organisations that are identified with the committed stage of sustainability are more in touch with stakeholder issues such as the attitudes of customers and employees towards environmental pollution, energy use and waste management.

As with many developmental qualities, the stages described in Table 8.1 emerge inclusively in that later stages are built on, and are inclusive of, the core capacities of previous stages. For example, organisations at the postconventional stage which are committed to imbedding broad-ranging sustainability principles and practices will also retain the capacity to function efficiently and conform to regulations. These conventional stages in turn include the pre-conventional requirements to survive and compete as an organisation in a competitive marketplace. Stage-based capacities build on and support each other and are not exclusive to each other. The inclusive emergence of stages of sustainability means that later stages have a greater capacity for engaging with the complexities of large and intricate environmental and social systems. The more ambitious the type of sustainability aimed for, the more complex the organisational culture and structure needed to achieve those ambitions will be (van Marrewijk & Werre, 2003).

The developmental holarchy lens is generally structured according to the pattern of pre-conventional, conventional and postconventional stages, where there is progressive inclusion of formative stages within later stages. The inclusive emergence of these stages means that transformation has

Table 8.1 Stages of Organisational Sustainability (Based on Dunphy, Griffiths & Benn, 2003; and van Marrewijk & Werre, 2003)

Basic Stages of Organisational Sustainability	
Pre-conventional stages of sustainability	1. Subsistent organisation: Sustainability seen as a matter of survival. The values base is one of working hard and getting by without doing obvious damage to individuals or environments. Survival and maximisation of profit regarded as the sole purpose of organisational activities.
	2. Avoidant organisation: Sustainability seen as an attack by oppositional groups. Ignorance of ethical standards and legal responsibilities and apathy towards the negative impact of organisational activities on workforce and community until profits are affected.
Conventional stages of sustainability	3. Compliant organisation: Sustainability seen as an impost. Values conformity and compliance to traditional ethical and legal standards. Supports industry regulation as a way of circumventing more demanding regulations regarding sustainability. Reactively responds to regulatory laws.
	4. Efficient organisation: Values sustainability as a source of cost saving. The "business case" for sustainability. Sees broader sustainability demands as imposing on an individual's freedom to do business.
Postconventional stages of sustainability	5. Committed organisation: Values sustainability as balancing social, economic and environmental concerns. Is committed in principle and goes beyond legal compliance. Sees organisations as connected with other communities within a societal network.
	6. Sustaining organisation (local): Values sustainability as a way of developing the organisation and its stakeholders. Develops transformational strategies for moving towards triple bottom-line goals that support host communities whatever the regulatory environment.
Post-postconventional stages of sustainability	7. Sustaining organisation (global): Sustainability is embedded within all aspects of the organisation and is seen in global and intergenerational terms. Sustainability refers to multiple layers of purpose including physical, economic, environmental, emotional, social and spiritual.

a general direction towards more complex and more integrative forms of organisational sustainability. However, there can be considerable variation in the developmental pathway for any particular organisation. Organisations have many developmental options for navigating through the challenges of achieving sustaining forms of activity. They can retain conventional modes of minimal compliance and pursue system efficiencies for cost-saving goals, or they can regress into pre-conventional forms of rejection and avoidance to pursue, what they regard as, the core purpose of wealth maximisation. As the consequences of the global financial crisis continue to unfold and economic pressures on organisations to compete and survive grow, many organisations will opt for conventional and pre-conventional forms of response. Others will create their own particular path towards more inclusive and just forms of sustainability. Over the next few years we will probably see a much greater range of organisational responses to these conflicting imperatives. Many organisations will aim for traditional profit growth and will be extremely conservative in their change planning, while others will transform markedly in response to global warming and human justice issues.

A comprehensive understanding of what constitutes a sustainable organisation or any other social system will need to incorporate understandings that include different forms of sustainability. The developmental holarchy lens is sensitive to these issues. The lens can be used to provide a basic template for assessing the general level of sustainability that an organisation operates from. There are, however, many factors that can qualify this assessment and there are several other lenses that are sensitive to these qualifications.

The Ecological Holarchy Lens and Sustainability

The developmental holarchy lens provides a window into what transformations are possible for the whole organisational system. However, organisations are made up of an ecology of subsystems and exist themselves within an inter-organisational, social and global environment. The ecological holarchy lens delves into this complex ecology of systems both within the organisational boundary[1] and beyond it (Santos & Eisenhardt, 2005). Its focus is not on qualitatively different forms of sustainability but on the ecological levels at which those forms are manifested.

Building on Starik and Rands's (1995) multilevel model of ecologically sustainable organisations, we can describe the various levels of organisational life as a web of relationships that involves individuals, groups, organisational subunits, the organisation, inter-organisational levels, political-economic levels and socio-cultural levels. Sustainability issues can be considered at each of these levels. Each of these levels draws inputs from its external environment, uses throughput processes to change those inputs into products and outcomes and exports those products as outputs into its external environment. These outputs include products, services and by-products. Of particular importance to sustainability issues in this multilevel organisational holarchy are the decision-making process and the influence that decisions have on the power of organisations to impact on natural and social environments. Decisions made at each of these levels all feed into this impact.

At the individual level, we have issues of job design, workplace duties and responsibilities and the training, supports and technologies available to individuals to develop and maintain sustainability values and practices in their work situation. At the group and subunit levels, sustainability issues become a question of formal systems and practices that have become established within the accepted standards of performance. At the organisational level, explicit policies, goals and public positions on issues of sustainability are decided and declared. Leadership at the organisational level is also a fundamental indicator of an organisation's stance towards sustainability issues. All these levels relate to the internal levels of the ecology of an organisation. Turning to the external environment we find inter-organisational, industry, political-economic and social-cultural levels of sustainability involvement. These external levels of organisational involvement are often neglected in theories of organisational sustainability. This is unfortunate, because an organisation's involvement at the industry, community and political levels may be the most indicative aspect of its true attitude towards sustainability and the most important for proactive social action in meeting the challenging demands of sustainability (Senge et al., 2007). Some theorists propose that it is from this inter-organisational level that the most powerful levers for transformational change are effected (Boje, 2002; Grubs, 2000).

The Governance Holarchy Lens and Sustainability

The governance holarchy lens is used in theorising about a social system's decision-making and governance capacities. The term "governance" here is used in a general sense to refer to the multilevel "method or system of government or management of the organisation" (Department of Family and Community Services, 2004). As with ecological holarchies, the focus of the governance lens can be on the organisational system of managing itself (autopoiesis) or it can be on the organisation within its broader socio-cultural setting. Because the governance lens is concerned with social agents' degree of regulatory power, it is sensitive to issues of political and social authority and influence, coercive power and to an entity's capacity to marginalise and oppress other players within its sphere of operations. Hence, the governance holarchy lens is often used by postmodern theorists of sustainability to uncover the coercive relationships and destructive assumptions involved in the unsustainable activities of organisations. This deconstructive focus can be a first step towards a more constructive critical attitude towards organisations and their internal and external power relations. Consequently, when power and administrative control is exercised in an inclusive manner, through such means as democratic representation, reciprocal leadership, bottom-up, consultative and participative processes, then the governance holarchy lens can shine a light on those types of governance that promote sustaining practices in the workplace.

Sustainability cannot be adequately addressed without reference to issues of social justice and to the reality of economic, social and cultural power that accompany such issues (Agyeman, 2005). Corporations, for example, are among the most powerful social entities in the world and many have larger economies than some nation-states (Luke, 2006). The global financial crisis is testament to the influence that organisational decisions can have on the general direction and specific goals of national and global economic development. Such matters are intimately involved with the healthy development not only of natural environments but human communities as well. Issues of social justice must also be part of the process of developing new views and community practices for achieving sustainability. The recent emergence of the "just sustainability" and "environmental justice" movements suggest that there is no sustainability without social justice and a regard for the concerns of host communities. For example, the "environmental justice" movement speaks of the need for:

> . . . equal protection and meaningful involvement of all people with respect to the development, implementation enforcement of environmental laws, regulations and policies and the equitable distribution of environmental benefits. (Commonwealth of Massachusetts, cited in Agyeman & Evans, 2004, p. 156)

The concept of a governance holarchy is relevant to these discussion of sustainability and transformation for several reasons. First, because organisations must involve some degree of hierarchical regulation, there is an inherent paradox built into the decision-making domain of the organisation that sets its strategic direction. That paradox centres around issues of securing the survival of the organisation while also meeting the challenges that come with adopting sustainability principles and practices. In meeting these challenges, organisational management must balance transformational goals with those of integration, stability and economic growth. This paradox creates a tension between short-term goals that emphasise economic benefits and long-term goals that allow for transformative potentials to be planned for and actively explored. The maximisation of wealth can mean very different things depending on the time frame of decision-making. Management decisions based on maximising intergenerational wealth will look very different to those that currently drive corporate objectives.

Second, the governance lens can connect issues of sustainability with those of positions of power in a governance structure and provide insights on how social privilege and identity politics relate to transformational perspectives. Where an organisational member sits in the decision-making and management hierarchy is strongly associated with their political, environmental and social views (Bernstein, 2005). The association between positions of organisational power and sustainability policies is an area that has been largely neglected in studies of organisational sustainability. The governance lens provides a means for conceptualising issues of power, privilege and the progressive policies that are needed for organisations to transform towards more justice-focussed views of sustainability.

Third, deploying the governance lens enables theorists to explore how an organisation's decision-making structures are associated with particular kinds of organisational cultures of (un)sustainability. That the governance structures of large transnationals are remote from local communities and natural environments may have much to do with the lack of importance that local views are given in the decision-making process. Such considerations lie behind transformational theories that call for the "flattening" or "delayering" of governance structures on sustainability grounds (Nooteboom, 2006). As organisations become larger and more complex the mechanisms by which organisational hierarchies and management systems can retain this connection with local issues becomes more problematic. This problem of grounding governance and decision-making at all organisational levels has been called "the democratic anchorage of governance" (Sorensen & Torfing, 2005), and this issue is highly relevant to the topic of a just sustainability. For example, the more levels in a governance holarchy the more chance there is of (i) dissociation between the upper and lower levels of decision-making (Bang, 2004), (ii) alienation of lower levels (Sarros et al., 2002), (iii) antagonism towards upper levels (Leavitt, 2005) and (iv) institutionalisation of systems of power and control (Badham & Garrety, 2003). Each of these problems means that the interconnectedness that needs to be present between stakeholders and organisational sources of control will be more difficult to attain. The resulting distrust and fragmentation stymies support for substantive change both among the members of the organisation itself and its potential partnerships with various stakeholder communities. Research on the relationship between new forms of governance (Amin, 2004; Winter, 2006) and important aspects of sustainability has much to gain from the application of the governance lens in its theory building.

The Internal–External Lens and Sustainability

Sustainability is not simply a characteristic of the isolated organisation but a complex mix that emerges from the myriad exchanges between organisational units and between the organisation and its external environment. The internal–external lens is sensitive to the connections that exist across boundaries. Both internal and external environments are intimately involved in the transformation equation and when either pole of the internal–external lens is omitted from a theory's explanatory ambit some form of reductionism will ensue.

Many different theories of organisational transformation can be located with regard to these distinctions (see Table 8.2). At the microlevel there are internal theories of transformations in individual staff members' behavioural and psychological approaches to sustainability. At the mesolevel there are theories of group change, both at the internal (organisational teams) and community levels (activist groups). Moving on to the macrolevel of the organisation, there are internal theories of whole-of-system change and external theories of environmental selection of organisations. At the

Table 8.2   Theories of Sustainability and Internal and External Change Factors

Sustainability through the Internal–External Lens		
Ecological holarchy lens	*Internal pole*	*External pole*
Microlevel (individual)	Sustainability via theories of employee behaviour and consciousness	Sustainability via theories of external leaders, stakeholders and activists
Mesolevel (group/team)	Sustainability via theories of group development, and team-based models of transformation	Sustainability via theories of local community involvement in organizational change
Macrolevel (organization)	Sustainability via theories of organizational evolution and structural contingency	Sustainability via theories of organizational ecology and environmental selection
Macro-macrolevel (regional/national)	Sustainability via theories of economic change at industry, regional and national levels	Sustainability via theories of international social movements and global change

macro-macrolevel level of societal transformation we have internal theories of industry and community sustainability and external theories of global change. This kind of meta-level indexing shows how the internal-external lens can contribute to mapping the current state of sustainability research.

The Transformation–Translation Lens and Sustainability

The transformation–translation lens offers the capacity to conceptualise the relationship between distinctive types of organisational change and sustainability. Transformation in this context is about the qualitative growth to a new mode of sustainable organising, new identity structures and new ways of functioning that support sustainable communities. The translation pole of this lens is concerned with transactions that legitimise and bolster the current level of sustainability of the organisation.

The sustainability challenges facing organisations require transformational responses so that qualitative shifts to new patterns of functioning can be undertaken. However, these radical shifts also require translational dynamics so that large-scale changes do not overwhelm the integrity and cultural identity of the organisation. When either of these aspects of change dominates the other, problems arise. Where translational dynamics are in the ascendancy, the organisational response to crises is dominated by a transactional management approach that is conservative,[2] reactive and compliant to enforced regulatory requirements (Hitchcock & Willard, 2006). Translational dynamics naturally tend to resist sudden change and are comparable to negative feedback systems. Contrastingly, transformational dynamics initiate sudden and radical change and can be regarded as following positive feedback mechanisms. Transformational theories of organisational sustainability emphasise the importance of radical organisational change, the necessity of transformational leadership and the need for routinising transformational changes (Buchanan et al., 2005).

All organisations must deal with transformational and translational imperatives. From a metatheoretical perspective, however, there is a lack of awareness over the role of these two forms of change. Translational change is largely identified with an increase in economic indicators rather than with qualitatively new forms or goals of organising. When translational views are dominant, authentic transformation of the kind described in the stage-based models of organisational sustainability is supplanted by a concern for ongoing economic growth. In his book *The Growth Fetish* (2003), social researcher Clive Hamilton described this obsession with endless cycles of production and consumption leading to ever-increasing growth. The transformational instinct is sublimated into a one-sided concern for quantitative increase rather than qualitative development. Organisations and their leaders see the importance of change but are unaware or avoidant of authentic transformational growth and focus instead on pure financial increase and and other translational forms of growth.

When transformational potentials are not recognised, translational activities must satisfy society's quest for innovation and growth. Organisational creativities and energies are subsumed by the drive to develop new products and services that conform with conventional (that is, translational) needs but which lack a capacity for meeting transformational objectives. In the financial services industry, the manufacturing of new products based on the demand for expansionary increase has contributed significantly to the recent global financial crises. From the perspective of the transformation–translation lens, such crises are to be expected and will occur again in various guises until translational economic growth is balanced by an appreciation for transformational growth.

There is also another imbalance at play here. Translational dynamics are rightfully ongoing and never-ending because they continuously stabilise identity structures and behavioural systems. These day-to-day transactions and exchanges create and recreate the organisational system moment by moment. However, they can never result in qualitative transformations of the kind required to deal with radically changing ecological and social environments. No amount of translation results in transformation. The danger here is that, in pursuing largely translational change strategies to address problems that require authentic transformation, organisations are locking themselves and their communities into ways of thinking and acting that exacerbate the problem. Unaware of the possibilities for transformation, organisations and their leaders look to translation growth and the creation of even more economic wealth as a solution to the sustainability dilemma. Timothy Luke calls this approach "sustainable degradation" (Luke, 2006). He argues that the "strategies of sustainable degradation" are offering justifications for ongoing translational growth to evade the deep cultural and structural changes that environmental sustainability actually calls for. There is an appearance of ecological issues being represented in managerial, commercial and judicial decision-making, but, as Luke contests (2006, p. 112):

> in reality, the system of sustainable degradation enables capital to extract even more value by maintaining the appearances of creating ecological sustainability while exploiting the realities of environmental degradation.

And so we have the vicious circle of increased economic activity being regarded as the solution to problems caused by increasing levels of production and consumption (Sonntag, 2000). In other words, organisations are ramping up their translational growth goals and activities to address problems largely caused by excessive translational growth. The potential benefits of true interior and exterior transformation are being eschewed in favour of endless boom/bust cycles of material wealth generation (Kimerling, 2001). By themselves, conservative approaches to change, which are naturally drawn to translational process and are suspicious, or unconscious of, transformative possibilities, will be unable to meet the urgent sustainability challenges we currently face.

One reason for organisations choosing translational strategies over transformational ones lies in the very difficult nature of achieving transformation itself. Transformation involves phases where old identities and behaviours are transcended and replaced by and integrated into new identities, behaviours and structural systems. As we have seen in the discussion on the transition process lens, these transitions will necessarily involve the experience of loss, confusion and emotional and social turmoil at all organisational levels. In contrast to this, the path of translational growth simply requires more of the same—more resources, more investment, more productive capacity and more consumption. One result of increasing translational activities is an ever-increasing need for inputs and the commensurate production of greater volumes of both intended and unintended outputs. Greater throughput efficiencies in such a system often result in even greater volumes of outputs being produced rather than any fundamental change in processes that are driving the system. The lack of consciousness around valid transformational goals and the ubiquitous pursuit of translational efficiencies and productivities mean that the sustainability crisis is being exacerbated by the very processes that are promoted as its solution.

The metatheoretical approach taken in this study sees a greater understanding of the transformation–translation lens as fundamental to a more realistic view of sustainability. The application of this lens sees the continued drive to improve and increase translational growth as a distraction from the main task of transformational growth. In many ways, translational growth masquerades as transformation. Sustainability is reframed as "sustainable growth", "sustainable profit margins" and "sustainable levels of production and consumption". These types of "weak" sustainability (Pennington, 2006) reframe concepts of transformation and radical change into a discourse based on incremental adaptation and more efficient wealth creation. They dilute the transformational imperative into a transactional imperative. The environmental and social challenges of radical development to new forms of organisation are placed within a context of maintaining profits, preserving the hegemony of economic values over other types of values and defending material wealth creation over other forms of well-being. The rapid changes we see occurring in the world of organisations can be considered a complex mix of both transformational and translational dynamics. It is critical, however, that they both be acknowledged and that their roles not be confused. Without including both in our explanations of sustainable development, we run the risk of producing inadequate understandings of both.

The Health–Pathology Lens and Sustainability

A final explanatory lens to be considered in the bipolar group is that of health–pathology. This lens can be used to consider how theories deal with the overall balance (health) or imbalance (pathology) that pertains to an organisational system. For example, the developmental holarchy can be combined with the health–pathology lens to explore pathological forms of each stage of sustainability. In their study of organisational change and paradox, Ford and Backoff (1988) discuss the influence of pathological development on subsequent growth. They point out that as development proceeds, new integrative powers are attained; however, the organising system also becomes much more complex and open to developmental vulnerabilities of many varieties. Emergence through lower levels can have significant consequences. Because lower levels are developmentally included within more complex levels of organising, they can influence those greater capacities and predispose them towards reproducing distortions and unhealthy forms of organising. This is particularly true during times of crisis.

Combining the health-pathology lens with the stages of organisational sustainability outlined in Table 8.1, we can describe healthy and pathological varieties of each of these stages. Pathological forms of the pre-conventional stages of "rejecting" and "avoidant" forms of organisation see sustainability as a matter of survival through the exploitation of human, environmental and social resources. Sustainability regulations are seen as an attack on commercial freedoms and there is a general ignorance of ethical standards, legal responsibilities and the negative impact of unsustainable practices. Pathological forms of the more conventional organisational forms of "compliant" and "efficient" are those that use public relations and image advertising to present an acceptable corporate face while privately flouting their responsibilities. They use the business case for sustainability and self-regulation to manipulate public opinion and evade sustainability issues. Pathological forms of "committed" and "sustaining" organisations are those that over-commit themselves to the point of threatening the survival of the organisation. Proselytising organisations are those where transformation towards sustainability is treated as a platform for converting others to some set of defined values. Organisations at these levels might also risk valuing the globalisation of sustainability values and systems to the detriment of local concerns for wealth creation and development.

The Learning Lens and Sustainability

Sustainable organising requires the adoption of innovative behaviours and new forms of consciousness. These changes do not emerge without some form of learning taking place. The strong connections between organisational learning and organisational sustainability have been pointed out by many theorists (Molnar & Mulvihill, 2003; Senge, 2003; Tilbury, 2004). Organisational learning has been shown to enhance corporate transformation towards systems of sustainable organising:

> Our research has shown that for those business corporations that make the commitment to sustainable development, the understanding and practice of the organisational learning disciplines will be the indispensable prerequisite of a successful transformation to sustainability. (Nattrass & Altomare, 1999, p. 5)

Theories that provide learning-based explanations of sustainable development emphasise the need for multilevel adoption of learning initiatives. At the individual level we have the notion of "personal mastery" where there is an investment in the "mental, physical and spiritual potential" of individuals within the organisation (Molnar & Mulvihill, 2003). The team level "allows groups of employees to grasp and understanding of sustainability concepts into focus on specific problems" (Molnar & Mulvihill, 2003, p. 172). At the organisational level, adopting a sustainability framework, such as *The Natural Step*, provides a shared focus for reordering priorities and restructuring systems towards new organisational goals. Hence, sustainability can be seen as a reciprocating system supported by individual and collective levels of learning. Such a system has both interior and exterior dimensions in that learning involves behavioural and psychological learning in both individual and social spheres of activity.

The learning lens can be used to explore new ways of conceptualising sustainability. In the context of single-loop learning, individuals and groups develop "know what" knowledge that reinforces the current paradigm of thinking and acting. Single-loop learning is translational not transformational. For example, an organisation at the efficiency level of sustainability implements some new technological innovation to incrementally improve existing waste management procedures. The cost savings flowing from such innovations affirm and legitimise the efficiency stage of sustainability that the organisation identifies with and acts from. The organisation learns that cost-saving and efficiency goals can be achieved through reinforcing sustainability practices. However, this type of learning does not stimulate a more radical assessment of waste production.

With double- and triple-loop learning a more evaluative assessment of current practices are explored and transformation is made possible because of the capacity to critique the long-term sustainability of organisational practices. In an empirical study of organisational sustainability and single- and double-loop learning, Bernd Siebenhüner and Marlen Arnold found that "radical changes could not be found without corresponding learning processes according to the double-loop mode" (2007, p. 345). The combination of the learning cycle and the notion of transformational levels opens up many opportunities for researching sustainability from a learning perspective that go beyond questions of mere efficiency or technological innovation.

The Perspectives Lens and Sustainability

Perhaps the most significant contribution from postmodern theorists to explanations of organisational transformation is the inclusion of "standpoint" theories that include voices and perspectives that have previously been neglected in organisational research (Kuepers & Weibler, 2008). These lenses systematically introduce perspective-taking and can be crossed with other lenses to provide insights from all the key individuals and groups involved in the transformation experience.

A particularly important lens from the standpoint category is that of personal perspective. Until recent years, the third-person inquiry method has dominated the organisational literature on sustainability. More recently, however, the postmodern concern for first- and second-person inquiry has led to a reappraisal of un/sustainability by giving voice to the lived experiences of individuals and communities. Whereas a modernist inquiry method assumes the value of third-person objective accounts, the postmodern use of the perspectives lens focuses on the first-person voice of those who aren't usually heard, on the second-person relationship of "the other" and on the assumptions that underlie the objective study of the third person. Hence, we have first-person stories from individuals and collectives who personally experience the unsustainability of destructive industrial and commercial practices. Such stories often come from community members of the developing world and they give voice to the impact of unsustainable activities on natural and human ecologies. Worthy of particular mention here are the views of indigenous peoples and how their perspective can contribute to a deeper understanding of a truly global sustainability (Spittles, 2004).

The Stakeholder Lens and Sustainability

The stakeholder lens offers explanations for transformation that focus on the roles of the various people involved in an event or situation. This lens opens up the issues of power and influence and the inclusion and/or exclusion of different interest groups within the purpose, decision-making and goal-setting centres of an organisation. With regard to organisations, stakeholder theory is juxtaposed with models that see the purpose of organisations as the maximisation of shareholder wealth or, more generally, as the pursuit of shareholder interests. In contrast, stakeholder theory is concerned with the interests not only of shareholders but employees, customers, suppliers and local and global communities and ecological systems. The aim of this approach is to achieve a "more equitable distribution of the benefits of corporate activity for non-shareholders relative to stakeholders" (Kaler, 2003, p. 71). Contemporary stakeholder theory now includes natural environments and the succeeding generations of people and natural ecosystems in what is called "extended stakeholder theory" (Zsolnai, 2006). Laszlo Zsolnai proposes that this enlarged, normative restatement of the stakeholder calls for a radical transformation of commercial organisations and global business systems (2006, p. 43) in that business should be (i) "sustainable, i.e. should contribute to the conservation and restoration of the natural world;" (ii) "pro-social, i.e. should contribute to development of capabilities of the members of society"; and (iii) "future respecting, i.e. should contribute to the enhancement of the freedom of future generations".

Zsolnai proposes a view of transformation that redefines the notion of the stakeholder. In broadening our circle of definition to include communities, the natural world and future generations, we are opening up an understanding of transformation that is driven by a more inclusive vision of organisational life; one that is imbedded within the natural and social world. Different stakeholder theories can be differentiated on the basis of their level of stakeholder inclusiveness and the extent to which their definition of "a stakeholder" includes non-traditional groups. As the circle of inclusion grows, the responsibility of business to consider the broader community and environmental impact of its actions also grows (Steurer et al., 2005). Stakeholder-based theories provide a way of seeing how varying spheres of participant stakeholder inclusion can drive different conceptualisations of sustainability. The stakeholder lens opens the researcher to the boundaries of self-interest and the ways in which the values and goals of organisations are connected to people and communities who have a stake in their functioning. The inclusion of non-traditional groups such as community members and ecological environments opens up broader explanations of how sustainability might be achieved and it has significant implications for organisational governance and decision-making processes.

The Mediation Lens and Sustainability

Transformational change towards sustainability is not only about the internal capacities of organisations. Sustainability theorists have pointed out repeatedly that organisations do not exist in isolation from their social environment (Marshall & Toffel, 2005). But more than this, the social environment is as much the source of transformation as any internal organisational resource. The structures and cultures that together constitute new forms of sustainability lie as much in the social depth of the organisation's surroundings as they do within its own boundaries. Institutionalising the changes leading to authentic sustainability will, for perhaps the large majority of organisations, require the mediation of new types of social consciousness, moral sensitivity and economic practices from the outside to the inside of the organisation. Consequently, as Kersty Hobson argues, theories of sustainability will need to include "the institutional and cultural mediation of individual and collective responses to environmental concerns" (2006, p. 292). Change research from this perspective recognises the impact of social and institutional contexts and does not assume that choices are made by isolated rational agents. Hobson argues that mediational approaches bring "considerable critique to bear on the models of behaviour change that underpin prevailing sustainable development strategies" (2006, p. 292). The assumption that change originates through the actions of individuals, which Hobson sees as dominating both academic and public policy circles, "advances impoverished and simplistic representations of the subject and of society" (2006, p. 292). A less impoverished view of "the subject and of society" can discern the channels by which individual and groups communicate and interact in complex networks of co-creating identities and realities. Societies change not only because each individual comes to a rational decision to change their behaviour but also because of public expectations, cultural worldviews expressed in the media and the views and actions of community, business and political leaders (Margolis & Hansen, 2002).

The lens of social mediation opens up new ways of understanding the determinants of transformation. For example, organisations need support in their transitions by mediating factors such as leading-edge public expectations, innovative inter-organisational networks, community visions, informed media and Internet communities, social activists, consumer advocates and progressive government regulation (Senge et al., 2007). Left to their own innate capabilities, single organisations, even those with sympathetic views towards sustainability, will not be able to transform in the radical ways necessary for the establishment and maintenance of advanced forms of sustainability (Laszlo & Seidel, 2006). The transformative depth that lies in the inter-organisational and socio-cultural environment needs to be recognised so that it can be utilised to effect change. It is the mediation of these networks of exchange relations that supports the emergence of new archetypes of organisational identity and behaviour.

Some of the key means for the social mediation of sustainable development are scientific research, public education and awareness of sustainability issues, government legislation and regulation, public media such as the press and electronic media, inter-organisational bodies that support sustainability initiatives, non-governmental bodies that report on organisational behaviour and international networks that encourage organisational change towards sustainability. Each of these areas plays a fundamental role in shaping a society's expectations and requirements of organisations regarding their stance towards sustainability. And for each of these agents of social mediation, communication is the crux. An extensive body of literature sees radical organisational change primarily as the transformation of its communicative interactions (Giddens, 1993; Luhman, 1990) and that interactions that form communications and conversations are the essential modality by which the capacity to organise emerges (Taylor & Every, 2000).

The Alignment Lens and Sustainability

Many different theoretical approaches to sustainability make use of the concept of alignment (Cartwright & Craig, 2006; Freeman, 2006; Hobson, 2006). The basic principle guiding these theories is that close alignment leads to greater efficiency and effectiveness but may not necessarily lead to transformational change. In contrast, misalignment leads to ongoing inefficiencies and ineffectiveness but may also provide the triggering motivation for radical change.

The alignment lens can be focused on the organisation's internal structure or it can be used to consider the degree of (mis)matching between the organisation and its environment. The range of sustainability issues considered through the alignment lens includes values (Boxelaar et al., 2003), corporate governance (Cartwright & Craig, 2006), research and development (Scott, 2001), consumer behaviour (Weber, 2003), social justice (Schwing, 2002), competitive advantage (Gottschalg & Zollo, 2007) and corporate reputation (Freeman, 2006). With all of these topics it is the degree of alignment and/or misalignment that is taken as the explanatory concept for transformational change.

The Streams Lens and Sustainability

The streams lens is in evidence when theorists focus on particular domains of organisation theory to explain change. For example, theorists are employing a streams lens when, to explain transformation, they focus on the field of technology, knowledge management, leadership, industrial relations, innovation or economic conditions. The streams lens is useful in the sustainability context when the contributions of each of the core organisational streams are considered necessary for transformation. Taking Porras's streams model for example, we might investigate the transformations required in an organisation's structural organising arrangements, human and social factors, technology and physical setting for sustaining forms of organisation to be pursued.

A narrow application the streams lens becomes reductionist when it sees change as being caused or driven solely by one particular domain of organisational activity. Regarding all solutions to sustainability problems as dependent on technological innovation is an example of this type of conceptual myopia. This type of stream reductionism or, as Wilber (2006) calls it, "line absolutism" can be seen, for example, in the focus on technological solutions to global warming through such as means carbon sequestration, clean coal technology and nuclear power. In contrast, the subjective mindsets and beliefs systems that underlie the problem are considered peripheral issues (Reidy, 2005). A more integrative approach sees sustainability as a multidimensional characteristic that involves many streams of organisational life, including its consciousness, behavioural, cultural and social systems aspects.

METATHEORETICAL FRAMEWORKS FOR SUSTAINABILITY

The preceding discussion has described the relevance of some integral lenses for our exemplar topic of organisational sustainability. This has provided a starting point for describing the integral metatheory for organisational transformation. The following section carries this explicative process further by showing how lenses can be systematically combined to develop metatheoretical frameworks for sustainability.

Developmental and Ecological Holarchy Lenses

Combining the developmental and ecological holarchy lenses provides a model for exploring types of sustainability present within each ecological level of the organisation and/or its social environment. This means that pre-conventional, conventional and postconventional stages of sustainability can be examined at the individual, group, organisational and societal levels (see Table 8.3). When organisations set out on the path of radical transformation, there will be key individuals, groups and organisational units that either enthusiastically support or energetically resist the take-up of new values and practices. The conflicts that arise from these misalignments can be crucial for successful, whole-system transformation towards sustainability. Such conflicts are to be expected because transformation to new forms of sustainable organising will necessarily involve a qualitative shift in values, worldviews and imbedded organisational practices. At the very least, recognising that there will be differences in these values and behaviours between different levels of the organisation can provide a basis for understanding why, where and how such conflicts emerge. For example, individuals and teams which still function from a "compliant" or "efficient" stage will have difficulty in moving to a "committed" stage of sustainable organising and, as such, they will come into conflict with other individuals and groups who are supportive of more integrative levels of sustainability. This mosaic of varying values, worldviews, behaviours and imbedded practices can be usefully considered using this mapping approach.

One benefit of combining ecological and developmental holarchy lenses to form a multilevel framework for organisational sustainability is in disclosing the emergent interactions that occur between various organisational levels. This framework makes it possible to track the aetiology of transformations in attitudes, behaviours, policies, practices and cultures as they emerge at multiple sites, both within and outside the organisation. Several theorists have pointed to the connections between sustainability and micro–macro issues (Griffiths & Petrick, 2001; Kinlaw, 1993). In their article entitled "Weaving an Integral Web", authors Starik and Rands state that (1995, p. 909):

> Sustainability and sustainable development have multilevel and multisystem characteristics . . . and the achievement of sustainability requires an effective integration of these multiple levels and systems. For us, integration involves the assumptions that (a) an ecologically sustainable world requires ecologically sustainable societies, cultures, political and economic systems, organisations, and individuals and that (b) achievement of sustainability by an entity at any one of these levels require simultaneously recognising and addressing the actions of and interactions with entities at each of these levels.

A comprehensive picture of how sustainability emerges from the interaction of "entities at each of these levels" will also include the developmental stages of sustainability awareness and behaviour that each of these entities displays in their interactions. Connecting the micro, meso and macro worlds with a developmental lens that is attuned to radical change in sustainability consciousness and behaviours makes it possible to follow the transformational currents that are propagated through these levels via such processes as structuration (Giddens, 2000), coevolution (Bleischwitz, 2007) and relationism (Ritzer & Gindoff, 1992). Combining lenses and applying the resulting frameworks to extant sustainability theory is one of significant contributions that an integral metatheory for sustainability offers to researchers in this field.

Table 8.3 Sustainability Mapping Using Ecological and Developmental Holarchy Lenses

| | | Sustainability Stages for the Developmental Holarchy Lens | | | | | | |
| | | *Pre-conventional stages* | | *Conventional stages* | | *Postconventional Stages* | | *Post-postconventional* |
Organisational Levels for Ecological Holarchy Lens		Stage 1 Rejecting	Stage 2 Avoiding	Stage 3 Complying	Stage 4 Efficiency	Stage 5 Committed	Stage 6 Local Sustaining	Stage 7 Global Sustaining
Micro	Individual Dyad	rejecting individual(s)	avoidant individual(s)	compliant individual(s)	efficient individual(s)	committed individual(s)	sustaining individual(s)	
Meso	Group Subunit	rejecting group	avoidant group	compliant group	efficient group	committed group	sustaining group	
Macro	Organisation	rejecting organisation	avoidant organisation	compliant organisation	efficient organisation	committed organisation	sustaining organisation	
Macro-macro	Industry	rejecting industry	avoidant industry	compliant industry	efficient industry	committed industry	sustaining industry	
	Political/Economy	rejecting economy	avoidant economy	compliant economy	efficient economy	committed economy	sustaining economy	
	Social-cultural	rejecting society	avoidant society	compliant society	efficient society	committed society	sustaining society	
	Global	rejecting world	avoidant world	compliant world	efficient world	committed world	sustaining world	

The AQAL Framework and Sustainable Development

Wilber's AQAL framework has been used to develop an "All Quadrants" approach to sustainable development (Brown, 2005). This model describes sustainability primarily in terms of the stage-based development of the individual domains of personal consciousness and behaviour and the collective domains of culture and social systems. The AQAL sustainability model stresses that (Brown, 2005, p. 17):

> mindfulness of individual consciousness (belief system, mental model, motivations, etc.) is vital when attempting to address all the major influences on a sustainable development initiative.

The assumption is that a healthy transformation towards behavioural and structural sustainability is not possible without a concomitant transformation in consciousness and culture. Applying the quadrants framework to organisational sustainability discloses four essential domains. Neglecting any of these domains over the long term results in the impoverishment of the lives of individuals and of the organisations, the communities and the natural environments in which they work. If this neglect continues unabated, that impoverishment will contribute to the unsustainable forms of growth that are currently accepted as the norm. Sustainability, then, is the balanced, long-term "coevolution" of these four quadrants. With regard to the consciousness quadrant, organisational sustainability is influenced by conscious intentions, knowledge, attitudes, feelings of efficacy/helplessness and motivations to care for the viability of natural and social environments. The behavioural quadrant is the site of personal actions that promote sustainability. These include actions that promote or hinder sustainable lifestyles, work practices that encourage or discourage compliance, behavioural goals that support or hinder sustaining forms of work. The cultural quadrant addresses worldviews, systems of meaning making and values that relate to sustainability. This quadrant is exemplified in the contesting of, for example, the maximisation of shareholder wealth and/or the optimisation of well-being for multiple stakeholders. In the social quadrant, sustainability is conceptualised as a function of social systems, administrative functions and organisational structures. This is the most common form of conceptualising sustainability and most research has focused on designing systems and managing functions from this domain.

The quadrants model has been applied to the field of environmental ecology by integral theorists Sean Esbjörn-Hargens and Michael Zimmerman (2009). These authors point out that each domain co-creates and supports the others and that all need to be included when developing theories, practices and research projects that target sustainability issues. Esbjörn-Hargens (2005) has shown that ecological theories can be usefully categorised into one or other of these four domains. The same applies to sustainability where theories often focus exclusively on either subjective consciousness (Elgin, 1994), culture and intersubjectivity (Lewis, 2003), objective behaviour (Sonntag, 2000) or organisational systems (Stowell, 1997). Leaning too heavily on any one of these quadrants will result in a reductionist approach to sustainability. Transformation will only flow from a four quadrants involvement that creates and supports radical change in consciousness and behaviour at both the microlevel of individual activity and the macrolevel of organisational and inter-organisational systems.

An Ecological Framework for Sustainability

A comprehensive form of the ecological holarchy lens enables us to see the crucial role being played by small groups, teams and committees in the development of sustaining forms of organisation. This lens includes the mesolevel of group-focused phenomena in understanding the emergence of more environmentally aware values and worldviews. In addition to this, an ecological holarchy does not stop at an organisation's boundary but includes inter-organisational, industry-level, environmental, societal and global levels (Starik & Rands, 1995). Factoring in ecological levels beyond organisational boundaries enables the broader industry and societal environments to be included in the analytical mix. All these distinctions are lost when we think of an organisation's multilevel ecology simply as an individual–collective polarity.[3]

A detailed form of the ecological holarchy lens has been applied to the area of commercial business by the integral theorist Daryl Paulson (2002). His integral business model crosses the levels of individual, team, company, industry and world environment with the AQAL quadrants and developmental holarchy lenses. The resulting model incorporates the subjective and objective aspects of individual and collective life at each of these ecological levels. A feature of the model is that it includes both internal (intra-organisational) and external (inter-organisational) ecological levels. A further refinement of this way of using the ecological holarchy lens is described in Figure 8.1.

The figure includes multiple levels of organisational ecology and, instead of relying on a simplified individual–collective bipole, crosses multiple levels of organisational ecology with the interior–exterior lens to form a multilevel scalar approach to both psychological and behavioral forms of sustainability. As with the basic quadrants framework, there exist subjective and intangible realities as well as objective and tangible realities for each of these ecological levels. Sustainability can be conceptualised in terms of "inner and outer worlds" (Bradbury, 2003) for each ecological level that we might wish to include. This means that both the subjective and objective, at a variety of points in the ecological holarchy, can be included in formulations for more comprehensive and multilevel explanations of sustainability. In particular, the introduction of the mesolevel of the ecological

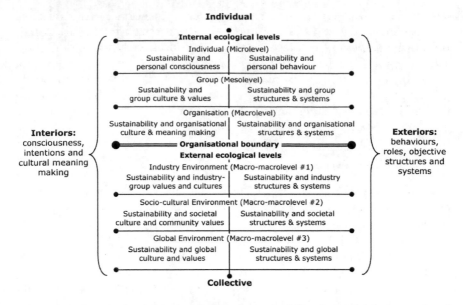

Figure 8.1   Interior and exterior forms of sustainability for multiple internal and external levels of organisational ecology.

holarchy in Figure 8.1 highlights the role of groups, teams and committees in the emergence of new forms of sustainability. It is at this group level that innovative and experimental forms of behaviour and culture can be trialled and evaluated.

While the emergence of new values and ways of working can be more easily established with small group settings, the mesolevel is, as is the case with microlevel innovation, dependent on support from management and control structures of the organisation. This brings into the picture the governance holarchy lens which, as we have already seen, considers levels of management, decision-making and strategic and political power and how these impact on transformative potential. Sustainability initiatives and experiments, like all transformative practices, need flexible environments that allow for trail-and-error testing in order to prosper. Experimentation through individual- and group-level initiatives needs to be provided with a space and allowed to create innovative ways of meeting sustainability objectives that might otherwise fail or not prove successful in the short term. Material support, emotional encouragement and proactive leadership by management is crucial for the creative generation of new ideas and methods (Hart, 2005; Placet, Anderson & Fowler, 2005). Their emergence in institutionalised and organised settings is typically a fragile and tremulous thing. The mesolevel of the groups might metaphorically be regarded as a midwife for the emergence of sustainability initiates for the transformation of personal intentions and behaviours and collective cultures and systems. Theories that focus on these local, mesolevel efforts offer an important perspective that needs to be recognised in any integral approach to organisational sustainability.

An Agency–communion Framework for Sustainability

The agency–communion lens looks at the task versus relational nature of organisational life. While these two aspects of organising are complementary and mutually enhancing, often agentic and task-focused forms of organising take precedence over more relational forms. Although the power of relationships has been recognised in organisational development as a fundamental tool for change (Joyce, 2003), it remains highly under-utilised as an avenue for guiding transformation (Gergen, McNamee & Barrett, 2001).

One useful way of considering the agency–communion lens within a sustainability context is to combine it with the ecological holarchy and internal–external lenses. This combination of lenses generates a framework for considering the balance between tasks and relationships both inside and outside the organisation. The framework indicates that transformation towards more sustaining organisational practices requires both sustaining tasks and sustaining relationships within the organisation and with the organisation's community stakeholders. It shows the importance of relationships in the sustainability equation and that a single-minded focus on tasks, to the exclusion of communal and relational processes, may alienate potential collaborators.

Both people-oriented (communal) and task-oriented (agentic) goals need to be imbedded within multiple organisational levels if sustainability is to be a truly transformational process. For this reason the technical and economic sides of sustainability cannot be dealt with in isolation from the human side of social justice and relationships. Sustainability can be pursued at the microlevel of interpersonal communication and collaboration, at the mesolevel of group projects and decision-making and at the macrolevel of organisational systems and policies. Agentic and communal activities are particularly important at the inter-organisational level where industry environments that support transformation towards sustainability can be created. It is through agentic leadership and communal networking at the inter-organisational levels that the potential for rapid societal responses to international and global challenges can be realised.

Learning and Developmental Holarchy Lenses

The crossing of learning and developmental holarchy lenses forms a framework for theorising about multiple levels of transformational learning. In the context of sustainability, Molnar and Mulvihill (2003) have called this kind of transformational learning "Sustainability-Focused Organisational Learning" (SFOL). The pursuit of SFOL requires the questioning of "core business values and basic assumptions" and the opportunity for employees to have import into the organisation's core values and long-term vision is "a crucial part of SFOL". SFOL combines the idea of organisational learning with the transformation of core values to propose a model of radical change that includes multiple levels of learning.

Similarly, Halme (2001) has described two different types of learning that can occur in inter-organisational sustainability networks. "Lower-level learning" produces "transactional outcomes" and facilitates improvement in sustainability practices but does not challenge the underlying systems and philosophies of the network members. The second type of learning Halme refers to as "higher-level learning". High-level learning produces "transformational outcomes" which fundamentally change the way the organisation and its members think and act with regard to sustainability issues. Transactional learning cannot produce the types of shifts necessary for movement to occur through the basic stages of organisational sustainability described, for example, by Dunphy, Griffiths and Benn (2003).

Solutions to sustainability problems that are caused by deeply held values and which are performed through institutionalised systems of practice cannot be found via single-loop or incremental learning. Only generative learning approaches such as double- and triple-loop learning, which require frame-breaking insights and behaviours to be experienced and institutionally implemented, can result in such transformations. This, however, is not a simple process of linear progression through successive stages. Development, regression and stagnation can occur over time as an organisation struggles to balance translational with transformational modes of learning in a sustainability context.

The Social Mediation and Developmental Holarchy Lenses

An informative way of theorising about sustainability is to see how relational and communicative processes mediate transformation though the stages of organisational sustainability. This is significantly different to the developmental approach where internal organisational capacities are seen as the progenitors of qualitative change. In fact, these two approaches, developmental and mediated theories of change, complement each other in fundamental ways and an authentic conceptualisation of transformative growth will not be possible without the use of *both* these lenses.

Table 8.4 shows how the explanatory lenses of developmental holarchy and social mediation can be combined to provide a mediational model of organisational sustainability. The first column maps out the major developmental/transformational stages of organisational sustainability as they exist for a particular organisation. The second column offers a brief description of mediating agents of transformation that exist in the organisation's environment. The third column identifies the core values that are being mediated between the organisation and its ecological and socio-cultural environment.

Mediating agents communicate transformational depth from the environment to the organisation's internal culture and structure. For example, organisations at the compliant stage of sustainability will eventually be faced with external signals, exemplars, ideas and models—from stakeholders, markets and public media—calling for greater efficiency, cost minimisation and competitive rationales for adopting sustainability initiatives. These mediations support internal innovations that challenge the old forms of compliance thinking and stimulate the adoption of efficiency-related values, behaviours, systems and ways of thinking throughout the organisation. Hence, transformation has come about not only through internal motivations but through the mediation of exterior agents and structures (Nardi, 1996).

The application of the mediation lens introduces a more critical analysis of organisational responses to sustainability. Utilising this lens to study and build theory shifts the explanatory focus onto the inter-organisational environment and to how transformation can be viewed within the competitive and interdependent environment of contemporary socio-cultural life. Through focusing on the exchanges between an organisation and its social milieux, the mediation lens is well suited for analysing the theoretical treatment of issues such as relationality, power and social influence. These types of mediational analyses are sorely lacking among current explanations of transformational processes in general and the urgent issue of global sustainability in particular.

Table 8.4 Mediating Means for Transformation towards Sustainability

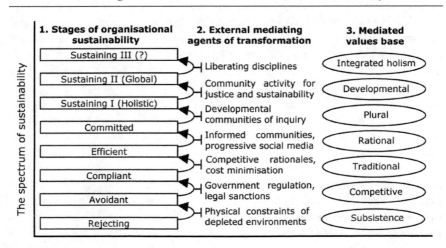

Metatheoretical Frameworks Using the Alignment Lens

One way of applying the alignment lens is to look at how the facets of other lenses are configured (see Table 8.5). Taking the interior–exterior lens for example, we can look at the alignment between interior values and cognitive mindsets and exterior organisational structures and behaviours. Where these interior and exterior qualities are closely aligned, there will be a high level of coherence between organisational culture and behaviour and there will be strong levels of commitment to the current stage of organisational sustainability. Where there are significant misalignments, there will be high motivation to change either interior values and mindsets or exterior behaviours and systems of work. Actual behaviours and operations can often lag behind espoused values and intentions simply because it is easier or merely expedient to verbally commit to principles than to operationally apply them. In such cases, organisations live with the ongoing dissonance and tensions that result in systemic problems of low morale, diminished loyalty and lack of cohesiveness. Alternatively, values can be aligned with organisational operations activities through bringing the organisation's mission, vision, policies and plans in line with its actual activities and operations.

The alignment lens can also be usefully employed to consider the disconnections between the organisation's internal and external environments. The degree of alignment between, for example, organisational values and community values can have serious implications for an organisation's approach to issues of sustainability and change. The current community interest in issues of global warming is seeding changes in consumerist values that may have very significant impacts on fundamental organisational goals. There are several options available to organisations and their leaders to meet this challenge. One type of response, seen in the behaviour of some multinational corporations, has been an attempt to modify private and public attitudes and values so that they fit more conveniently with the values and goals of those corporations. The use of lobbyists, privately funded research programmes, advertising and public relations campaigns have proven to be very successful in shaping community values and individual attitudes. A current example of this type of reframing of values can be seen in the nuclear industry's current attempt to be seen as a "green" energy producer that is meeting concerns over global warming. These types of managed responses are more about seeking competitive advantage through the alignment of organisational reputations with community values. Much of corporate public relations activity is geared towards this type of strategy. The approach here is to align values only at a superficial level so that the pressure for transformational change can be circumvented.

The opposite response is, of course, to change organisational values so that they conform more closely to community expectations. Many

Table 8.5 Integral Lenses and Forms of Alignment

Integral lenses	Forms of alignment	Options for transformation towards sustainability
Internal–external	organisational values and community values	lobby industry groups to adopt sustainability practices and principles organisation to adopt progressive community values align organisational reputation with actual policies and behaviour
Interior–exterior	espoused organisational values and actual behaviour	align espoused values to behavioural realities implement staff development to align behaviours with values leaders to model expression of values with taking real action
Ecological holarchy	organisational policies and individual members' beliefs	staff selection process to align personal and organisational values committee decision-making to be informed by sustainability values all staff to be involved in formulating organisational vision
Stakeholders	the interests of different stakeholder groups	allow wider range of decision-making contributions from major stakeholders, e.g. customers, suppliers, community stakeholders undertake a review of stakeholder attitudes towards sustainability
Developmental holarchy	alignment between different transformational stages	perform values audit and identify next stage of transformation identify sustainability practices and attitudes and take steps to implement those through changes in structure and culture
Organisational streams	technological initiatives and corresponding cultural capacities	ensure that organisational technologies and systems streams (e.g. monitoring, accounting, manufacturing, training) are aligned with cultural streams (e.g. mission, values and communications)

companies are moving to adopt sustainable energy principles and practices in response to community values. And, in some instances, organisations are acting as leaders in adopting transformational values and practices that provide leading-edge examples of sustainability to the rest of the community (Anderson, 2003; Esbensen, 2006). Many non-government organizations, for example, are at the leading edge of community and national attempts to meet sustainability challenges in the environmental, social and economic arenas (Courville & Piper, 2004).

Mismatches can also occur between organisational levels. The gap between organisational goals and individual members' personal attitudes and beliefs is often the site of much contention and efforts to promote change (Boswell, 2006). It is here that the phenomenon of external whistle-blowing can arise. When there is a serious misalignment between organisational activities and the beliefs of individual members, those members can act to inform the community of the situation. Where organisations have not been meeting their social and environmental responsibilities, individuals can be motivated to inform authorities, the press or community members of ethical and legal transgressions. The protection of whistle-blowers may be one of the most important signs that an organisation is serious about moving to a new values base.

The use of the alignment lens can unlock new pathways for conceiving how transformation to sustainable organising can be achieved. It can aid in understanding the complex dynamics that currently exist within organisations as they deal with the dissociations and dislocations that exist internally and externally. The alignment lens can also be used at multiple scales of focus, from the very microlevel of individual values to the macrolevel of global development. At the broader level of global sustainability, the most obvious source of misalignment that feeds into the unsustainable nature of current economic and social organising are the gaps between the developed, developing and underdeveloped nations and between rich and poor within those nations. These misalignments lie at the heart of many of the seemingly intractable problems associated with global sustainability. Theories of organisational sustainability have their part to play in analysing these problems and the use of the alignment lens can open up many fruitful insights into understanding and addressing the fault-lines and misalignments that characterise global development and sustainability issues.

The Spirituality Lens Combined with Other Integral Lenses

The spirituality lens, because of its multiparadigm nature, can be used to consider sustainability from a number of conceptual orientations. These include: (i) spirituality as an advanced stage of sustainability, (ii) spirituality as a ubiquitous process that underlies all sustainable relationships and (iii) spirituality as an integrative rather than merely growth-focused endeavour.

Spirituality as an advanced stage

In his book entitled *Sustainability and Spirituality*, John Carroll (2004) writes, "'Sustainability' is an all too common word describing a condition which these days seems to hardly exist". The scientific literature on sustainability grows daily while, at the same time, the belief systems and unsustainable practices that drive economic activity seem to be, if anything, more entrenched than ever. The current focus on dealing with the growing global economic crisis exacerbates this problem. Long-term sustainability issues are taking a back seat to the short-term need to stimulate unsustainable economic activity. While there are many innovative theories and encouraging practical sustainability initiatives being made, the pathway to a sustaining global future seems more elusive than ever. There is a growing uncertainty over whether humanity as a whole can achieve the level of transformation required (Sachs, 2006). Sustainability advocates and researchers are reassessing the feasibility of such radical and widespread transformational change. For such a transformation to take place, a fundamental reorientation of organisations and societies will need to occur at the individual, societal and global levels (Lowe, 2007).

Radical transformation of this order goes to the very heart of our personal and collective understanding of core purpose and ultimate meaning. Evaluating these issues brings in questions of spirituality and some sustainability theorists draw strong connections between spiritual transformation and the level of change required to achieve global systems of sustainable development.

There are some forms of spirituality that have much in common with the deep level of transformation that authentic sustainability requires. Both are revolutionary in nature in that they challenge the conventional behaviours and moral assumptions of mainstream society. Carroll goes so far as to say, "Spirituality, deeply held spiritual beliefs, religion, religious faith, however we might define these things, are all necessary to achieve real sustainability" (2004, p. 166). This perspective looks to the leading edge of concepts of sustainable development. It looks to the most ambitious understandings of sustainability as a profound shift in individual and collective orders of being and doing. It is from this developmental perspective that we have the notion of "cosmocentric consciousness, or spiritual intelligence" (Dunphy et al., 2003) as being the most advanced stage of organisational sustainability. A spiritual view of sustainability looks to a movement away from economies based on production and consumption and towards economies based on "reverence" (Tudge, 1995) and "integrity" (Elgin, 1994). The models for these types of transformational economies often come from communities with an explicit spiritual, and often religious, base (Carroll, 2004; Findhorn-Community, 2003). The spirituality lens enables us to conceptualise and research emergent forms of sustainability that are adopted within these spiritual communities.

Spirituality as a ubiquitous process

While spirituality and sustainability can be associated with a revolutionary reorientation to our relationships with the natural and social worlds, there is also a more mundane, less ascetic but no less authentic application of the spirituality lens. This understanding of spirituality has to do with a relationally grounded sense of spirituality as an inherent aspect of *every* worker's experience and of the dynamics of *every* organisational workplace (Chile & Simpson, 2004). This is an understanding of spirituality as process, as a way of energising and enthusing the life that contributes to human organising. Here spirituality is connected to relationality and to interpersonal process. Martin Buber described this form of spirituality as arising from "the sphere of the between" and "the space between" (Buber, 1947). The idea here is one of ongoing opportunity for deepening dialogue and encounter with the other and that this opportunity continually arises out of "the space between" people in the process of relating to one another. This dialogue occurs not only between people, but also between people and their natural environments. Encountering "the other" in this context also includes being with environments in both their pristine and degraded forms, in wilderness and in urban environments and in the harshness and splendour of nature and the ugliness and beauty of built environments.

In explaining sustainability through the lens of spirituality it is important to remember that different views of the spiritual can themselves be appropriated within organisations to merely reinforce established practices of control and conformity (Boyle & Healy, 2003). There exist many different forms of spirituality and many of these act to maintain conventional practices and offer anything but the transformational challenge to the unsustainable practices that many organisations currently engage in. In fact, an integral approach regards the process-based understanding of spirituality as a translational form of activity that, while enlivening and providing inspiration for everyday work, can easily be co-opted to legitimate conformist organisational cultures and their associated systems of operating. This is particularly true when the transformational aspect of spirituality is not acknowledged or overtly included within theories of sustainability and spirituality. Transformation is inherently challenging. It involves a step into the unknown "where one wrestles with one's own contradictions" (Inayatullah, 2005, p. 578). Without stage-based understandings of transformation the spirituality of process can become a tool for reinforcing traditional conventions. Modern and postmodern insights are rejected in favour of traditionalism. As Inayatullah (2005, p. 577) puts it:

> For spirituality to become part of the global solution it will have to become transmodern, moving through modernity, not rejecting the science and technology revolution and the Enlightenment, not acceding to post-modernity (were all values and perspectives are relativised) or to the pre-modern (where feudal relations are supreme).

Spirituality as integrative rather than growth-focused

To integrate means to make whole, to complete, to retain balance and to bring together what was previously fragmented. The word *religion* also means to reconnect and to unite things that were previously separate. Spirituality is sometimes regarded as a basic human instinct for wholeness and completion (Wilber, 2006). In this sense the lens of spirituality focuses on those fragmented theoretical and conceptual elements and disconnects that might be brought together to form a more holistic understanding. The topic of sustainability is ripe territory for integrative and reunifying endeavours (Mudacumura, Mebratu & Haque, 2006; Singh, 1995). A spirituality lens that is more concerned with integration moves our attention away from the growth-based explanations of change and technological innovation towards integrative conceptualisations of sustainability. Hence, the particular interest in agricultural sustainability, urban gardens, simpler lifestyles and in forms of organisational sustainability that make use of such things as biomimicry and substituting biological systems for man-made technological systems (Hawken, Lovins & Lovins, 1999).

Integrative theories of sustainability tend to employ the spirituality lens to uncover the feminine and nurturing aspects of development as opposed to the more masculine and growth-based aspects (Frenier, 1997). Such approaches are calling for integrative visions rather than purely growth-based planning. Integrative futures seek to develop and rediscover nature-based technologies, economies and lifestyles that reclaim core human values and eschew growth-based visions of the future. These translational understandings of growth look to solve sustainability problems through hyper-technologies and commercial worldviews that do not challenge the values that currently drive economic growth.

The foregoing sections in this chapter have presented: i) detailed descriptions of integral lenses as applied to the exemplar topic of organisational sustainability and ii) combinations of lenses to form metatheoretical frameworks for investigating sustainability theory. Table 8.6 presents each of the integral lenses and their unique contributions to explaining transformation within the sustainability context. The identification of these lenses has been based on the detailed analysis of theories from many research paradigms. Any of the lenses shown in Table 8.6 can be flexibility combined to develop new metatheoretical frameworks and typologies. The relatively large number of lenses means that the researchers' creativity is an essential element of the research process for developing these multi-lens frameworks. While conceptual flexibility is crucial in metatheoretical research, this flexibility is also constrained by the need to retain internal consistency in the relationships within and between lenses. For example, irrespective of what lenses are combined, they each still need to retain their defining characteristics – that holarchical lenses retain their definitive levels, bipolar lenses retain both poles, cyclical lenses their key phases, relational lenses their mediating focus, standpoint lenses their range of perspectives, systems lenses their key dynamics and multimorphic lenses their multidimensionality and mult-lens capacity. It is crucial that these defining characteristics are retained when lenses are combined.

So far in this chapter I have applied many integral lenses and metatheoretical frameworks to the exemplar topic of organisational sustainability. Hopefully, this has helped to give a sense of how these lenses can be used to

Table 8.6 Integral Lenses and Their Contribution to Conceptualising Organisational Sustainability

Integral Lenses	"Organisational sustainability is explored as ..."
1. Deep structure	fundamental structures versus surface features
2. Developmental holarchy	a spectrum of organisational archetypes
3. Ecological holarchy	a multilevel system of social ecologies
4. Governance holarchy	a multilevel system of decision-making
5. Interior-exterior	interior meaning-making and exterior behaviour
6. Transformation-translation	radical and transactional change
7. Internal-external	relative to some key boundary
8. Agency-communion	agentic autonomy and communal relations
9. Health-pathology	healthy and unhealthy types
10. System dynamics	feedback systems and equilibrium dynamics
11. Learning	cycles of learning and knowledge acquisition
12. Transition Process	dynamic transitions between organisational states
13. Inclusive emergence	cycles of inclusion and integration
14. Evolutionary	cycles of innovation, selection and reproduction
15. Mediation	a process of social communication
16. Alignment	the concordances between separate domains
17. Relational exchange	interactions between entities and environments
18. Stakeholder	the standpoint of multiple stakeholders
19. States of consciousness	a function of states of consciousness
20. Personal perspectives	the vantage points of the 1st, 2nd and 3rd persons
21. Postmodern	a contest between socially constructed views
22. Spirituality	ultimate purpose, deep meaning and relationship
23. Streams	multidimensional domains of organising
24. Types	ideal types derived from key organisational dimensions

give insights into sustainability issues. In the next section I present a more general description of the integral metatheory for organisational transformation. My main purpose in setting out this very abstract presentation is to show that these ideas can be generalised beyond the organisational change domains. The implication of this generalisability will be discussed in the final chapter.

AN INTEGRAL METATHEORY FOR ORGANISATIONAL TRANSFORMATION

In the following pages an abstract and generalisable form of the metatheory is presented. This presentation is informed by the work of management theorist John Mathews (1996) and his research on "holonic organisational architectures". The aim here is to represent the integral metatheory using the holarchical lens as a scaffold for accommodating all the constituent lenses.

Four Orders of Holonic Relations

The holarchical group of lenses performs a pivotal role in metatheorising, particularly because this type of research brings together so many different conceptual orientations to a topic. Using the holon construct as a scaffolding concept for assembling other lenses offers a non-reductive system for representing and evaluating complex ideas about organisational life. In an article entitled "Holonic Organisational Architectures", Mathews (1996) provides a detailed analysis of the various descriptive levels at which a holonic analysis of change can be presented. Introducing his framework, Mathews points out that organisational holarchies and their constituent holons can be regarded as layered systems and subsystems that possess their own identity and intelligence (1996, p. 39):

> The basic conceptual core of holonic systems is the holon, which is an autonomous, independent, intelligent operating entity that is both a system in itself, possibly containing subsystems that can also be characterised as holons, and at the same time a subsystem of a broader systemic entity—as described in such telling clarity by Koestler. The holon is endowed with its own identity, processing intelligence, and the capacity for self-activity and reflection.

Matthews outlines three "orders of description" that can be applied to any holonic system. First, there is the order of description that pertains to the characteristics of a single, autonomous holon with its "own identity" and "self-activity". This is the "intra-holonic order" of description and its domain is all those qualities that relate to single holons. Second, there is the order of description that refers to relationships between holons, that is, those relational, communicative and mediating processes and subsystems that arise when two holons engage in some shared event. This is the "inter-holonic order" of description. Third, when theorists focus, on holarchical systems, they are considering a more general "systemic order" of analysis. Mathews's model stops at these three, but I add a fourth order of analysis. This is the inter-systemic order which applies to relationships between holonic systems. While further orders of analysis might be possible, these four provide a sufficient base for describing the general metatheory.

The Intra-holonic Order

In the intra-holonic order the focus is on the characteristics of a single holon.[4] Any number of relevant variables or qualities can be superimposed onto the holon construct. For example, the leadership theorist Russ Volckmann (2005) uses the holon for holding together multiple factors in his theory of executive leadership. He juxtaposes different dimensions relating to purpose, commitment, resources, competence, innovation and entrepreneurial capacity and assesses how these dimensions play out within "the executive leader". Working within the intra-holonic order of description, theorists can confer any number of defining qualities on the holons of interest. As the ecologists Allen and Starr put it, "What a holon shall contain is determined by the observer" (cited in Checkland, 1988, p. 237). The intra-holonic order of description allows theorists to move down into the details of how one holon will behave according to the particular lenses they employ in their analysis. However, because holons are always part of a larger system, a more complete analysis will involve inter-holonic and systemic orders of analysis.

The Inter-holonic Order

The inter-holonic order of description focuses on the interaction between holons, for example, the interpersonal, inter-group and inter-organisational relationships that create the social environment of organisational life. The inter-holonic order of analysis is interested in the mediational and communicative processes that flow between holons. Transformation arises from mutualising activities *between* holons rather than from the innate qualities *within* a holon. The social mediation lens can be used to disclose these inter-holonic realities.

An example of this approach is Taylor and Every's (2000) theory of "the emergent organisation". In this approach communication is not about the transmission of "one person's knowledge to others", rather it is a mutualising process that permits all parties "together to construct interactively the basis of knowledge" (2000, p. 3). And so communication creates the world of organising or rather, as the authors put it, "organisation emerges in communication". From this perspective, organisational transformation comes about as a result of new forms of interactive meaning-making rather than from the development of some pre-existing structure located within the organisation or its members. The organisation and its process and structures are continually being renegotiated and recreated through the media of language and texts as situated in interpersonal settings. From these negotiations, relationships of decision-making, control, power and authority are created and reshaped in various forms of organising hierarchies and heterarchies, i.e. forms of organising holarchies. This is why mediational (inter-holonic) forms of descriptive analysis are often employed in theories using a postmodernist or social constructionist perspective (see, for example, Deetz, 1995). Such approaches analyse organisational change through language, communication and message transmission and are sensitive to the relationships that define organising holarchies as constituted by mediating artefacts and systems.

The Systemic Holonic Order

The systemic order of description focuses on the relationship between holons and the holarchy or whole system in which they are imbedded. Of relevance here are lenses that deal with systems of relationships (which are always more than the sum of their constituent intra- and inter-relationships). Questions concerning transformation move from the intra-level of single holons and inter-level of two holons to the systemic level of the holarchy and its relations with its constituent holons and the environment in which it operates. The governance lens, for example, provides a window into the nested systems of decision-making and regulation that all organisations must have to retain their identity and operational cohesion.

The Inter-systemic Order

Mathews's model of first-, second- and third-order characteristics of holonic systems can be amended with a fourth order of description. This is the inter-systemic order that moves beyond the relationships that exist within a holonic system, to also consider multiple systems of holons and holarchies in dynamic environments. At this order of description, holarchic systems can be represented as multi-lens frameworks which combine lenses from each of the holon categories described in Table 7.1.

Figure 8.2 provides a graphical representation of the four orders of holonic description. In each of these orders the holon construct holds together concepts in non-reductive relationship. That is, it provides a window into conceptualising complexity without reducing that complexity either to some unfathomable whole or to some aggregate of parts. The model shows the flexibility of the holon construct for dealing with social events at multiple orders of complexity. Mathews notes, "The principal virtue of holonics systems lies in their flexibility and adaptability" (1996, p. 42), and it is these qualities that enable holons to marry lenses at very different levels of scope (simple and complex systems) and scales of focus (micro- and macrolevels).

Change theorists tend to emphasise one order of description to the exclusion of others depending on their general orientation. This results in

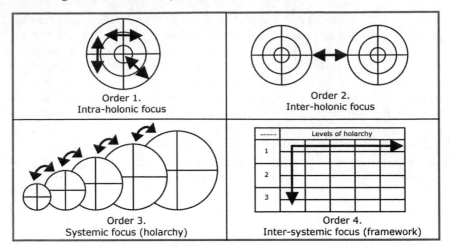

Figure 8.2   Four orders of holonic description.

a type of restricted explanatory range that supports the parochial nature of the debates often seen between proponents of different research paradigms (De Cock & Jeanes, 2006; Payne, 2000). Developmentalists, who typically focus their explanations of change at intra-holonic orders of description (e.g. on the unfolding structures of personal consciousness), find that the inter-holonic and systemic orders lack an understanding of the interiors and of cognitive, intentional, cultural and emotional qualities. Such topics are characteristic areas of developmental research. Alternatively, postmodern theorists emphasise the inter-holonic domain of communication, social mediation, language and texts. Systems-level theorists explain emergence through social interaction, communicative processes and the impact of power in organisational relationships. Mediation theorists see developmental explanations of change as overly concerned with cognitive and individualist explanations. At the systemic order of holon description theorists look at the overall patterns of change, regulatory dynamics and structuring forces. Systems-level theorists can move across both individual and social systems but often miss the need to ground their theorising in subjective and intersubjective social realities. They need intra-holonic and inter-holonic lenses to provide a more humane explanation of transformative change. All orders of description, and their associated paradigms of developmentalism, mediational and systems approaches, are in a position to benefit from a broader awareness of these different orders of description and their application in building theories of change.

An Integral Metatheory for Organisational Transformation

The holonic model just described can be used to present a more general presentation of the integral metatheory for organisational transformation.

Mindfull of the very abstract nature of these concepts, it is useful to present these ideas pictorially. Figure 8.3 presents bipolar and cyclical lenses that are commonly used at the intra-holonic level. For example, a researcher may be interested in the team-level dynamics of transformational change (transformation–translation lens) and want to consider the impact of within-boundary and cross-boundary communications (internal–external lens) and how the team responds through its group culture and collective behaviour (interior–exterior lens). This type of lens uses combinations of these bipolar lenses to develop categorical models and typologies.

Figure 8.3 also shows the cyclical group, system dynamics, transition process, evolutionary and learning lenses applied to a particular holon.[5] To illustrate this we might imagine a researcher investigating how hands-on, reflective and social learning (learning cycle lens) interact with the crisis, transformation and integration phases of organisational change (transition process lens) to produce innovations that can be selected and reproduced throughout an organisation (evolutionary lens).

Relational lenses are usefully represented at the inter-holonic order of description. The inter-holonic order describes encounters between holons and what emerges out of that relational space for different situational contexts and environments. Figure 8.4 shows the relational group of lenses for holons engaged in mediated relationships (social mediation lens) as they exchange with each other at different holonic levels (exchange relations lens) and as they move in and out of alignment with each other (alignment lens). Relationships, interaction and connection are thematic characteristics of the spirituality lens and, although it has relevance to other orders, the inter-holonic order is an appropriate domain for situating conceptual approaches based on the spirituality lens. The decentring lens is also relevant to inter-holonic relations in that the postmodern concerns with communication, interaction and power are all relational in nature.

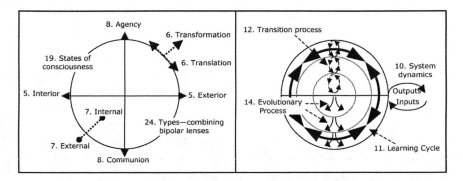

Figure 8.3 Bipolar lenses and cyclical lenses applied at the intra-holonic order.

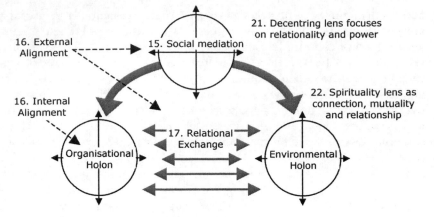

Figure 8.4   Relational lenses applied at the inter-holonic order.

Serial systems of holons form holarchies (Koestler, 1967). These series can be defined by temporal progression (developmental holarchy), spatial inclusion (ecological holarchy) or regulatory inclusion (governance holarchy). Figure 8.5 shows the three forms of holarchy found in theories of organisational transformation. Also represented here are the lenses of deep structure and inclusive emergence which, combined with the developmental lens, form a powerful set of lenses for investigating discontinuous change in organisations. Figure 8.5 also depicts the stream lens within this developmental context.

The systemic order of description and representation is also where holarchies can be used as scaffolding systems for bringing together bipolar

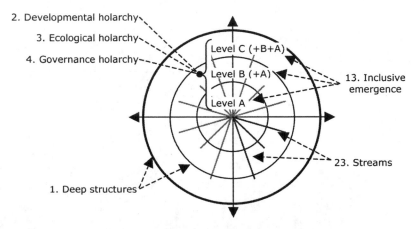

Figure 8.5   Holarchic lenses applied at the systemic order.

and cyclical lenses. Wilber does this with his quadrants framework and always represents the interior–exterior and individual–collective lenses within a holonic context.

Table 8.7 shows the inter-systemic order for describing metatheoretical lenses. It shows the relationships between the stakeholder lens and the perspectives lens. The framework describes how the personal perspectives of various stakeholder groups might be studied according to an ecological holarchy of, for example, individual owner/CEO, organisational stakeholders (staff, customers, suppliers), community stakeholders (local communities) and global stakeholders (biosphere, next generations). Each level of stakeholder from the inner circle of owners and executive management to the community to the intergenerational and environmental circles has its own perspective on, and experience of, transformational endeavours such as the pursuit of sustainable development. An inter-systematic inquiry into these perspectives is required for a comprehensive approach to transformation. Each cell in this inter-systemic framework can be regarded as a holon and so can be studied via intra-systemic, inter-systemic and systemic holonic orders of analysis. The full range of bipolar, cyclical, interactive and standpoint lenses can be subsequently brought into the picture depending on the research questions of interest. The health–pathology lens can be used to consider balanced and unbalanced aspects of any of the contents of these cells.

The diagrams representing intra-systemic, systemic and inter-systemic orders of holonic description are suggestions for the application of integral lenses at various orders of holonic description. The diagrams provide a

Table 8.7 Standpoint Lenses Applied at the Inter-Systemic Order of Analysis

18. Stakeholder Lens	20. Perspectives Lens			9. Health
	1st-Person Inquiry	2nd-Person Inquiry	3rd-Person Inquiry	
Ownership Circle of Stakeholders: The inner circle of owners, executive management, major shareholders	Experiential study of executive stakeholders	Relational study of executive stakeholders	Objective study of executive stakeholders	Balanced/ Unbalanced
Business Circle of Stakeholders: The middle circle of small shareholders, employees, suppliers and customers	Experiential study of staff, customers, etc.	Relational study of staff, customers, etc.	Objective study of staff, customers, etc.	Balanced/ Unbalanced
Community Circle of Stakeholders: The outer circle of local communities and environments	Experiential study of community stakeholders	Relational study of community stakeholders	Objective study of community stakeholders	Balanced/ Unbalanced
Intergenerational & Ecological Circle of Stakeholders: The intergenerational and global circle of present and future communities	Experiential study of global stakeholders	Relational study of global stakeholders	Objective study of global stakeholders	Balanced/ Unbalanced

general picture of the flexibility of the integral metatheory for transformation and some directions for combining relevant lenses within holonic contexts. In being aware of these different orders of description we can also see that research paradigms often work within some orders while neglecting others and that, consequently, theories will make use of certain metatheoretical lenses to the exclusion of others. The integrative metatheory described here opens up a more generous landscape for theorising about transformational change.

9 Evaluating the Big Picture

> Metatheorising is in an enviable intellectual position to adjudicate between rival traditions' competing and theoretically pertinent discursive and empirical claims. By clarifying the analytical standards often implicit in intra- and inter-tradition disputes and devising more ecumenical and persuasive criteria of its own, metatheorising can establish a foundation for reasoned evaluations of work associated with a host of competing paradigms. (Colomy, 1991, pp. 282–283)

EVALUATING INTEGRATIVE METATHEORY

This chapter will evaluate the integrative metatheory for organisational transformation and also show how metatheoretical frameworks can be used to evaluate other theory and metatheory. One of the main uses of metatheory building is in the critique of extant middle-range theory (Whetten, 1989) as well as other metatheory (Colomy, 1991). Depending on its conceptual scope, metatheory can be used to compare and contrast highly abstract ideas across many different theories and research paradigms. This adjudicative capacity will also be explored in a critique of AQAL, which has acted as a metatheoretical resource for this study.[1] For example, having derived a set of conceptual lenses from the multiparadigm review and analysed their various relationships, it is now possible to review AQAL in its use of such lenses.

The evaluation of the metatheory for organisational transformation is based on established criteria for "good" theory building (Wacker, 1998; Whetten, 1989). Although these criteria were developed for evaluating middle-range theory (Merton, 1957), they are also relevant to metatheory building in that the process steps involved in theory development are similar across different levels of conceptual abstraction (Meredith, 1993). As Wacker says: "a basic underpinning of all theory building is that theory is built on existing theory" (2004, p. 645). What will be different is the relative importance of these criteria. For example, the criteria of comprehensiveness and abstraction level are critically important in metatheory building whereas parsimony is less crucial. Wacker (1998) suggests that it is more important that too many explanatory concepts are included at the theory building stage than too little. In other words, comprehensiveness needs to be weighted more heavily than parsimony in metatheory building, at least in its initial phases.

IMPLICATIONS—"METATHEORISING FOR ADJUDICATION"

Evaluating Theories of Organisational Transformation

Ritzer (2001) has noted that many of the most important contributions to theory building in the social sciences have been based on the evaluation of other theories. He sees metatheoretical frameworks as not only useful for developing insight into the range of theoretical perspectives within a field but also that "systematic metatheorising allows us to more adequately evaluate and critically analyse extant theories" (1991a, p. 302). As previously noted, Paul Colomy (1991) calls this type of research "metatheorising for adjudication" (M_A) to delineate it from Ritzer's other forms of multiparadigm research. Colomy says that "a primary task of metatheorising involves not only understanding extant theories but evaluating them" (1991, p. 281). Colomy describes M_A as (1991, p. 269) "oriented towards devising and applying explicit, universalistic criteria to adjudicate the competing claims issued by rival social scientific traditions".

AQAL has also been used to perform this type of evaluative reassessment of extant theory. The principle of non-exclusion obliges the integral theorist to not only include but also to critically evaluate theories and situate them within an integrated metatheoretical framework. For example, theorists have battled for many decades over whether social events are best explained through micro- or macrolevel interactions (Ritzer, 2001). Yet it has been convincingly argued for several decades that multilevel research needs to acknowledge the validity of all these perspectives (Yammarino & Dansereau, 2008). If a theory relies solely on micro- or macrolevels in its explanations it is being reductionist and imbalanced in some fundamental way.

As indicated in a previous chapter, it is precisely within this evaluative context that the health–pathology lens can be applied. An integral metatheory can take the shortcomings of particular theories into account and make diagnoses and adjudications based on, for example, the lenses that they neglect or the conceptual partialities that they might be prone to. There are several forms of partiality that integral metatheorising can draw attention to and these can be described according to the main groups of explanatory lenses found in this study (see Table 9.1).

- Holarchy category: Partiality is commonly seen in the omission of certain levels of a holarchy. For the developmental holarchy lens it is usually postconventional levels that are omitted; for the ecological holarchy it is the mesolevel or group level; and for the organising or governance holarchy is often the "lower" levels which are assumed to not possess any organising potential.

Table 9.1 Healthy and Pathological Forms of Conceptual Lenses

Lens Categories	Healthy Form	Pathological Form	Type of Partiality	Examples of Partiality
Holarchy	full spectrum: all levels of the holarchy are included	partial spectrum: only some holarchical levels are included	holarchical reduction	omission of postconventional stages of development
Bipolar	balanced: both poles included	imbalanced: only one pole included	bipolar reduction	methodological individualism which assumes individuals create social reality
Cyclical	entire cycle: all phases of the cycle are included	incomplete cycle: only some phases of the cycle are included	process reduction	transformational cycle with "no pain", i.e. omits chaos/grief phases
Standpoint	multiple standpoints: all major perspectives and standpoints included	privileged standpoints: only dominant perspectives included	viewpoint reduction	top-down management theories—all organising power comes from the top echelons
Relational	mediated and unmediated interactions are included	Only mediated interactions are included	nature–nurture reduction	environmentalism which assumes that transformation is totally context dependent
Multimorphic	multiparadigm system: multiple lenses in a relational system	disconnected pluralism: unrelated multiple lenses	system reduction	methodological pluralism which assumes no way of evaluating multiple views

- Bipolar category: The most common form of reductionism here is to assume that social realities can be explained through only one pole of a particular lens, for example, that social phenomena can only be explained by individual agency *or* collective structure. Another prominent example is the dominance of the exterior (functional/behavioural) pole over the interior (interpretive/consciousness) pole in explanations of change.

- Cyclical category: In the cyclical group of lenses, some phases of the transition cycle or learning cycle can be neglected to result in various kinds of short-circuit reductionism. For example, in the transition cycle, some theories leave out the "dark night" phase of chaos, confusion and inactivity. The learning cycle can also be reduced to an incomplete number of phases as when the more abstract and conceptual phases of learning are emphasised to the detriment of the "hands-on", behavioural phases.

- Standpoint category: These lenses emphasise the multiperspective nature of social life. These "decentring" lenses take a critical standpoint towards dominant modes of explanation. The most common forms of pathology here are the neglect of marginalised perspectives that come from the periphery. Theorists often assume that a particular voice or perspective, often one that is politically, economically or managerially dominant, is the only significant voice in explanations of sustainable organising. For example, unsustainable organisational and economic practices have impacted most heavily on the poor and yet it is precisely these voices that have not been heard in the debates on trade, globalisation and climate change.

- Interactive category: The interactive lenses provide explanations about change that involve interaction between internal and external environments. Partiality here takes the form of relying on either unmediated (developmentalist) explanations or mediated explanations. Developmentalist approaches to organisational sustainability place too much causal emphasis on the interior structures of the organisation while purely mediational explanations tend to concentrate on the causal role of environmental factors.

- Multiparadigm lenses: Where multiparadigm sets of lenses are employed to develop "big-picture" explanations it is essential that they not simply be presented either as completely comprehensive in themselves or as a bag of eclectic and unrelated options. Metatheorising can become universalist when it stops critically examining the range, type and validity of the lenses it uses to build its metatheories. On the other hand, simply acknowledging the multiplicity of lenses without seeing the relationships and connections between them falls into a relativist position. This relativist approach to explanation lacks the capacity to not only discuss the boundaries and limitations of each form of explanation (or explanatory lens) but also identify their points of focus and strength.

To demonstrate these types of partiality, and the implications they can have on theory development, the following section will discuss some common types of reductionism that occur for the holarchical and the bipolar groups of lenses. Once again, organisational sustainability will be used as an exemplar topic for this discussion.

Reductionist Forms of Holarchical Lenses

Partiality and imbalance are seen most commonly in holarchies where a curtailed range of levels is employed. In the case of the developmental holarchy the full range of postconventional levels of development is frequently not included. This results in explanations of sustainability that leave out the postconventional levels of deep purpose, profound meaning making, moral transformations and leading-edge forms of community. Most discussions of organisational sustainability are concerned with conventional levels of development, with compliance, efficiency, technological innovation and commitment. The connections between justice, sustainability and postconventional forms of spirituality are neglected or regarded as peripheral. Theorists using non-reductive forms of the developmental lens find important roles for spirituality in exploring sustainability issues (Berry, 1999; Carroll, 2004; Christie, 2002). One of the most thorough treatments of organisational sustainability from a developmental holarchy perspective is the corporate sustainability model of Dunphy, Griffiths and Benn (2003). Towards the end of their book the authors introduce the idea of "cosmocentric consciousness", which they regard as a quality of both the individual member as well as the organisation (2003, p. 272):

> Cosmocentric consciousness, or spiritual intelligence, helps us connect to the emerging forms of the future. Without this kind of consciousness it is hard to find the future—with it, the future seems inescapable. The future is within us and around us. Its shape is already coalescing in our dreams, emerging from our play, emerging in the hasty decisions we make as we face overload at work. The future is forming here in our minds, already shaping the actions of our hands and moving our feet forwards. The world about us is also changing and we are connected with powerful forces that are already moving our world, and us, towards sustainability. The clues to a sustainable future are already there for us to find: in the next office, the factory up the street, the children's project at home, our own imagination. The future is a living presence now if we are prepared to respond to it.

Dunphy and his colleagues propose that seeking this "cosmocentric consciousness" or "spiritual intelligence" is a necessary element for transformation towards the truly sustaining organisation. This does not deny that conventional theories of sustainability contribute significantly to our knowledge. However, without including the full range of developmental potentials, including postconventional levels that involve capacities such as cosmocentric consciousness or spiritual intelligence, our understandings will remain at best partial and incomplete, and at worst unbalanced and stunted.

The ecological holarchy also often suffers from an undue abbreviation of levels. The most common form of this abbreviation is the micro–macro, or individual–collective, form of the ecological holarchy. Explanations that rely on this abbreviated bipolar model fall readily into reductionisms such as methodological individualism and collectivism. Strong forms of methodological individualism, such as agency theory and rational choice theory, still dominate much of economic theory (Zwirn, 2007) and, by association, influence much research into organisational change (Cao, Clarke & Lehaney, 1999). These biases have a significant impact on theories of sustainability. Where individuals are seen as the explanatory source of change there is a tendency to neglect the social forms of influence such as peer groups, cultural norms, social conventions, government regulation and community values. Alternatively, where change is pursued purely through collective means, the part of the individual is undervalued. Approaches to change that come from the collective pole can also induce forms of unwilling compliance and passive resistance that can actually be counter-productive for achieving sustainability objectives in the long term (Maxwell, 2007).

Both these reductionisms treat the ecological holarchy lens as a bipolar variable with individual agents at one end and collective wholes at the other. In fact, the "individual" and the "collective" occupy arbitrary levels on a social scale that consists of multiple levels. One level that is frequently omitted is the mesolevel of the group. New research has shown that this level has particular significance in transformation (West, Markiewicz & Trimpop, 2004). It is at the group level where sustainability initiatives and experiments can be trialled that are not possible in more structured environments. While mesolevel studies of transformation for sustainability are becoming increasingly common (Bleischwitz, 2007; Brunetti, Petrell & Sawada, 2003; Welsh & Murray, 2003) there is still a significant gap in the theoretical literature on this topic.

Reductive forms of the governance holarchy lens also distort our understandings of how organisations can transform towards greater sustainability. A common distortion of the governance lens assumes that organisations are best managed from the top down and that leadership flows from the upper echelons to the lower. Distortions like this reinforce Taylorist theories of management that result in coercive and depersonalised governance structures (Richardson, 1996). They also support views of change that attribute the chief responsibility and power for change to executive levels of management. Such understandings drive the phenomenon of CEO turnover where organisational renewal is equated with obtaining a new CEO who imposes top-down transformation (Billiger & Hallock, 2005). At the other end of this spectrum of governance distortions there are bottom-up perspectives that equate transformation with the flattening and delayering of the governance structure. Delayering theorists reason that fewer layers of decision-making and managerial intervention will create more participative and responsive organisational forms (Egelhoff, 1999). While flattening strategies are often centred on removing middle management layers for efficiency rather than transformational reasons, the move to flatter governance structures has its merits. Nevertheless, it is also true that "relayering" of the organisation often takes place (Littler, Wiesner & Dunford, 2003) and that some form of hierarchy is a fundamental aspect of all social organising, decision-making and strategic action. This point is made by organisational behaviour theorist, Harold Leavitt (2005, p. 55):

> Despite persistent (and perhaps, hopeful) rumors to the contrary, hierarchy is alive and well—and it's not going away anytime soon. . . . For better or for worse, the pyramid remains the dominant design of organizations in today's world, just as it was in yesterday's. To be sure, hierarchies have changed in important ways. Many have flattened, teamed, and otherwise modernized. And their inevitable authoritarianism has been veiled and perfumed to obscure its unattractiveness. Yet beneath the veils, almost all large human organizations are still top-down, authority-driven structures. Bosses are still piled on bosses. People lower down still report to those higher up. Those organizations are still loaded with control systems, performance evaluations, and a host of other constraints on their people's behaviour. And large hierarchies are still plagued by a variety of human and productive flaws.

The organising holarchy is a dynamic and multilevelled aspect of organisations that involves bottom-up, top-down and reciprocal dynamics (Chakravarthy & Gargiulo, 1998). Reliance on any one of these facets results in a reductive and unbalanced understanding of organising processes and how they might contribute to more sustaining forms of organisation.

Bipolar Group

A key issue in evaluating the use of bipolar lenses is whether a theory includes both poles of those lenses in its explications. Taking the agency–communion lens as an example, the leadership and management literature emphasises the agentic end of the spectrum. A relative dearth of theory has been developed for explaining the communal and relational aspects of leadership (Mintzberg, 2006). This focus is not only apparent at the microlevel of the individual but also at other organisational levels. Research into the goal-focused behaviour and strategic agency of the meso- and macrolevels of group and organisational activity has also been the predominant concern. This point has been taken up by Gladwin, Kennelly and Krause (1995, p. 898) in an article on the shift in conceptual paradigms that has occurred in sustainability studies. Under the heading "Agency to Communion", the authors ask the following questions:

> Has the body of management theory inadvertently encouraged this diminishment of communion and enlargement of hyper-agency (i.e., excessive concern with autonomy and self-preservation)? Do theories emphasise organisational freedom over union, rights over responsibilities, independence over interdependence, and what works (efficiency) over what is worth pursuing? Have management theories, when implemented, pushed organisations into a pathological agency, where severance from communities (both human and ecological) sets forces in motion that eventually destroy the communities upon which organisations ultimately depend?

The poles of the agency–communion dimension are often associated with the gender dimension. Organisational theory shows a concerted emphasis on the masculine and its agentic values, worldviews and forms of activity and a neglect of the feminine and its associated worldviews of relationality and interdependence. Gladwin and his colleagues ask a pertinent question related this issue (1995, p. 898): "Are positive contributions to sustainability more likely to arise from organisations that are more female versus male in their value spheres?" Perhaps the issue is how to recognise that a balance between the two is essential for building truly sustaining forms of organisations. Without that balance, theories of organisational life that are systematically blind to concepts of communality, relationality, mutuality and interdependence will continue to produce inadequate explanations and reinforce understandings that lead to reductionist and pathological commercial practices (Ghoshal, 2005).

The interior–exterior lens is another bipolar dimension that can be used to assess shortcomings in extant sustainability theory. Bradbury's observation that sustainability is about both "inner and outer worlds" deals specifically with this issue. As long ago as 1979 Burrell and Morgan noted that the majority of organisational theories came from objective and functionalist orientation. While the interpretive and the experiential now play a greater role in organisational theory, the majority of theorists continue to rely on behavioural and structural modes of explanation. This exterior approach to theorising is also present within the field of organisational sustainability where technological and systems-based research dominates interior approaches concerned with cultural and psychological realities. One result of this bias has been a lack of awareness about the role of values, consciousness and cultural pressures in driving unsustainable practices and systems. Again, Gladwin and his colleagues ask an insightful question regarding this issue. Under the heading of "Exterior to Interior" they ask (1995, p. 898):

> Sustainability, like human medicine, mixes both descriptive and normative or action-guiding content. Has our domain become devoid of ideas dangerous to greed, short-sightedness, indulgence, exploitation, apathy, narrowness, and other values inconsistent with sustainability (Orr, 1994)? In short, the study of sustainability must shift from objectivity to subjectivity, from exterior nuts and bolts to interior hearts and minds.

A balanced metatheory for sustainability would aim to integrate both exterior "nuts and bolts" and interior "hearts and minds". The theoretical partiality for the exterior, which is evident in most conceptualisations of sustainability, is also reflected in our predilections for technological rather than psychological or ethical solutions to the problems caused by profligate practices.

A final example of lens reduction in the bipolar group comes from the application of the transformation–translation lens. The defining poles of this dimension refer to qualitative and discontinuous transformation and incremental and continuous translation respectively. Focusing one-sidedly on either end of this dimension can result in significant conceptual misunderstandings about the change process. For example, in not recognising the ongoing process of incremental change and continuous transaction, theorists, consultants and managers can rely too heavily on dramatic and radical restructuring. Karl Weick (2000) has warned against a reliance on transformational approaches in solving the challenges facing contemporary organisations, particularly when such solutions come at the expense of supporting an emergent and evolutionary approach that appears through localised initiatives and everyday transactions. Translational change includes things like everyday decision-making, informal negotiations, interpersonal communications and the coordination of mundane activities. These are all crucial for the healthy maintenance of social cohesion and organisational productivity. However, translational change is not sufficient to meet the challenges of a transforming social environment. When the necessity for radical change is not recognised, an organisation can quickly become out of touch with the realities of its markets, customers, ethical responsibilities and the consequences of its actions on natural environments.

An organisation that possesses the capacity to balance both transformational and translational requirements has been called an "ambidextrous organisation" (O'Reilly & Tushman, 2004). Such an organisation can respond to the need for both stability and for significant reorganisation and development. Both sides of this dimension are needed in theory development and in the practical work of developing successful organisations which provide healthy and challenging working environments. Yet many researchers continue to develop theory about one side of this polarity and exclude the other to the detriment of a more inclusive understanding of transformation (see, for example, the debates between Theory E and Theory O researchers in Beer & Nohria, 2000).

AN EVALUATION OF THE INTEGRAL METATHEORY FOR ORGANISATIONAL TRANSFORMATION

Ritzer has made the point that metatheory needs to be evaluated by "standards indigenous to metatheorising" (1991a, p. 310). By this he means that metatheory building cannot be evaluated directly by empirical studies but by the logical criteria and methods involved in analysing its own database, that is, other conceptual models. In this section three sets of criteria will be used to evaluate the integral metatheory for organisational transformation: (i) Ritzer's criteria for assessing the quality of metatheorising projects, (ii) Wacker's "virtues" of good theory and (iii) Whetten's criteria for theoretical contributions.

Nesting

Ritzer's criterion of "nesting" is important because it ensures that metatheoretical propositions are grounded in theory and on the core assumptions that characterise different paradigms. For example, the method developed for this study grouped, or in Ritzer's terms nested, theories according to their dominant explanatory themes for transformation. While many theories included themes that cut across paradigms, this nesting process at least ensured that a very broad range of paradigm perspectives were included in the development of conceptual lenses. The bracketing technique used to identify lenses within paradigm categories provided a methodological means for ensuring that the nesting criterion was included in the study.

By "nesting" Ritzer is also referring to the historical relationship between one theory and another. This approach to understanding the development of theory has connections with "the history of ideas". Although some historical aspects of the development of theories of organisational transformation were described in Chapter 4, a chronological analysis of theories and themes of transformation was not included in this study. A metatheoretical investigation of how theories of transformation have developed over time could contribute significant detail to the conceptual analysis performed here (see, for example, the work of White, 1973).

Linkage

Once the nestedness of theories has been considered, Ritzer's second criterion of "linkage" between theories comes into play. Linkage is the process by which numerous conceptual elements are analysed and synthesised so that points of linkage can be found and shared discourses, viewpoints and orienting strategies identified and described. Weinstein and Weinstein (1991, p. 140) point out, "Metatheory treats the multiplicity of theorizations as an opportunity for multiple operations of analysis and synthesis". The bridging and bracketing techniques, which were used to identify the set of 24 integral lenses, accommodated this linkage criterion by connecting theories both within and across paradigm categories (as discussed in Chapter 5).

Comparative Techniques

Ritzer sees metatheorising as possessing an "inherently comparative character" (1991a, p. 312). The comparison, contrast and calibration of theories have been frequently used here to derive generalised patterns. For example, the developmental holarchy, learning and transition process lenses were each identified through a comparative analysis of many theories. Comparisons such as these not only serve to identify conceptual lenses for understanding and explaining organisational transformation, they also help to map out the detail of those lenses. For example, the comparative study of stage-based models of transformation presented in Appendix C identifies the full range of transformational potentials that theorists have explored to date. In the case of the transition process lens, comparative analyses identified a much greater level of detail for describing the phases of transitioning. Such comparisons have been a hallmark of metatheoretical studies and to this point they have relied on qualitative methods to perform these comparisons. The lack of application of quantitative methods to this comparative task has been a significant weakness in the research methodology of conceptual meta-studies.[2] Metatheorising stands to gain considerably from a more rigorous application of both quantitative and qualitative methods.

Conservation and the Integral Metatheory

Conservation refers to the idea of not replacing one theory with another unless "there is good reason to believe all other theories are lacking in some virtue" (Wacker, 1998, p. 365). In the case of metatheorising, we need not replace one metatheory with another unless there is significant weakness in existing frameworks. What has been attempted here in building an overarching view of organisational transformation is an appreciation of the insights of other theorists and metatheorists while also evaluating their limitations.

Perhaps the most distinctive feature of integral metatheory is its appreciation of other theory and metatheory. In practice this means that scientific theories are regarded as contributing unique insights and that the accumulation of knowledge is not a process of replacing one theory with another but of seeing how theoretical pluralism contributes to knowledge development. This is fundamentally a conservative position, one that is not focused on what is "lacking" and therefore to be replaced, but on what is contributed and needs to be conserved. The metatheory for organisational transformation proposed here has identified and applied core conceptual contributions from many theories of organisational change. In this way their insights have been conserved in the frameworks that can be derived from the metatheory.

There is a danger, however, that when the conservative side of metatheorising stops being flexible and creative, the situating of theories and lenses can become a process of typing and categorisation. The AQAL framework may be particularly prone to this problem because of the prescriptive manner in which it is used. The fundamental task of metatheorising is not to be able to categorise theories within some pre-existing overarching framework but to ensure that the unique contributions of middle-range theories are accommodated with the metatheory. In other words, the primary research goal is to identify the unique lenses that theorists and research paradigms offer and to integrate them within the metatheoretical system rather than to categorise theories. In fact, any middle-range theory can be accommodated within some facet of a metatheoretical lens. Any theory, for example, can be regarded as dealing, at least to some extent, with psychological interiors, behavioural exteriors or a combination of both and so can be located somewhere within the interior–exterior lens. However, this type of categorisation is only valid once we can demonstrate that we have captured the definitive lenses of that middle-range theory. Locating theories that use mediation lenses within a metatheory that only possesses developmental lenses is not valid metatheorising. This falls into the *a priori* forms of metatheory that Ritzer (2001) warns against.

The approach presented here has attempted to conserve the unique lenses of extant middle-range theories of transformation and accommodate them within the integrative metatheoretical system. The process of combining different conceptual lenses displays the potential flexibility of metatheory and how it can call on the creative skills of the researcher. While categorisation and the generation of typologies is a worthwhile theoretical activity (Doty & Glick, 1994), metatheory building has much broader creative potentials than that.

Uniqueness of the Integral Metatheory

The criterion of uniqueness looks at the level of distinctiveness that a conceptual framework possesses. Although it is not often recognised as such, metatheory building occupies a very distinct position within scientific research disciplines (Ritzer, 1991c). Most importantly, metatheorising builds knowledge at a level of deep abstraction and generalisability.

The current study has constructed overarching theoretical frameworks at a high level of abstraction while also retaining strong connections with the pool of individual theories that the metatheory draws on. One way that it has done this is through the development of a more detailed metatheory building method (see Chapter 4). This method has uncovered a rich source of data for metatheory development. From this data, the metatheory building method developed here derived 24 integral lenses and their relationships. This level of methodological detail has never been attempted before in metatheoretical research. The result of this more detailed method has been the identification of several metatheoretical lenses that have not been previously identified or used in large-scale theory building for organisational studies. These include the ecological and organising holarchy lenses, the learning lens, the mediation lens and the alignment lens. It is hoped that identifying these explanatory orientations and describing the relationships they have with other lenses will contribute to the development of further middle-range theory.

Parsimony in the Integral Metatheory

Parsimony is an important principle in metatheory building. It requires that metatheorists keep to a minimum the number of explanatory factors included in the metatheoretical system. Only those factors that are essential for explaining the phenomena of interest should be retained. However, while parsimony is a desirable aim in metatheory building, it is crucial that this type of research favour the inclusion of multiple concepts as these can always be weeded out, when and if they are found to be redundant. David Whetten addresses this when he says (1989, p. 490):

> When authors begin to map out the conceptual landscape of a topic they should err in favour of including too many factors, recognising that over time their ideas will be refined. It is generally easier to delete unnecessary or invalid elements then it is to justify additions.

There is the further possibility that several of the lenses may be derived from combinations of other lenses. For example, the stakeholder, decentring and ecological holarchy lenses have some common characteristics and they might be different versions of a more fundamental discourse. The same could be said of the lenses in the interaction group. The alignment lens might be explained by some combination of the mediation and relational exchange lenses. At this point I would argue that these lenses do offer some important and unique insights and that retaining them all is justified.

Generalisability of the Integral Metatheory

Generalisability refers to the scope or coverage of a theory and the applicability of findings to other areas of research. The more areas to which theory can be usefully and validly applied, the better the metatheory. Describing the metatheory via the exemplar topic of sustainability has shown that it can be gainfully applied to fields of organisational research. The level of abstraction of the integrative metatheory is significant and, as Wacker notes (1998, p. 366), "High abstraction level theories (general or grand theories) have an almost unlimited scope". Consequently, it is likely that the ideas presented here will have some relevance to other areas within the organisational and management field and to social sciences.

It is not coincidental that several of the conceptual frameworks reviewed here have much in common. The same sense-making conceptual tools arise repeatedly and independently across many different fields of social research and so it is arguable that the lenses identified here may be generalisable beyond organisational transformation. There are, however, some cautionary points that need to be made regarding the generalisability of integral lenses and frameworks to different cultural contexts. The integral metatheory for organisational transformation proposed in this study was based primarily on the work of theorists from North America, Europe and Australia. Being conscious of this limitation opens up the opportunity for inter-cultural forms of metatheorising that can accommodate lenses derived from non-Western and indigenous cultures. Such perspectives are likely to present unique explanatory lenses that can add valuable insights into transformational phenomena. In particular, the viewpoints of indigenous peoples will have particular relevance to the topic of sustainability and to the social transformations required for achieving intergenerational sustainability at a community level.

The quality of generalisability assumes that the patterns and systems that are interpreted as being present in one situation are also present in other situations. Because metatheorising functions at such high levels of abstraction, there is a danger that patterns and concordances can be too easily read into the description of complex social theories and across multiple fields of human experience. This issue is particularly relevant when patterns within natural, non-human systems are also interpreted as occurring within human, social systems. In her review of punctuated equilibrium models of transformation, Gersick (1991, p. 33) calls for caution when:

> applying models from one research domain to another too freely or literally. Human systems, self-aware and goal-directed, have the capacity to 'schedule' their own opportunities for revolutionary change (as with time-triggered transitions), to solicit outside perspectives, and to manage their histories in ways that are inconceivable for unconscious systems. Much as theories from different domains have to offer each other, it would be a mistake to import constructs uncritically, rather than to use them to provoke questions about how they might apply in other settings. The punctuated equilibrium paradigm offers a new lens through which theorists can make fresh discoveries about how

managers, workgroups, organisations, and industries both develop over time and react to changes in their environments.

The danger of developing invalid lenses that are not generalisable across human and non-human systems is a particular problem when reviewing theories coming out of the systems and new sciences research paradigms. While theories from these paradigms continue to make important contributions to the study of organisational transformation, there needs to be a conservative approach to transferring their explanatory factors from the natural and system sciences across to a complex area of human activity like social transformation.

Level of Abstraction of the Integral Metatheory

The abstraction level of a construct is its independence from situational and temporal particulars. When a theoretical system has a high abstraction level it has the capacity to "integrate many relationships and variables into a larger theory" (Wacker, 1998, p. 365). Metatheories are intended to do precisely this and so it is vital that overarching approaches should possess considerable abstractness. One way of demonstrating this capacity is to assess the range and number of conceptual elements that have been included from other theories. The integral approach to organisational transformation demonstrates this characteristic of inclusiveness. For example, abstractness is a definitive quality of the holon construct. It is the holon's capacity to include both holistic or atomistic forms of analysis which enables it to provide non-reductive explanations of social happenings.

Abstractness can also be a barrier to understanding and applying metatheoretical concepts. Metatheories need to demonstrate their practical implications and applied utility and the abstract nature of this form of research has been a major barrier to the general comprehension and recognition of metatheorising. This problem is particularly relevant to the goals of this study where the multifaceted topic of organisational transformation has been the domain for integrating many abstract change-related concepts. In Ritzer's typology of forms of metatheorising, the overarching variety, M_O, is the most abstract. However, the work of Bill Torbert has shown that communicating metatheoretical ideas is possible in organisational studies. The application of Torbert's DAI to such diverse and down-to-earth issues as timely decision-making (Torbert et al., 2004) and collaborative management research (McGuire, Palus & Torbert, 2007) is testament to the practical value of this form of conceptual research.

Internal Consistency of the Integral Metatheory

The virtue of internal consistency is particularly crucial for assessing the quality of a conceptual system. Of particular importance in building metatheory is the consistency in the relationships within and between the metatheoretical lenses. For example, if each lens actually provides a unique window into conceptualising some phenomenon then there should be minimal conceptual redundancy between those lenses. The facets of one lens should not be highly associated with the facets of another lens. This means that lenses should be relatively independent of each other and be capable of combining to create insightful explorative frameworks.[3] Unfortunately, once they have been established, metatheories tend to fall into the trap of assimilating new lenses within their existing system and the internal consistency of the relationships between lenses fails as a result.

Definitions are another major issue for maintaining internal consistency. Middle-range theorists have been critical of metatheory because of the imprecise definitions given to the many abstract terms involved. However, abstraction is actually a required quality for developing metatheories and so lack of clarity in definition needs to be separated as much as possible from the level of abstraction of the concepts involved. Subsuming concepts such as "structure" and "culture" within other even broader concepts exemplifies the difficulty faced by metatheorists working at this level of abstraction. While these concerns over concept stretching and definitional clarity are valid, they should not be used as arguments against the use of highly abstract, "second-order concepts" in the first place (Elkana, 1988).

Has the Metatheory Identified New Factors?

David Whetten offers three criteria for judging "what is a legitimate, value-added contribution to theory development" (1989, p. 492). These are the addition of new factors, new conceptual relationships and credibility. Whetten suggests that one way to contribute to theory building is to bring together disparate or previously unassociated explanatory factors to increase a theory's conceptual scope (1989, p. 493):

> Theoretical insights come from demonstrating how the addition of a new variable significantly alters our understanding of the phenomena by reorganising our causal maps.

The same can be asked of the integrative metatheory proposed here. Has the metatheory introduced new "variables" (lenses) and new combinations of variables for the analysis of transformation? Numerous factors, identified from the multiparadigm review phase of the research, have been brought together here for the first time into one conceptual system. For example, I have described how the organisational ecology lens, the interior–exterior and internal–external lenses can be combined to construct a framework for investigating subjective and objective aspects of multiple levels of organisational sustainability. Most theories of transformation adopt one or two lenses and develop their explanations based on the distinctions that flow from them. Even where more integrative attempts are made, only a few of the more important lenses, for example the developmental and the interior–exterior lenses, are included within the frameworks proposed. Take, for instance, Sarason's (1995) integrative model of organisational transformation which includes only the micro–macro and systems dynamics lenses. The exception to this is the developmental action inquiry model of Torbert and his colleagues (Fisher et al., 2003; Torbert et al., 2004). Their approach brings together a number of lenses including the developmental, ecological and governance holarchies, interior–exterior, mediation, learning, perspectives and transition process lenses.

One particularly underutilised lens is that of social mediation. The inclusion of this lens within an integral approach to organisational transformation adds significantly to its capacity for critically analysing theory and the application of theory to such areas as public policy and social change. When new explanatory factors such as the social mediation lens are used in conjunction with other lenses, powerful conceptual models become available for exploring transformational phenomena.

Relationships Between Factors

Another of Whetten's criteria for judging theoretical contributions is the identification of conceptual relationships. He states that (1989, pp. 492–493), "Relationships, not lists [of factors], are the domain of theory". The integral metatheory for organisational transformation not only identifies numerous explanatory lenses but also analyses, describes and depicts their internal and external relationships. For example, I have dealt at some length with the relationships within and between lenses so they could be brought together into a coherent meta-system. Reductionist forms of these lenses were also described through investigating the internal relationships between lens facets. The study of the metamorphological relationships between categories of lenses is a particularly important domain for metatheoretical research. There is potential here for seeing how our theorising may be systematically distorted in predictable ways and, subsequently, for researching how these distorted lenses might be better formulated. Given the power of theory and metatheory to shape social realities, metatheoretical research and the study of areas like the metamorphologies of concepts deserve much more attention than they currently receive.

The Credibility of the Proposed Metatheory

Whetten (1989, p. 491) notes that: "During the theory development process, logic replaces data as the basis for evaluation". This criterion for judging the value of a metatheoretical contribution is concerned with the "logic underlying the model" and with "the underlying psychological, economic, or social dynamics that justify the selection of factors and the proposed causal relationships" (Whetten, 1989, p. 491). The major underlying assumptions that have informed the metatheorising undertaken are those of appreciative meta-inquiry (Edwards, 2007) and Wilber's IMP (see Chapter 4). These assumptions consist of (i) an appreciative stance towards the contributions of scientific theories and cultural forms of knowledge (Wilber's "nonexclusion" principle), (ii) a historical perspective towards the accumulation of knowledge (Wilber's "unfoldment" principle) and (iii) a recognition that theory building is but one aspect of a process that includes method, interpretation and analysis (Wilber's "enactment" principle).

The assumption of an appreciative stance assumes that all relevant, well-articulated and rigorously researched theories can contribute important insights. This is a positive and inclusive form of scholarship that recognises the plurality of perspectives on social reality. The impact of this assumption can be seen in a large number of explanatory lenses identified in this study. Unfoldment assumes that knowledge unfolds through history and through all cultures and that that emergence is reflected in the accumulation of scientific knowledge. Unfoldment assumes not only the relevance of interdisciplinary and cross-cultural knowledge for metatheory building research, but that such endeavours evolve over time. This principle is seen in the developmental emphasis that I have taken here for the study of organisational transformation. The third assumption is enactment. Enactment assumes that each ontological domain will have its own associated epistemology and methodology. In other words, the "data" of a particular social reality can only be uncovered when an adequate system of knowing and a relevant method of practice are in place. This assumption means that the absence of a particular lens will result in a limited encounter with the practical realities of a situation. For example, if an organisational theory focuses purely on internal dynamics and does not include external factors such as market forces, inter-organisational networks and community attitudes it will never uncover all the facts needed to develop holistic explanations of change.

The value of these principles for metatheoretical research becomes clearer when overarching models that do not use these principles are examined. Taking the non-exclusion principle as an example, the multiparadigm framework of Burrell and Morgan included only two explanatory dimensions of lenses—radical versus regulatory change and subjective versus objective orientation. While this framework has spurred much theoretical discussion and some research, it has not continued to develop as a viable metatheory into the twenty-first century. The underlying lack of an appreciative position, and the consequential inability to accommodate further lenses, may have played some part in its demise. In contrast, the integrative methodology proposed here has the potential for continued growth and ongoing accommodation of emerging theoretical viewpoints.

A CRITIQUE OF THE AQAL FRAMEWORK

> But I should say that I hold this integral critical theory very lightly. Part of the difficulty is that, at this early stage, all of our attempts at a more integral theory are very preliminary and sketchy. It will take decades of work among hundreds of scholars to truly flesh out an integral theory with any sort of compelling veracity. Until that time, what I try to offer are suggestions for making our existing theories and practices just a little more integral than they are now. (Wilber, 2005)

Metatheory building is an inherently recursive process. It relies on the iterative refinement of its propositions and frameworks through critical analysis and self-reflection. Susan Lynham's (2002) statement that a theory is always "a theory in progress" also holds true for metatheory. The "ongoing refinement and development" of theoretical frameworks form the basis for establishing any social science discipline (Dubin, 1978). This does not only refer to theory testing through the gathering of empirical evidence but also to metatheory building and conceptual research (Meredith, 1993). Conceptual development of a theory ensures that it is kept "current and relevant and that it continues to work and have utility in the practical world" (Lynham, 2002, p. 234). The following critique of AQAL is a step in this process of refinement and development.

AQAL is an innovative and comprehensive metatheoretical systems and, for this reason, it has acted as an important resource for the development of an integrative metatheory for organisational transformation. In the course of performing this role, it has become clear that there are several discrepancies between the list of lenses identified through the multiparadigm review and those described in AQAL. There are also other differences including lens relationships, the flexibility of the metatheory and definitional issues.

Definitional Clarity

To this date, the complete set of conceptual elements that constitute the AQAL framework has still not been fully defined. In Chapter 4 I described several conceptual elements that are frequently used in AQAL analyses but are not formally included within its five definitive categories of quadrants, levels, lines, states and types. One of the most important tasks in theory building is the detailed description and definition of the central elements of the metatheory. AQAL metatheory has been found wanting in this regard. For example, one of the most commonly used lenses in AQAL, personal perspective, is not among the set of core elements and yet perspectives perform a central role in the metatheory's most current form. By not formally including such lenses as perspectives, the relationships between lenses also suffer from a lack of clarity. For example, the relationship between quadrants and perspectives is unclear. Improving descriptions of the defining elements of AQAL would help in clarifying these issues.

Discrepancies Between AQAL and the Multiparadigm Review Lenses

The number of conceptual lenses derived from the multiparadigm review is considerably larger than those found in AQAL. This is surprising given that the multiparadigm review performed here only surveyed theories from the field of organisational transformation whereas AQAL purports to cover much more territory. There could be several explanations for this discrepancy between lenses. The first is that AQAL is missing some important conceptual viewpoints and that a significant revision of AQAL is called for. A second reason could be that the additional lenses identified in this study might not actually provide further explanatory viewpoints and, consequently, could be subsumed within existing AQAL components. A third reason could be that AQAL has not yet been adequately described and so it does not fully account for all of the explanatory lenses it currently uses. This comes back to the issue of definitional clarity previously raised.

Taking this third point first, we might ask: What are the basic lenses that are included within the current presentation of the AQAL framework? In Chapter 3 it was noted that AQAL can be summarised as "quadrants, levels, lines, states and types" and that these amounted to six fundamental explanatory lenses: (i) the interior–exterior, (ii) individual–collective, (iii) stage-based developmental holarchy, (iv) multimodal streams, (v) states of consciousness and (vi) types. All six were found among the conceptual lenses used by multiparadigm theorists in their explanations of transformative change. Apart from these explicitly identified elements there are also a number of other theoretical components which are used extensively in integral analyses but are not formally described by Wilber as part of the AQAL framework. These unofficial lenses are set out in Table 9.2.

It is unclear why these concepts are not explicitly included by Wilber in his formal statement of AQAL. It is certainly not because these additional elements play a minor role in AQAL analyses. It may be that these additional lenses can be regarded as corollaries that derive their explanatory power from the core components of quadrants, levels, lines, states and types. However, the multiparadigm review did not find this to be the case. To give but one instance, many change theorists conceptualise transformational issues through the use of the transitional process lens without any reference to discontinuous change or to stage-based development. Theorists from the developmental schools, on the other hand, often describe transformation without any reference to transitional phases. If two lenses can be used independently by separate research paradigms to explain the same event, then both should be recognised as stand-alone lenses that are each worthy of formal inclusion within a larger metatheoretical framework.

The reason for not formally including several important lenses in AQAL may be more straightforward. As explained earlier, the inclusion of each additional lens makes the framework considerably more complex. It may well be that Wilber has kept the number of elements in AQAL to a minimum for reasons of parsimony and simplicity. However, the importance of developing a parsimonious set of lenses should not be confused with the task of formally defining and including within a metatheory all of its major conceptual components. Theory building principles require a level of definitional clarity that AQAL has not addressed.

Table 9.2 lists both formal and informal AQAL lenses with those found in the multiparadigm review of theories of organisational transformation. There are nine lenses identified in the multiparadigm review that are not included in any way, formally or informally, in AQAL. These additional lenses are core explanatory concepts for many transformation theorists. It is interesting to note that several of these lenses come from the relational and standpoint categories and they include social mediation, stakeholders and decentring. It is notable that these groups of lenses are based on situational as opposed to dispositional explanations. They typically see events as thoroughly relational and interactive. These are fundamental ways of explaining social reality and yet they are not included in AQAL metatheory. Why has AQAL not included mediation in its explanatory toolkit? To address this question, I will look in more detail at the lens of social mediation.

One of AQAL's most important explanatory lenses is the developmental holarchy lens. This lens sees transformation as the unfolding of successive deep structures or features of consciousness. Wilber developed this lens from extensive comparisons of many stage-based theories of human

Table 9.2 Comparison of AQAL and Organisational Transformation Lenses

Lenses formally included in AQAL	*Lenses used but not formally included in AQAL*
• interior–exterior	• perspectives
• individual–collective	• agency–communion
• developmental levels	• transformation–translation
• developmental lines	• inclusive emergence
• states of consciousness	• exchange relations
• types	• health–pathology
	• transition process
	• internal–external
	• spirituality

Conceptual lenses neither formally nor informally included in AQAL	
• social mediation	• stakeholder
• learning	• decentring
• system dynamics	• evolutionary process
• alignment	• governance holarchy

development including those of Jane Loevinger, Jean Piaget, Lawrence Kohlberg and numerous theorists of postformal reasoning. It is notable, however, that in developing his view of human development, Wilber has completely neglected one of the most important schools of human development. This is the school of Lev Vygotsky, which has come to be known as Cultural Historical and Activity Theory (CHAT) (Cole & Wertsch, 1996). The focus within this tradition is not on development as an unfolding set of internal psychological structures. Rather, the CHAT research paradigm sees development as the mediation of structures from the social exterior to the individual interior. As Vygotsky expressed it, "The central fact about our psychology is the fact of mediation" (1982, p. 166). And yet the concept of mediation and the sociogenetic understanding of development as an outcome of social mediation are absent from Wilber's metatheorising. There is no reference to social mediation, Vygotsky or any theorist in the CHAT school in any of Wilber's copious writings. This omission has serious implications for how AQAL explains developmental processes that rely on situational and relational ways of understanding.

There are other lenses not included in AQAL, for example, the learning and decentring lenses, which are highly critical of stage-based approaches to human development. The notion of transformation as a discontinuous transformation of internal capacities currently dominates AQAL-informed explications of development. This needs to be augmented by incremental, situational and meditational notions that recognise the role of communicative processes, relationships and social power in understanding radical change. The analysis of social power is a topic that has not been at all prominent within AQAL analyses and once again, this may be due to the lack of these mediating, relational and decentring lenses that are such a definitive aspect of postmodern approaches to organisational life and social transformation.

Discrepancies in Lens Relationships

The relationships between lenses identified in the multiparadigm review have some notable differences from those described in AQAL. These involve relationships between: (i) the individual–collective lens and other lenses, (ii) personal perspectives and other lenses and (iii) holons/holarchies and other lenses.

AQAL's individual–collective lens is a reduced form of the ecological holarchy lens. A more complete description of this lens within organisational settings might involve the holarchical levels of individual, dyad, triad, group, department, organisation, community, society, nation and global community. A minimal representation of this holarchy should include at least three or four levels—individual (microlevel), group (mesolevel), organisation (macrolevel) and environment (macro-macrolevel). Problems arise in lens relationships when the ecological holarchy is reduced to the two levels of individual and collective. For example, in spite of Wilber's clarifications (Wilber & Zimmerman, 2005) it is unclear whether the four quadrants refer solely to an individual or to the encounter between an individual and its social environment. This confusion arises because the individual–collective lens is a scalar dimension that can apply to one, two, three or large collectives of social entities (holons). In using the reduced version of this multi-level holarchy, the individual–collective lens is mistakenly represented as a bipolar lens that can be applied to one holon when it should always refer to a holarchy. One implication of this confusion is that AQAL never shows holons in relationship. Consequently, interactive lenses such as mediation and decentring play small roles in AQAL analyses of social phenomena.

A compounding issue here is the conflation in AQAL between the perspective lens and the quadrant lenses. Certain perspectives are associated with certain quadrants despite there being no metatheoretical evidence or logical necessity that this is the case. These lenses provide independent and unique tools for investigating the interior, exterior and relational perspectives of ecological levels. Table 9.3 presents a non-reductive application of these lenses to organisational levels.

In missing the intermediate mesolevels of organisational ecology, AQAL is susceptible to reducing the genesis of transformation to either the microlevel

Table 9.3 A Metatheoretical Framework Combing Perspectival, Interior–Exterior and Ecological Holarchy Lenses

Ecological levels	1st person perspective ("I/We")	2nd person perspective ("You")	3rd person perspective ("He/She/It/They")
Microlevel (individual)	interiors / exteriors Discloses personal data about "I/Me"	interiors / exteriors Discloses interpersonal data about "You"	interiors / exteriors Discloses impersonal data about "He/She/It"
Mesolevel (group)	interiors / exteriors Discloses intra-group data about "Us/We"	interiors / exteriors Discloses inter-group data about "You"	interiors / exteriors Discloses group data about "Them"
Macrolevel (organisation)	interiors / exteriors Discloses intra-organisational data about "Us/We"	interiors / exteriors Discloses inter-organisational data about "You"	interiors / exteriors Discloses organisational data about "Them"
Macro-macrolevel (environment)	interiors / exteriors Discloses macro-environmental data about "Us/We"	interiors / exteriors Discloses macro-environmental data about "You"	interiors / exteriors Discloses macro-environmental data about "Them"

of the individual or the macrolevel of the collective. For example, under the section title, "The Nature of Revolutionary Social Transformation", Wilber (2003a) discusses the emergence of social revolution with reference to the rise of new technology. He states that "what generally happens is that a technological innovation begins in the mind of some creative individual . . . —James Watt and the steam engine, for example". Transformation is seen as having its genesis in the subjective insights of an individual genius. This reduction of "social transformation" to the innovative thoughts of one individual is representative of methodological individualist explanations for change (Fernando, 2001). In contrast to Wilber's view, other explanations of the development of the steam engine emphasise the collective interactions that occurred over many decades that culminated in its emergence. In an article on this topic, Mimi points out that (2006, p. 10):

> History books tend to connect just one person's name with the invention of a remarkable new machine or the discovery of a new technology. But, the reality behind new ideas usually presents a different, and more complicated, picture.

To this point, Wilber has chosen to emphasise the microlevel of the individual as the source of transformative energy and it may be that the inherent developmentalism of AQAL has contributed to this bias. Inclusion of the mesolevel provides a completely new way of seeing the rise of innovation and, more generally, the evolution of emergent capacities.

The final area of discrepancy among lens relationships relates to the holarchy category of lenses. AQAL includes only one form of holarchy— the developmental holarchy. In contrast to this, the multiparadigm review and the subsequent analysis of explanatory themes found that theories of organisational transformation employ at least three forms of holarchy. These holarchies are built on the criteria of developmental emergence, ecological inclusion and governance (or organising capacity). Each of these is a valid means for describing the nature of holons and holarchic relationships. While Wilber recognises that there are different types of holarchies (Wilber & Zimmerman, 2005), AQAL employs only the developmental variety in any comprehensive fashion. One possible reason for this is that AQAL has largely used the holon construct at the intra-holonic order, that is, for "what happens inside individual holons, according to internal structure" (Mathews, 1996, p. 41) and has neglected the inter-holonic and systemic orders of analysis where the ecological and governance holarchies are more likely to be applied.

The omission of a governance holarchy is a particular drawback in AQAL analyses of organisations. Without some dedicated lens for considering the holarchic nature of governance, organising and decision-making structures tend to be seen as either top-down or bottom-up arrangements. That there is little analysis of power relations in AQAL analyses of social events is a serious limitation and the omission of a governance holarchy is one contributing factor to that shortcoming.

CONCLUSION

I have argued elsewhere (Edwards, 2008a, 2008b) that the evaluation of integrative metatheory is an important but largely ignored activity in the social sciences. There are considerable dangers in overlooking the need for the critical assessment of metatheories. As Anthony Giddens has pointed out, metatheories can be extremely powerful cultural artifacts and they can shape society as much as, or even more than, any technological revolution. In this chapter I have provided two modest means for evaluating overarching metatheory. One has relied on the application of criteria taken from the metatheoretical literature as well as criteria borrowed from middle-range theory building. The other has been to evaluate one of the metatheoretical resources for this study (AQAL) by comparing the basic data sources for constructing metatheory, that is, the core elements of middle-range theory. Much work needs to be done to provide a more rigorous and formal basis for these kinds of evaluations.

10 Towards an Integral Meta-Studies

[W]e are small creatures in a big world of which we have only very partial understanding, and that how things seem to us depends both on the world and our constitution. We can add to our knowledge of the world by accumulating information at a given level—by extensive observation from one standpoint. But we can raise our understanding to a new level only if we examine that relation between the world and ourselves which is responsible for our prior understanding, and form a conception that includes a more detached understanding of ourselves, of the world, and of the interaction between them. Thus objectivity allows us to transcend our particular viewpoint and develop an expanded consciousness that takes in the world more fully. (Nagel, 1986, p. 5)

ON METATHEORETICAL ORIGINS

In the preface to a later edition of his *The Origin of Species* Charles Darwin (1872) lists 34 authors who published views on the gradual modification of biological species before the appearance of the first edition of his own famous work in 1859. Two of these authors, W. C. Wells and Patrick Matthew, described the process of natural selection in some detail several decades before Darwin and Wallace published their own celebrated theories. Darwin was not aware of many of these writings before publishing his own views but he was very much aware of the diversity of ideas on evolution that existed in such fields as animal husbandry, natural history and the geological sciences of his day. Although he does not indicate his reasons, I believe that Darwin provides this list to give some impression of the complexity involved in the emergence of new ideas. Darwin was a humble man and he wished to acknowledge that his ideas had many predecessors. Great breakthroughs in science are as much about familiarity with the climate of multiple contending ideas as they are about the sudden production of the individual work of genius. In this sense, all good theory is metatheoretical in origin. All theory of some value emerges through the contestation and combination of precursory ideas. The metatheorising I have described here is merely the formalisation of this implicit aspect of research. In drawing attention to the importance of metatheory, I hope that this fundamental aspect of doing science will be seen for what it is, be more openly acknowledged and be performed with greater methodological rigour.

Integrative metatheorising is an ambitious project. It is based on the premise that the appreciation of diverse theoretical perspectives offers a new way forward in the development of science. It seeks to find insights through the connection of knowledge rather than the specialisation of knowledge. The Big Pictures that emerge from this process stand in contrast to the goals of mainstream social science which are almost exclusively concerned with the building and testing of middle-range theory. Given the disastrous outcomes of some of the totalising theories of the nineteenth century, the subsequent focus on ideas of the middle-range is understandable. But middle-range theory will not resolve global problems. Global problems of the scale that we currently face require a response that can navigate through theoretical pluralism and not be swallowed up by it. In saying that, twenty-first-century metatheories will need to be different from the monistic, grand theories of the past. They will have to be integrative rather than totalising, pluralistic rather than monistic, based on science and not only on philosophy, methodical rather than idiosyncratic, find inspiration in theories from the edge more than from the centre and provide means for inventing new ways of *understanding* as much as new technologies.

In the preceding chapters I have proposed a method for how an integrative metatheory can be developed and described some examples of what a pluralistic Big Picture might look like. In this final chapter I want to broaden the discussions from an overarching model of *theories* of transformation to also consider the Big Picture on questions about *method, interpretation* and *data-analysis*. The development of meta*theory* should not be isolated from the other essential phases of doing science. Integrative Big Pictures will need to be grounded in a system of knowledge acquisition that also has a place for complementary studies in method, data-analysis and hermeneutics. In fact, there are prototypes of each of these metalevel branches of scientific study already in existence. The time is now ripe for a more general description of their place in the development of metalevel scientific studies.

TOWARDS AN INTEGRATIVE META-STUDIES

Formal science is more often associated with the empirical testing of ideas than with their initial construction or inspiration. Testing a theory involves a complex mixture of research design, method, data collection, analysis and interpretation. Theory, method, data and interpretation are the four walls within which we accommodate the details of scientific evidence. In the same vein, to develop overarching forms of scientific investigation, we need to critically review theory to build metatheory, review methods to develop meta-methods, review data to perform meta-data-analysis and review interpretive systems to create meta-hermeneutic models. While meta-data-analysis has been developing quickly within the medical and health sciences since the 1970s, each of the other metalevel branches of study is in the very early stages of development and attempts to bring them together to describe a system of meta-studies are only just beginning to emerge.

Drawing on some formative descriptions of disciplinary-based meta-studies, in the following pages I sketch out the possibility of an integrative meta-studies that could have application across many forms of social science. From the discipline of sociology, Shanyang Zhao describes a general structure of meta-studies as a second-order form of research that "transcends or goes beyond" other forms of study (1991, p. 378). Zhao's general meta-studies includes "metatheory", "meta-methodology" and "meta-data-analysis". From the field of qualitative health research, Barbara Paterson and her colleagues describe a meta-studies that entails the analysis and "scrutiny of the theory, method, and data of research in a substantive area" (Paterson et al., 2001, pp. 5–6). Discussions of meta-hermeneutics (Colby, 1987; Habermas, 1983), meta-methodology (Chandler & Torbert, 2003; Karlsson & Wistrand, 2006) and the burgeoning field of meta-(data)-analysis (Glass, 1976) can also be included in the mix. From these and other metalevel analyses of the major families of social science research (Denzin & Lincoln, 2005; Esbjörn-Hargens, 2005a, 2005b; Mingers & Brocklesby, 1997), I believe it is possible to map out a structure for an integrative meta-studies in which metatheory, meta-method, meta-data-analysis and meta-hermeneutics all play their part (Edwards, 2008a, 2008b, 2008c). We have then the possibility of recognising and developing not only integrative metatheories but also integrative forms of meta-methodology, meta-data-analysis and meta-hermeneutics. Together, these metalevel investigations constitute an integrative meta-studies—the science of integrating knowledge from the mutualising worlds of theory, method, data and interpretation (see Figure 10.1).

There are already innovative examples for several of these branches of integrative meta-studies. Throughout this book I have referred to Wilber's AQAL and Torbert's DAI as seminal examples of integrative metatheories. But these scholars have also produced perhaps the two most detailed examples of integrative meta-methodologies. Wilber's IMP provides a framework for describing eight irreducible categories of research methodologies (see Esbjörn-Hargens, 2005b). Wilber (2006) proposes that all research methods can be located within these eight categories. Torbert proposes a meta-methodology derived from three lenses—time, perspectival practice and perspectival voice. As with his metatheory, Torbert's central goal in proposing his meta-methodology is not to categorise methods in an overarching framework but to inform and broaden a researcher's immediate world of transformational inquiry. The focus is on mapping many methods into an action-oriented process of discovery. Where Wilber seeks to formalise a metalevel Big Picture that can situate other methods, Torbert wants to expand the practice of research inquiry itself. In many ways the two approaches complement each other.

There have also been integrative innovations in the meta-data-analysis area. Meta-synthesis is an integrative approach to meta-data-analysis that has been recently developed to collate findings from qualitative research studies in health (Sandelowski, 2006; Thorne et al., 2004).[1] All this suggests that metalevel studies are being pursued within isolated sub-fields and that there is an opportunity now to bring these metalevel inquiry systems into a more coherent overview. It is important to distinguish between forms of meta-studies that are distinctly *integral* and those that are more localised in character. Research in any of these meta-studies activities becomes integrative when it: (i) is consciously and explicitly performed within an appreciative context that can move across and within various disciplines; (ii) adopts systematic research methods and principles; (iii) uses, as conceptual resources, other integrative frameworks such as Wilber's AQAL, Bhaskars's meta-reality (2002b), Torbert's DAI (1999), Schumacher's system of knowledge (1977), Nicolescu's transdisciplinary studies or Galtung and Inayatullah's (1997) macrohistory; (iv) is characterised by its inclusiveness and emancipatory aims.

Figure 10.1 maps out the basic structure for an integrative meta-studies. Metalevel researchers can, of course, move across all of these branches of studies, but usually both individual researchers and their paradigm-based communities of inquiry tend to specialise in one or two domains. Metatheorists are very rarely meta-methodologists (Paul Meehl being a prominent exception to this). Practitioners of meta-hermeneutics (including many postmodern interpretivists) are wary of entering the territory of metatheory (even though their metalevel discussions assume the existence of such territories). As we have seen, there are also strong barriers between the metalevel and the middle-range level of research, for example, between middle-range theorists and metatheorists.

An interesting feature of this map of scientific territories is that researchers from one domain often have limited understanding of the contributions from other domains. So when researchers make forays into foreign domains, problems can arise in, for example, their claims about the veracity or usefulness of those other branches of knowledge. We see this when

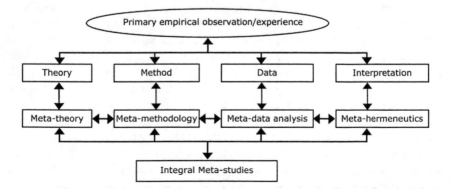

Figure 10.1   The structure of integral meta-studies.

theorists denounce metatheorists for being too abstract, or when meta-interpretivists (postmodernists) assure us that metatheory is impossible or always hegemonic, or when metatheorists make factual claims about the world of empirical data.

Metatheorising can also encroach on the territory of other branches. For example, metatheory building is based on the analysis of extant theory and does not deal directly with empirical data. Consequently, it cannot validly make conclusions about empirical data based on its metatheorising (that is the task of meta-data-analysis). If it does so, it is stepping outside its realm of expertise. To put this another way, metatheory is primarily about other theory and not about the prediction or evaluation of first-order empirical data. As Ritzer (2006) has pointed out, it is entirely possible and, in fact, desirable that middle-range theory be developed from metatheory (this is Ritzer's M_p). But in doing that, the new middle-range theory will require empirical testing. Metatheory can be used to develop metaconjectures about empirical events but these will then need to be evaluated through middle-range theory testing or meta-data-analysis.

These types of meta-domain encroachment can also be seen in the other strands depicted in figure 10.1. Meta-hermeneutics, which is one of the most important fields of research for postmodern scholars, often strays into the realm of metatheorising and makes claims, based on its own analysis of interpretive frameworks, about the value, or even possibility, of developing metatheory. This particular form of meta-domain encroachment has plagued meta-studies in general, and metatheorising in particular, for several decades now. The main point of figure 10.1 is to show that there is a place for various kinds of metalevel studies just as much as there is for scientific studies of the middle range. These metalevel domains need to be recognised by the mainstream and by their fellow metalevel colleagues as contributing valid and useful forms of scientific activity.

The meta-studies framework also highlights the gaps that are present in specifically integrative metalevel research. Integrative meta-studies has started to develop metatheoretical and meta-methodological branches but has not yet ventured into the domains of integrative meta-data-analysis or meta-interpretive analysis. Integrative meta-data-analysis could bring a synthesising perspective to the large-scale evaluation of empirical literature, including both qualitative and quantitative studies. The sophisticated techniques of meta-analysis and meta-synthesis have been instrumental in the opening up of new fields such as evidenced-based medicine and nursing. An integral meta-data-analysis has the potential to develop evidence-based approaches in interdisciplinary and transdisciplinary approaches to social policy, developmental studies and health sciences.

The study of systems of interpretation has been an important area of work for many postmodernist writers. Integrative meta-hermeneutics has the potential to offer an integrative and constructive focus rather than a decentring and deconstructive intent. Integral meta-hermeneutics can show how the interpretive turn can also uncover integral pluralisms as well as relative pluralisms.

There is one preliminary and rather speculative observation that I would like to make about the content of the different domains of theory, method, data and interpretation. One of the most noticeable commonalities between the metatheories and meta-methods of both AQAL and DAI is that the same or very similar lenses used in their metatheoretical frameworks are also present in their meta-methodological frameworks. I gain the same impression when reviewing other metalevel literatures, particularly in the methodological domain (Denzin & Lincoln, 2005). It could be that the metatheoretical lenses identified in metatheory building research are being used at the metalevel study of methods, data-analysis techniques and interpretive frameworks. If this is the case, the same metatheoretical lenses might be informing all branches of the scientific enterprise and they may be fundamental dimensions for shaping all forms of knowledge acquisition.

INTEGRAL META-STUDIES AND
ORGANISATIONAL TRANSFORMATION

There are many implications of this integral meta-studies framework for the study of organisational transformation. I have elaborated here on the metatheoretical implications but there are also meta-methodological, meta-analytical and meta-hermeneutical implications. With regard to method, there is good reason to support the development of an integrative form of mixed-methodology. Sean Esbjörn-Hargens (2005b) has made a notable contribution to the emergence of this field and this has important implications for the study of transformational phenomena.

When we use objective methods to study organisations we can miss the relational and subjective realities that underpin observable behaviours and measurable outcomes. Confusion or poor communication about the purpose of change can then get translated as "resistance". More subjective methods reframe employee resistance against transformational process as a question of poor planning, coercive management or top-down management. The methodological divide is reflected in the division between functionalist and interpretivist research paradigms. An integrative meta-methodology has room for objective, relational and subjective methods of data collection and thereby overcomes the limitations of single methods. Understanding the reactions of organisational members to the need for transformation has much to gain from a mixed method approach. The method of Open Space Technology proposed by Harrison Owen (2000) is one transformational method that opens up a more relational and participative space for developing transformational aspirations. An integrative meta-methodology has much to offer in the study of such methods.

Meta-data-analysis is a branch of meta-studies that has had little application to the study of organisational change although there are important studies emerging in this area (Pettigrew, Woodman & Cameron, 2001). An integrative form of meta-data-analysis could accumulate findings from both qualitative and quantitative sources to examine a host of important transformational issues. For example, one paricularly useful question to ask is how successful transformational change programmes have been in terms of objective change and subjective experience. I have commented several times on the alignment problems that are created when transformational programmes target one aspect of the organisation, for example, technological systems, while leaving other aspects unaddressed, for example, organisational culture. An integrative analysis of data from empirical studies of these misalignments could contribute significantly to our understanding of the differential impacts of organisational transformation.

Integral approaches to the study of interpretive systems have much to offer transformation research. It is frequently commented that different theoretical schools tend to use different methods and interpretive frameworks. Researchers employing functionalist theories tend to use quantitative methods and objectivist epistemologies, while theorists from interpretive traditions adopt qualitative methods and subjective or relational epistemologies. An integrative meta-hermeneutics could move across all of these boundaries and constructively appreciate the diversity of meaning-making systems. Organisational transformation research is not only marked by theoretical diversity but also by a diversity in interpretive frameworks and the development of ways of connecting those systems would, at the very least, benefit the communication of findings between the various research paradigms.

GLOBAL CRISIS OR BUSINESS OPPORTUNITY

Significant change towards sustaining forms of organisation will not happen without the input of new theories and metatheories of transformation. However, in the current climate of economic insecurity, the interest in transformation is being reprioritised to take a back seat to issues of stability. This is a serious mistake. When turbulent change dominates the environment, the reactive instinct to maintain stability has to be balanced by a more insightful awareness. In a world that urgently needs to reduce its dependency on carbon-based fuels, we see governments desperately trying to stimulate the same old patterns of production and consumption that are driving global warming. The growing economic fallout from the world financial crisis is reinforcing the fundamental paradox of global marketism[2]—that we base our aspirations and dreams for the future on economic expansion when, in fact, the resources and environments that sustain that expansion are bounded. Technological innovation is held by many to be the solution to this paradox, but global warming, peak oil, the world food shortage, the global water crisis and the

Jevons effect are only a few of the problems that will not be fully resolved through a reliance on our technological inventiveness. The global challenges we face in the twenty-first century will require new ways of seeing as well as new ways of doing. If that challenge is not met by transformational change in organisations of all kinds then it will not be met at all.

The turbulence in financial and commercial environments over the past year will be seen by many organisations and business consultants as a chance for taking a deep breath, a time for gathering energies to acquire even greater rewards on the other side of this temporary downturn in economic conditions. From this view, the various crises emerging on the global stage are regarded as occasions for taking stock so that businesses can return to the fray with renewed energy. It is often mentioned that the Chinese word for "crisis" is a combination of the characters for danger and opportunity. But is opportunity really the first thing to look for in times of deep crisis? Might not the real danger be that after a short hiatus we will once again promote and reproduce organisations and commercial systems with the same values and goals as those that are degrading our capacity for planetary and intergenerational sustainability. Victor Mair, professor of Chinese language and literature at the University of Pennsylvania has a different interpretation of the Chinese word for crisis:

> Those who purvey the doctrine that the Chinese word for "crisis" as composed of elements meaning "danger" and "opportunity" are engaging in a type of muddled thinking that is a danger to society, for it lulls people into welcoming crises as unstable situations from which they can benefit. Adopting a feel-good attitude toward adversity may not be the most rational, realistic approach to its solution. (Mair, 2008)

Mair tells us that crisis in Chinese actually means "a dangerous moment, a time when things start to go awry". Large business and government enterprises might be tempted to look at the current turmoil as just another opportunity for developing strategies for accumulating economic wealth or political power. In which case, crisis is reframed as an opportunity to do more of the same. In metatheoretical terms organisations will emerge from the global downturn with renewed vigour for translational growth when what is required is transformational change on a global scale. Einstein's oft quoted observation that problems can never be solved at the level of thinking that created them is highly relevant here. The global economic crisis will not be solved in the long-term by rescuing financial systems that will once again provide credit or high-risk financial products for investing in unsustainable business activities. A more scientific way of developing new perspectives on truly sustainable forms of growth is called for and the vantage point of meta-level studies is one way of achieving that. Metatheorising offers the capacity to evaluate not only middle-range theory but the distortions in theory which create ideology and the imbalanced forms of organisational activity which pursue narrow and damaging conceptualisations of growth. I have briefly touched on the possibilities of the scientific study of lens facets and the types of reductionisms and conflations that result from the application of distorted conceptual lenses. The reason that these analyses are important is that conceptual lenses are not only filters for interpreting social realities, they are tools that create and shape those realities. Economic and organisational theories are not impassive bystanders to the real events of organisational life. As Kenneth Gergen and Barbara Zielke argue, theories constitute ways of life; theory is "a form of discursive action, and is thus itself a practice" (2006, p. 306). When theories are based on conceptual perspectives that do not take account of fundamental orientations to an issue they reproduce and imbed imbalanced and unhealthy forms of organisation. Global sustainability, and the organisational transformation that is required to pursue it, will not be achieved by regaining confidence in fundamentally inadequate systems and the reductive concepts they are based on. The ideas presented here offer some scientific ways of critiquing the partialities of the metatheories that currently drive many forms of global activity. As well as the critique of current ideologies, we urgently need scientific approaches to developing Big Pictures that are more balanced, more integrative and more conscious of the distortions that all systems of thought are subject to.

THE POWER OF BIG PICTURES

A number of important issues related to metatheorising have been explored here: the need for an integrative metatheory for organisational transformation; the development of a general research method for metatheory building in organisational studies; the application of metatheoretical frameworks to organisational sustainability; how metatheoretical research can be performed to develop new ways of thinking about old problems; and the notion of situating metalevel scientific activities within the context of an integrative meta-studies.

In developing an integral metatheory for transformative change I hope to have shown how metatheory can meet the challenge posed by theoretical pluralism. Metatheory building is a constructive process that fosters conceptual connection and interplay. Andrew Van de Ven and Marshal Poole, in a seminal article on change theories entitled, "Explaining Development and Change in Organizations", make the point that (1995, pp. 515–516):

> It is the interplay between different perspectives that helps one gain a more comprehensive understanding of organizational life, because any one theoretical perspective invariably offers only a partial account of a complex phenomenon. Moreover, the juxtaposition of different theoretical perspectives brings into focus contrasting worldviews of social change and development. Working out the relationship between such seemingly divergent views provides opportunities to develop new theory that has stronger and broader explanatory power than the initial perspectives.

It is this creation of knowledge with "stronger and broader explanatory power" through "the interplay between different perspectives" that has been the central theme of this book. Organisational studies is representative of many social sciences in that it has lacked an integrative response to theoretical pluralism. In the course of developing the metatheory I have identified the major paradigms and theories of organisational transformation and, in particular, their core explanatory lenses. Burrell and Morgan (1979) showed, through their work on adapting sociological paradigms to the analysis of organisations, that new understandings and explanations can be generated when metatheoretical frameworks are used to situate and compare the core conceptual lenses from otherwise disparate theories and models. This contextualising function of metatheory building is not simply a categorising exercise but also provides knowledge about the relationships between theories. Metatheory is inherently evaluative of theory. When developed from a representative sampling of theories from many different research paradigms, it can identify dominant as well as neglected and emergent perspectives that are often hidden and marginalised.

I hope that the ideas presented here will contribute to a revisioning of the way theorists, researchers and teachers have understood organisational transformation. More than 20 years ago, in the first review of theories of transformation in organisational settings, Levy and Merry said,

> Progress in the domain of second-order change is constrained by a lack of adequate conceptual frameworks. Analytical reasoning that probes the dimensions and processes of such a crucial phenomenon has utility, for it begins to inform and guide practice, and to stimulate inquiry and, hence, enhance theory building (1986, p. 269).

This point is still valid. The number and diversity of theories being proposed, tested and applied has resulted in a highly diverse and even fragmented knowledge base for the study of organisational transformation. The development of a metatheoretical perspective can, at the least, engender a deeper appreciation for, and understanding of, this diversity. As Benjamin Lichtenstein comments:

> By uncovering assumptions that have been mostly unexplored in dynamic models of organisational change, a connection between various approaches to organisational development and change will become apparent. Moreover, I argue that identifying this correlation will lead to a paradigm of self-organising that may be useful for understanding transformative change. . . . A primary contribution of this new paradigm would be to integrate numerous empirical studies into a single framework, which can then be used by researchers and practitioners to more clearly understand the dynamics of transformation, and launch transformative change in organisations. (2000, p. 527)

While Lichtenstein is referring here to the integration of empirical studies, the same holds true for the integration of concepts and theories within an accommodating metatheory. I would also point out that my aim has not been for the development of "a single framework" for transformation. For metatheorising to become a real domain of scientific research it needs lots of contending metatheories. Ultimately the goal of metatheorising in a field such as organisational transformation is to develop visions, tools and interventions that promote the likelihood of lasting organisational change, both theoretically and practically, at a time when such changes are desperately needed. And this can only be done by active scientific communities engaged in appreciative and critical inquiry.

Metatheorising is a form of research that has been neglected and not well understood. My hope is that this book will raise awareness of the potential benefits of metatheoretical research in organisational studies. The integrative approach pursued here has sought to link and situate multiple paradigms of organisational change. The intent has been to find perspectives for connecting theories while at the same time honouring their distinctive contributions. Both Big Pictures and Little Pictures are needed in the accumulation and utilisation of knowledge. Integrative knowledge complements and generates specialised science just as the proliferation of theories calls for the development of systemic knowledge. Overarching approaches serve to bring greater conceptual coherence to social disciplines that are often characterised by a plethora of seemingly incommensurate theories. As Lewis and Kelemen succinctly put it (2002, p. 263):

> Multiparadigm research seeks to cultivate diverse representations, detailing the images highlighted by varied lenses. Applying the conventions prescribed by alternative paradigms, researchers develop contrasting or multi-sided accounts that may depict the ambiguity and complexity of organizational life.

I have proposed here "varied lenses" and developed "multi-sided accounts" with the aim of furthering our Big-Picture views of what transformational change is, what it might be and how it might contribute to a more sustaining world. The ambiguity, complexity and ultimate mystery of transformation will always be there and will continue to provide opportunities for deepening our understanding of organisational life. Whether we take up those opportunities or hold fast to our current modes of thinking and doing is the challenge that lies before us. The promise of integral metatheorising is that it offers a scientific response to meeting this challenge.

Appendices

Appendix A   A Phase-Based Comparison of Learning and Educational Theories

Learning Theories	Learning Cycle phases			
	Doing and Handling	Thinking and Experiencing	Interpreting and Understanding	Validating and Expressing
AQAL Quadrants	behavioural (upper right)	intentional (upper left)	cultural (lower left)	social (lower right)
DAI Territories of Experience	action (2nd territory)	intentionality (2nd territory)	planning (2nd territory)	outcomes (2nd territory)
Education (Dewey, 1938/1997)	experiential continuity		situational interaction	
Learning models (Juch, 1983)	doing	sensing	thinking	addressing
Experiential learning cycle (Kolb, 1984)	concrete experience	reflective observation	abstract conceptualisation	active experimentation
Validity claims (Habermas, 1984)	truth	truthfulness (sincerity)	comprehensibility	rightness (legitimacy)
Forms of knowledge (Bhaskar, 1986)	performative	experiential	epistemological	propositional
Learning as technology (McCarthy, 1987)	doing something with it	taking it in	ordering and naming it	expressing it
Organisational learning (Miller, 1996)	experimental	analytic-structural	synthetic	interactive-institutional
Knowledge Strands (Wilber, 1998)	injunction	apprehension		validation
Organisational learning cycle (Dixon, 1999)	information generation	experiential integration	collective interpretation	social action
2-phase learning (Greenaway, 2002)	do/experience		review/reflect	
Organisational knowing (Choo, 2002)	action selection	knowledge creation	sense-making	
Organisational learning schools (Bell, Whitwell & Lukas, 2002)	economic school	developmental school	process school	management school
Organisational learning (Akgun, Lynn & Byrne, 2003)	acquisition	thinking emotion	sense-making collective memory	dissemination implementation
Organisational transformation (Spitaletta, 2003)	action	observe	orient	decision
Systems learning (Mingers, 2006)	action	appreciation	analysis	assessment
Organisational learning cycles (Tsai & Lee, 2006)	care why	know why	know what	know how
Organisational learning cycles (Rosendaal, 2006)	scanning and problem solving	abstraction	diffusion and absorption	impacting

Appendix B Process Models of Organisational Transformation

Transition Phase Description	Archetype Tracks (Greenwood & Hinings, 1988)	Revolutionary change (Simsek & Louis, 1994)	Resistance (Mariotti, 1996)	Worker performance (Bupp, 1996)	Transitional change (Grant, 1996)	Spiral Dynamics (Beck & Cowan, 1996)	Managing Diversity (Cox & Beale, 1997)	Diversity and Transformation (Dreachslin, 1999)	Rhizomic Model (Chia, 1999)	Steps in Transformation (Kotter, 2006)
12. Creativity at new level				Creativity	Creativity			Revitalisation of individuals & systems	Immanence	
11. New baseline level	Archetype coherence	New normalcy period	Re-emergence	Accomplishment	Accomplishment	The new Alpha: new stage of life conditions achieved, return to a steady state of functioning				Institutionalise new approaches
10. Integration of capacities								Transformation of whole system		Consolidating
9. Transform to new paradigm		Revolution					Action to address issues and implement solutions		Logic of "otherness"	
8. Leaving the old paradigm										Short-term wins
7. New opportunities	Embryonic archetype coherence		Readiness	Opportunity	Opportunity	Delta Surge: time of energy and release, old barriers are overcome	Understanding of opportunities and costs		Loosening of structures	Empowering others Communicating the vision
6. Emergence of possible solutions			Openness	Exploration Acceptance	Acceptance and letting go			Exploration of alternatives Assessment of challenges	Heterogeneous transformation	Creating a vision Form a guiding coalition
5. State of shock	Schizoid incoherence		Resignation Depression	Grief Chaos	Depression and incompetence	The Gamma Trap: feelings of hopelessness, anger, and barriers to progress	Awareness of problems and deficiencies		Inherent flux	Establishing a sense of urgency
4. Crisis climax			Bargaining Anger	Anger						
3. Building crisis	Embryonic archetype incoherence	Confrontation of anomalies	Denial	Shock/denial	Denial and minimisation Shock and immobilisation	Beta Condition: uncertain times				
2. Ambiguities & anomalies	Archetype coherence							Discovery of anomalies		
1. Baseline (paradigm)		Normalcy	Equilibrium			Alpha fit: stability and status quo				

Appendix C   A Comparison of Stage-Based Models of Organisational Transformation

Stage	Byrd (1982)	Nelson & Burns (1984)	Beck & Cowan (1996)	Bleich (1996)	Barrett (1996)	Fisher, Rooke & Torbert, (2003)	Lester (2003)	Cacioppe & Edwards (2005b)
8			Holistic, spontaneous		Spiritual	Liberating disciplines (ironist) — Post-postconventional		Integral
7b			Systemic, developmental, world-centric	Boundaryless	Society	Foundational community of inquiry (magician) — Postconventional		Visioning
7a					Community		(Decline)	Contributing
6			Egalitarian, sociocentric	Stakeholder value	Meaningful	Collaborative inquiry (strategist)		
5b	Renewing	High performance	Individualist, meritocracy	Professional	Transformative / Mental	Social network (individualist) — Conventional	Renewal	Achieving
5a		Proactive				System productivity (achiever)		
4c	Consolidating	Responsive	Authoritarian, absolutist	Technocrat		Experiments (expert)	Success	Organising
4b	Controlling							
4a	Planning							
3b	Organising		Egocentric, exploitative	Shareholder value	Self-esteem	Incorporation (diplomat)		Asserting
3a				Ownership				
2	Staffing	Reactive	Tribalistic, peer group focus, compulsive		Relationship / Emotional	Investment (opportunist) — Pre-conventional	Survival	Bonding
1b			Instinctive, survival-sense		Survival / Physical	Conception (impulsive)		Surviving
1a							existence (birth)	

Notes

NOTE TO CHAPTER 1

1. Meaning both theory and metatheory.

NOTE TO CHAPTER 2

1. The definition of "micro", "meso" or "macro" levels is an arbitrary process that depends on the researcher's frame of reference in comparing different levels. The general convention is, however, that the sphere of individual interaction is referred to as the microlevel, group activity is the mesolevel and the organisation as a whole (and anything larger) is referred to as the macrolevel.

NOTES TO CHAPTER 3

1. The same might also be said of the fervour with which rational economics has been adopted since the 1980s (the results of which are feeding into many of the global problems we face today).
2. Ritzer differentiates between what he sees as scientific forms of developing overarching metatheory (M_O) and unscientific forms of speculative big pictures (O_M). He admits that the charge of totalising might have some relevance to the imaginative speculation that characterises O_M but is not relevant to the conceptual analyses performed in M_O studies.

NOTES TO CHAPTER 4

1. While AQAL and DAI are metatheories, they also have their meta-methodological systems. For AQAL it is Integral Methodological Pluralism (IMP) (Wilber, 2006) and for DAI it is "Transforming Inquiry" also called the "27 flavours of action research" (Chandler & Torbert, 2003).
2. Why this might be so will be discussed in Chapter 9.

NOTES TO CHAPTER 5

1. Sometimes metatheorists also perform empirical research data as part of M_P, but this is not M_O, or metatheory building. The issue of concern here is the methodical process by which metatheory building is done.

2. See Table 6.1 in the following chapter for the complete list of paradigms of transformative change and some representative theories and research articles.

NOTE TO CHAPTER 6

1. Causal focus refers here to the "why" researcher's interest in identifying the permitting, enabling, precipitating and triggering conditions that are associated with transformation.

NOTE TO CHAPTER 7

1. This is precisely how Burrell and Morgan identified the dominance of functionalist approaches in organisation theory.

NOTES TO CHAPTER 8

1. Organisation boundaries are becoming ever more flexible and "virtual". However tenuous the nature of these boundaries, there remain definitive lines of demarcation between organisations and environments which designate internal and external aspects of organisations (see Santos & Eisenhardt, 2005).
2. The term "conservative" here refers to organisational structures and cultural values that maintain the current paradigm of thinking and acting rather than any specifically political position.
3. Wilber's AQAL framework currently suffers from this lack of analytical specificity and this issue will be taken up in the following chapter where a critique of AQAL will be presented.
4. Intra-holonic order does *not* mean within an individual. The prefix intra- can refer to any holon, be it an individual, a team, an organisation or a community.
5. While this example has applied these cyclical lenses at the intra-holonic level they might just as easily be applied at the inter-holonic level.

NOTES TO CHAPTER 9

1. Torbert's DAI will not be evaluated here, although some of the findings on AQAL are also generally relevant to other metatheories including DAI.
2. There has, of course, been extensive use of quantitative methods in research involving meta-analysis.
3. AQAL has particular problems in this regard and I will explore this idea in more depth in a later section.

NOTES TO CHAPTER 10

1. Of course, meta-analysis is now an established research technique in mainstream health studies but the objective there is integrative monism rather than integrative pluralism (see Chapter 3). In other words, (monistic)

meta-analysis seeks one right answer rather than the valid contributions of many perspectives, which is the goal of an integrative meta-data-analysis.
2. It seems rather anachronistic to refer to market capitalism here when the command economy of China is so closely intertwined with traditional capitalist economies.

References

Abbott, AD (2001) *Chaos of Disciplines*. University of Chicago Press, Chicago.

Adams, JD (ed.) (1984) *Transforming Work: A Collection of Organizational Transformation Readings*. Miles River Press, Alexandria, VA.

Adriaanse, A (2005) 'Interorganizational communication and ICT in construction projects: A review using metatriangulation', *Construction Innovation*, vol. 5, no. 3, pp. 1471–4175.

Agyeman, J (2005) 'Where justice meets sustainability', *Environment*, vol. 47, no. 6, pp. 10–23.

Agyeman, J & Evans, B (2004) '"Just sustainability": The emerging discourse of environmental justice in Britain?' *Geographical Journal*, vol. 170, pp. 155–164.

Akbar, H (2003) 'Knowledge levels and their transformation: Towards the integration of knowledge creation and individual learning', *Journal of Management Studies*, vol. 40, no. 8, pp. 1997–2022.

Akgun, AE, Lynn, GS & Byrne, JC (2003) 'Organizational learning: A socio-cognitive framework', *Human relations*, vol. 56, no. 7, pp. 839–868.

Alexander, J (1991) 'Sociological theory and the claim to reason: Why the end is not in sight', *Sociological Theory*, vol. 9, no. 2, pp. 147–153.

Allen, B (2003) 'Transforming IT', *Optimize*, Vol. 20, January, pp. 20–27.

American-Heritage (2000) *Dictionary of the English Language*. Available from: http://www.bartleby.com/am/ (accessed December 16, 2008).

Amin, A (2004) 'Regulating economic globalization', *Transactions of the Institute of British Geographers*, vol. 29, no. 2, pp. 217–233.

Anderson, R (2003) 'Introduction: Envisaging the prototypical company of the 21st century', in *Ants, Galileo, and Gandhi: Designing the Future of Business through Nature, Genius and Compassion*, ed. S Waage. Greenleaf, Sheffield pp. 17–30.

Andrews, D (2006) 'Sustainability and spirituality', *Rural Sociology*, vol. 71, no. 1, pp. 166–168.

Applebaum, SH & Wohl, L (2000) 'Transformation or change: Some prescriptions for health care organizations', *Managing Service Quality*, vol. 10, no. 5, p. 279.

Armenakis, AA & Bedeian, AG (1999) 'Organizational change: A review of theory and research in the 1990s', *Journal of Management*, vol. 25, no. 3, pp. 293–315.

Arnold, MB & Gasson, JA (1954) *The Human Person: An Approach to an Integral Theory of Personality*. Ronald Press Company, New York.

Arvidsson, A, Baume's, M & Peitersen, N (2008) 'The crisis of value and the ethical economy', *Journal of Futures Studies*, vol. 12, no. 4, pp. 9–20.

Ashburner, L, Ferlie, E & FitzGerald, L (1996) 'Organizational transformation and top-down change: The case of the NHS', *British Journal of Management*, vol. 7, no. 1, pp. 1–16.

Aurobindo (1993) *Integral Yoga: Sri Aurobindo's Teaching and Method of Practice*. Lotus Press, Twin Lakes, WI.

Avolio, BJ (2007) 'Promoting more integrative strategies for leadership theory-building', *American Psychologist*, vol. 62, no. 1, pp. 25–33.

Bacharach, SB (1989), 'Organizational Theories: Some Criteria For Evaluation', The Academy of Management Review, vol. 14, no. 4, p. 496.

Bacharach, SB, Bamberger, P & Sonnenstuhl, WJ (1996) 'The organizational transformation process: The micropolitics of dissonance reduction and the alignment of logics of action', *Administrative Science Quarterly*, vol. 41, no. 3, pp. 477–506.

Badham, R & Garrety, K (2003), ''Living in the Blender of Change': The Carnival of Control in a Culture of Culture', Tamara : Journal of Critical Postmodern Organization Science, vol. 2, no. 4, p. 22.

Bagozzi, RP & Yi, Y (1991) 'Multitrait-multimethod matrices in consumer research', *Journal of Consumer Research*, vol. 17, no. 4, pp. 426–439.

Baker, B (1999) 'The dangerous and the good? Developmentalism, progress, and public schooling', *American Educational Research Journal*, vol. 36, no. 4, pp. 797–834.

Ball, P (2004) *Critical Mass: How One Thing Leads to Another*. Farrar, Straus and Giroux, New York.

Bamford, CE, Rogers, PR & Miller, A (1999) 'Transformation of strategic types: An examination of the internal antecedents to organizational change', *Journal of Business Strategies*, vol. 16, no. 2, p. 135.

Bang, HP (2004) 'Culture governance: Governing self-reflexive modernity', *Public Administration*, vol. 82, no. 1, pp. 157–190.

Banner, DK (1987) 'The dark side of organization transformation', *Organization Development Journal*, vol. 5, no. 1, pp. 44–49.

Barbier, EB (2006) *Natural Resources and Economic Development*. Cambridge University Press, Cambridge.

Barrett, R (1998), Liberating the Corporate Soul: Building a Visionary Organisation., Butterworth-Heinemann, Boston.

Bartunek, JM & Ringuest, JL (1989) 'Enacting new perspectives through work activities during organizational transformation', *Journal of Management Studies*, vol. 26, no. 6, p. 541.

Baum, JAC & Singh, JV (1994) *Evolutionary Dynamics of Organizations*. Oxford University Press, New York.

Beach, LR (2006) *Leadership and the Art of Change: A Practical Guide to Organizational Transformation*. Sage Publications, London.

Beck, D & Cowan, C (1996), Spiral Dynamics: Mastering Values, Leadership, and Change, Blackwell., Oxford.

Becker, C (2004) 'Interdisciplinarity', *Symploke*, vol. 12, no. 1/2, pp. 191–208.

Beckhard, R (1969) *Organisation Development: Strategies and Models*. Addison-Wesley, Boston.

Beer, M & Nohria, N (2000) *Breaking the Code of Change*. Harvard Business School Press, Boston.

Belasen, AT (2000) *Leading the Learning Organization*. SUNY Press, Albany, NY.

Bell, E & Taylor, S (2003) 'The elevation of work: Pastoral power and the new age work ethic', *Organization*, vol. 10, no. 2, p. 329.

Bell, G & Warwick, J (2007) 'Towards establishing the use of holons as an enquiry method', *International Transactions in Operational Research*, vol. 14, no. 1, pp. 55–73.

Bell, SJ, Whitwell, GJ & Lukas, BA (2002) 'Schools of thought in organizational learning', *Journal of the Academy of Marketing Science*, vol. 30, no. 1, pp. 70–86.

Benefiel, M (2003) 'Irreconcilable foes? The discourse of spirituality and the discourse of organizational science', *Organization*, vol. 10, no. 2, p. 383.

Benefiel, M 2005, 'The second half of the journey: Spiritual leadership for organizational transformation', *Leadership Quarterly*, vol. 16, no. 5, p. 723.

Benn, S & Dunphy, D (2007) *Corporate Governance and Sustainability: Challenges for Theory and Practice*. Routledge, New York.

Bernstein, M (2005) 'Identity politics', *Annual Review of Sociology*, vol. 31, no. 1, pp. 47–74.

Berry, T (1999) *The Great Work: Our Way into the Future*. Bell Tower, New York.

Bhaskar, R (1986) *Scientific Realism and Human Emancipation*. Harvester Press, Sussex.

Bhaskar, R (2002a) *From Science to Emancipation: Alienation and the Actuality of Enlightenment*. Sage Publications, New Delhi.

Bhaskar, R (2002b) *Meta-Reality: Creativity, Love and Freedom*. Sage Publications, New Delhi.

Bhaskar, R (2002c) *Reflections on Meta-reality: Transcendence, Emancipation, and Everyday Life*. Sage Publications, New Delhi.

Billig, M (2004) 'Methodology and scholarship in understanding ideological explanation', in *Social Research Methods: A Reader*, ed. C Seale. Routledge, London, pp. 199–215.

Billiger, SM & Hallock, KF (2005) 'Mass layoffs and CEO turnover', *Industrial Relations*, vol. 44, no. 3, p. 463.

Bleicher, K (1994), 'Integrative management in a time of transformation', Long Range Planning, vol. 27, no. 5, pp. 136–144.Bleischwitz, R (2007) *Corporate Governance of Sustainability: A Co-Evolutionary View on Resource Management*. Edward Elgar, Cheltenham, UK.

Blom, R & Melin, H (2003) 'Information society and the transformation of organizations in Finland', *Work and Occupations*, vol. 30, no. 2, pp. 176–193.

Blumenthal, B & Haspeslagh, P (1994) 'Toward a definition of corporate transformation', *Sloan Management Review*, vol. 35, no. 3, pp. 101–106.

Bogdan, R & Taylor, SJ (1975) *Introduction to Qualitative Research*. John Wiley, New York.

Boje, DM (2000) *Holon and Transorganization Theory*. Available from: http://web.nmsu.edu/~dboje/TDholons.html (accessed September 1, 2008).

Boje, DM, 2006, Transorganizational Development, Online, available from: http://web.nmsu.edu/~dboje/TDtransorgtext.html.

Boswell, W (2006) 'Aligning employees with the organization's strategic objectives: out of "line of sight", out of mind', *International Journal of Human Resource Management*, vol. 17, no. 9, p. 1489.

Boxelaar, L, Warner, K, Beilin, R & Shaw, H, (2003) *Through the Looking Glass: Organisational Alignment for Sustaining Communities, Australian Academy of Science*. Available from: http://www.csu.edu.au/special/fenner/papers/ref/11%20Boxelaar%20Lucia.pdf (accessed March 21, 2007).

Boyle, MV & Healy, J (2003) 'Balancing mysterium and onus: Doing spiritual work within an emotion-laden organizational context', *Organization*, vol. 10, no. 2, pp. 351–373.

Bradbury, H (2003) 'Sustaining inner and outer worlds: A whole-systems approach to developing sustainable business practices in management', *Journal of Management Education*, vol. 27, no. 2, p. 172.

Bradbury, H & Lichtenstein, BMB (2000) 'Relationality in organizational research: Exploring the Space Between', *Organization Science*, vol. 11, no. 5, p. 551.

Brown, BC (2005) 'Theory and practice of integral sustainable development—an overview, part 1: Quadrants and the practitioner', *AQAL Journal of Integral Theory and Practice*, vol. 1, no. 2, pp. 2–39.

Brown, BC (2006) *The Use of an Integral Approach by UNDP's HIV/AIDS Group as Part of their Global Response to the HIV/AIDS Epidemic, (2006) Integral Institute*. Available from: http://www.integralworld.net/pdf/Brown. pdf (accessed May 24, 2008).

Brundtland, GH (1987) *Report of the World Commission on Environment and Development: Our Common Future*. United Nations, General Assembly Documents, A/42/427, New York.

Brunetti, AJ, Petrell, RJ & Sawada, B (2003) 'Team project-based learning enhances awareness of sustainability at the University of British Columbia, Canada', *International Journal of Sustainability in Higher Education*, vol. 4, no. 3, p. 210.

Bryman, A, Gillingwater, D & McGuinness, I (1996) 'Leadership and organizational transformation', *International Journal of Public Administration*, vol. 19, no. 6, pp. 849–872.

Buber, M (1947) *Between Man and Man*. Routledge and Kegan Paul, London.

Bubna-Litic, D (2008) 'Neophilia: A consuming passion or fabrication', in *ACS-COS 2008: The 3rd Australasian Caucus of the Standing Conference on Organizational Symbolism, Sydney*. Available from: http://www.business.uts.edu.au (accessed March 24, 2008).

Buchanan, D, Fitzgerald, L, Ketley, D, Gollop, R, Jones, JL, Lamont, SS, Neath, A & Whitby, E (2005) 'No going back: A review of the literature on sustaining organizational change', *International Journal of Management Reviews*, vol. 7, no. 3, pp. 189–205.

Buchanan, DA (2003) 'Getting the story straight: Illusions and delusions in the organizational change process', *Tamara: Journal of Critical Postmodern Organization Science*, vol. 2, no. 4, pp. 7–14.

Bupp, N (1996) 'The change curve', *High-Performance Work Organisation (HPWO) Partnership Seminar*. International Association of Machinists and Aerospace Workers, Placid Harbor, MD, pp. 4–11.

Burns, TR & Dietz, T (2001) 'Revolution—An evolutionary perspective', *International Sociology*, vol. 16, no. 4, pp. 531–555.

Burrell, G (1996) 'Normal science, paradigms, metaphors, discourses and genealogies of analysis', in *Handbook of Organization Studies*, eds. SR Clegg, C Hardy & WR Nord. Sage, London, pp. 642–658.

Burrell, G & Morgan, G (1979) *Sociological Paradigms and Organisational Analysis*. Heinemann, Portsmouth, NH.

Bushe, G (2001) 'Five theories of change embedded in appreciative inquiry', in *Appreciative Inquiry: Rethinking Human Organization*, eds. D Cooperrider, P Sorensen, D Whitney & T Yaeger. Stipes: Champaign, IL., pp. 117–127.

Byrd, RE (1982), 'Developmental Stages in Organizations: As the Twig Is Bent, So Grows the Tree', Personnel, vol. 59, no. 2, pp. 12-25.

Cacioppe, R (2000a) 'Creating spirit at work: Re-visioning organization development and leadership—Part 1', *Leadership and Organization Development Journal*, vol. 21, no. 1/2, pp. 48–54.

Cacioppe, R (2000b) 'Creating spirit at work: Re-visioning organization development and leadership—Part 2', *Leadership and Organization Development Journal*, vol. 21, no. 1/2, pp. 110–119.

Cacioppe, R & Edwards, MG (2005a) 'Adjusting blurred visions: A typology of integral approaches to organisations', *Journal of Organizational Change Management*, vol. 18, no. 3, pp. 230–246.

Cacioppe, R & Edwards, MG (2005b) 'Seeking the holy grail of organisational development: A synthesis of integral theory, spiral dynamics, corporate transformation and developmental action inquiry', *Leadership and Organizational Development Journal*, vol. 26, no. 2, pp. 86–105.

Cao, G, Clarke, S & Lehaney, B (1999) 'Towards systemic management of diversity in organizational change', *Strategic Change*, vol. 8, no. 4, p. 205.

Carayannis, EG (1999) 'Organizational transformation and strategic learning in high risk, high complexity environments', *Technovation*, vol. 19, no. 2, p. 87.

Carman, JM & Dominguez, LV (2001) 'Organizational transformations in transition economies: Hypotheses', *Journal of Macromarketing*, vol. 21, no. 2, pp. 164–180.

Carr, A & Zanetti, LA (1999) 'Metatheorizing the dialectic of self and other: The psychodynamics in work organizations', *American Behavioral Scientist*, vol. 43, no. 2, pp. 324–345.

Carroll, JE (2004) *Sustainability and Spirituality*. SUNY Press, Albany, NY.

Cartwright, W & Craig, JL (2006) 'Sustainability: Aligning corporate governance, strategy and operations with the planet', *Business Process Management Journal*, vol. 12, no. 6, p. 741.

Casey, A (2005) 'Enhancing individual and organizational learning: A sociological model', *Management Learning*, vol. 36, no. 2, p. 131.

Chakravarthy, B & Gargiulo, M (1998) 'Maintaining leadership legitimacy in the transition to new organizational forms', *Journal of Management Studies*, vol. 35, no. 4, p. 437.

Chandler, D & Torbert, B (2003) 'Transforming inquiry and action: Interweaving 27 flavors of action research', *Action Research*, vol. 1, no. 2, pp. 133–152.

Chapman, JA (2002) 'A framework for transformational change in organisations', *Leadership and Organization Development Journal*, vol. 23, no. 1/2, pp. 16–25.

Checkland, P (1988) 'The case for "Holon"', *Systems Practice*, vol. 1, no. 3, pp. 235–238.

Cheng, F-T, Chang, C-F & Wu, S-L (2004) 'Development of holonic manufacturing execution systems', *Journal of Intelligent Manufacturing*, vol. 15, no. 2, p. 253.

Chia, R 1999, 'A "Rhizomic" model of organizational change and transformation: Perspectives from a metaphysics of change', *British Journal of Management*, vol. 10, no. 3, p. 209.

Chia, R (2002), 'Time, duration and simultaneity: Rethinking process and change in organizational analysis', Organization Studies, vol. 23, no. 6, p. 863.

Chile, LM & Simpson, G (2004) 'Spirituality and community development: Exploring the link between the individual and the collective', *Community Development Journal*, vol. 39, no. 4, pp. 318–331.

Chiles, TH, Meyer, AD & Hench, TJ (2004) 'Organizational emergence: The origin and transformation of Branson, Missouri's musical theatres', *Organization Science: A Journal of the Institute of Management Sciences*, vol. 15, no. 5, pp. 499–519.

Choo, CW (2002) 'Sense making, knowledge creation and decision making: Organizational knowing and emergent strategy', in *The Strategic Management of Intellectual Capital and Organizational Knowledge*, eds. CW Choo & N Bontis. Oxford University Press, Oxford, pp. 79–88.

Christie, I (2002) 'Sustainability and spiritual renewal: The challenge of creating a politics of reverence', *Conservation Biology*, vol. 16, no. 6, pp. 1466–1468.

Clegg, SR, Clarke, T & Ibarra, E (2001) 'Millennium management, changing paradigms and organization studies', *Human Relations*, vol. 54, no. 1, pp. 31–36.

Clegg, SR & Ross-Smith, A (2003) 'Revising the boundaries: Management education and learning in a postpositivist world', *Academy of Management Learning and Education*, vol. 2, no. 1, p. 85.

Cogoy, M & Steininger, KW (eds.) (2007) *The Economics of Global Environmental Change: International Cooperation for Sustainability*. Edward Elgar Publishing, Cheltenham, UK.

Colby, BN (1987) 'Well-being: A theoretical program', *American Anthropologist*, vol. 89, no. 4, pp. 879–895.

Cole, M & Wertsch, JV (1996) 'Beyond the individual–social antimony in discussions of Piaget and Vygotsky', in *The Virtual Faculty*, ed. A Lock Available from: http://www.massey.ac.nz/~ALock/virtual/colevyg.htm (accessed February 14, 2009).

Collins, D (1998) *Organisational Change: Sociological Perspectives*. Routledge, London.

Collins, JC & Porras, JI (1997) *Built to Last: Successful Habits of Visionary Companies*. HarperCollins, New York.

Colomy, P (1991) 'Metatheorizing in a postpositivist frame', *Sociological Perspectives*, vol. 34, no. 3, pp. 269–286.

Cooper, DJ, Hinings, B, Greenwood, R & Brown, JL (1996) 'Sedimentation and transformation in organizational change: The case of Canadian law firms', *Organization Studies*, vol. 17, no. 4, p. 623.

Cooper, R & Burrell, G (1988) 'Modernism, postmodernism and organizational analysis: An introduction', *Organization Studies*, vol. 9, no. 1, p. 91.

Coulson-Thomas, CJ (1993) 'Corporate transformation and business process re-engineering', *Executive Development*, vol. 6, no. 1, p. 14.

Courville, S & Piper, N (2004) 'Harnessing hope through NGO activism', *Annals of the American Academy of Political and Social Science*, vol. 592, p. 39.

Cox, JW & Hassard, J (2005) 'Triangulation in organizational research: A representation', *Organization*, vol. 12, no. 1, pp. 109–133.

Cox, T & Beale, RI (1997) *Developing Competency to Manage Diversity*. Berrett-Koehler Publishers, San Francisco.

Crittenden, J (1997) 'What should we think about Wilber's method?' *Journal of Humanistic Psychology*, vol. 37, no. 4, pp. 99–104.

Csikszentmihalyi, M (2003) *Good Business: Leadership. Flow, and the Making of Meaning*. Penguin, New York.

Daniel, GC, David, JB & Gregory, AC (1997) 'A suggested ethical framework for evaluating corporate mergers and acquisitions', *Journal of Business Ethics*, vol. 16, no. 16, p. 1753.

Dansereau, F, Yammarino, FJ & Kohles, JC (1999) 'Multiple levels of analysis from a longitudinal perspective: Some implications for theory building', *Academy of Management Review*, vol. 24, no. 2, p. 346.

Darwin, C, (1872) *The Origin of Species by Means of Natural Selection*, ed. John Murray. Available from: http://darwin-online.org.uk (accessed April 20, 2009).

de Charon, L (2003) 'A transformational leadership development program: Jungian psychological types in dynamic flux', *Organization Development Journal*, vol. 21, no. 3, p. 9.

De Cock, C & Jeanes, EL (2006) 'Questioning consensus, cultivating conflict', *Journal of Management Inquiry*, vol. 15, no. 1, pp. 18–30.

Deetz, S (1995) *Transforming Communication, Transforming Business: Building Responsive and Responsible Workplaces*. Hampton Press, Cresskill, NJ.

Deetz, S (1996) 'Describing differences in approaches to organization science: Rethinking Burrell and Morgan and their legacy', *Organization Science*, vol. 7, no. 2, pp. 191–207.

Dehler, GE & Welsh, MA (1994) 'Spirituality and organizational transformation: Implications for the new management paradigm', *Journal of Managerial Psychology*, vol. 9, no. 6, pp. 17–18.

Dehler, GE, Welsh, MA & Lewis, MW (2001) 'Critical pedagogy in the "new paradigm"', *Management Learning*, vol. 32, no. 4, p. 493.

Del Casino, VJ, Grimes, AJ, Hanna, SP & Jones, JP (2000), 'Methodological frameworks for the geography of organizations', *Geoforum*, vol. 31, no. 4, pp. 523–538.

Dennis, PH & Harald, SH (1999) 'The conscious organization', *Learning Organization*, vol. 6, no. 4, p. 157.

Denzin, NK & Lincoln, YS (2005) *Handbook of Qualitative Research*, 3rd ed. Sage, London.

Department of Family and Community Services (2004) *Annual Report 2003–04*. Australian Government, Canberra.

Dervitsiotis, KN (2003), 'The pursuit of sustainable business excellence: Guiding transformation for effective organizational change', Total Quality Management & Business Excellence, vol. 14, no. 3, p. 251.Dewey, J (1938/1997) *Experience and Education*. Simon and Schuster, New York.

Diamond, M, Allcorn, S & Stein, H (2004) 'The surface of organizational boundaries: A view from psychoanalytic object relations theory', *Human Relations*, vol. 57, no. 1, pp. 31–53.

Dirsmith, MW, Heian, JB & Covaleski, MA (1997) 'Structure and agency in an institutionalized setting: The application and social transformation of control in the Big Six', *Accounting, Organizations and Society*, vol. 22, no. 1, p. 1.

Dixon, NM (1999) *The Organizational Learning Cycle: How We Can Learn Collectively*, 2nd ed. Gower, Brookfield, VT.

Djelic, ML & Ainamo, A (1999) 'The coevolution of new organizational forms in the fashion industry: A historical and comparative study of France, Italy, and the United States', *Organization Science*, vol. 10, no. 5, pp. 622–637.

Donaldson, L (1997) 'A positivist alternative to the structure-action approach', *Organization Studies*, vol. 18, no. 1, p. 77.

Doty, DH & Glick, WH (1994) 'Typologies as a unique form of theory building: Toward improved understanding and modeling', *Academy of Management Review*, vol. 19, no. 2, p. 230.

Dreachslin, JL (1999a) *Diversity Leadership*. Health Administration Press, Chicago.

Dreachslin, JL (1999b) 'Diversity leadership and organizational transformation: Performance indicators for health services organizations', *Journal of Healthcare Management*, vol. 44, no. 6, pp. 427–439.

Dubin, R (1978) *Theory Building*, 2nd ed. Free Press, New York.

Dunphy, D (2000) 'Embracing paradox: Top-down versus participative management of organizational change—a commentary on Conger and Bennis', in *Breaking the Code of Change*, eds. M Beer & N Nohria. Harvard Business School Press, Boston, pp. 123–135.

Dunphy, D, Griffiths, A & Benn, S (2003) *Organisational Change for Corporate Sustainability: A Guide for Leaders and Change Agents of the Future*. Routledge, London.

Dunphy, D & Stace, D (1988), 'Transformational and Coercive Strategies for Planned Organizational Change: Beyond the O.D. Model', Organization Studies, vol. 9, no. 3, pp. 317-334.

Dzurec, LC & Abraham, IL (1993) 'The nature of inquiry—linking quantitative and qualitative research', *Advances in Nursing Science*, vol. 16, no. 1, pp. 73–79.

Easley, CA & Alvarez-Pompilius, F (2004) 'A new paradigm for qualitative investigations: Towards an integrative model for evoking change', *Organization Development Journal*, vol. 22, no. 3, p. 42.

Edwards, MG (2005) 'The integral holon: A holonomic approach to organisational change and transformation', *Journal of Organizational Change Management*, vol. 18, no. 3, pp. 269–288.

Edwards, MG (2007) 'Towards an appreciative meta-inquiry', *Appreciative Inquiry Practitioner*, November, pp. 20–24.

Edwards, MG (2008a) 'Evaluating integral metatheory: A test case and a defence of Wilber's social quadrant', *Journal of Integral Theory and Practice*, vol. 3, no. 4, pp. 61–83.

Edwards, MG (2008b) '"Every today was a tomorrow": An integral method for indexing the social mediation of preferred futures', *Futures*, vol. 40, no. 2, pp. 173–189.

Edwards, MG (2008c) 'Where's the method to our integral madness? An outline of an integral meta-studies', *Journal of Integral Theory and Practice*, vol. 3, no. 2, pp. 165–194.

Egelhoff, WG (1999) 'Organizational equilibrium and organizational change: Two different perspectives of the multinational enterprise', *Journal of International Management*, vol. 5, no. 1, pp. 15–33.

Eggert, N (1998), Contemplative Leadership for Entrepreneurial Organisations: Paradigms, Metaphors and Wicked Problems, Quorum Books, London.Egri, CP & Frost, PJ (1991) 'Shamanism and change: Bringing back the magic in organizational transformation', *Research in Organizational Change and Development*, vol. 5, pp. 175–221.

Elgin, D (1994) 'Building a sustainable species-civilization: A challenge of culture and consciousness', *Futures*, vol. 26, no. 2, pp. 234–245.

Elkana, Y (1988) 'Experiment as a second-order concept', *Science in Context*, vol. 2, no. 1, pp. 177–196.

Elman, C & Elman, MF (2002) 'How not to be Lakatos intolerant: Appraising progress in IR research', *International Studies Quarterly*, vol. 46, no. 2, p. 231.

Elrod, PD & Tippett, DD (2002) 'The "death valley" of change', *Journal of Organizational Change Management*, vol. 15, no. 3, p. 273.

Elsbach, KD, Sutton, RI & Whetten, DA (1999) 'Perspectives on developing management theory, circa 1999: Moving from shrill monologues to (relatively) tame dialogues', *Academy of Management Review*, vol. 24, no. 4, p. 627.

Engels, F (2008) *Karl Marx*. Available from: http://www.marxists.org (accessed January 20, 2009).

Esbensen, T (2006) 'Renewables: Leading on the road to sustainability', *Refocus*, vol. 7, no. 3, p. 16.

Esbjörn-Hargens, S (2005a) 'Integral ecology: The *what*, *who*, and *how* of environmental phenomena', *World Futures*, vol. 61, pp. 5–49.

Esbjörn-Hargens, S (2005b) 'Integral research: A multi-method approach to investigating phenomena'.

Esbjörn-Hargens, S & Zimmerman, ME (2009), Integral Ecology: Uniting Multiple Perspectives on the Natural World, Integral Books, Boston.

Falkenberg, J, Stensaker, IG, Meyer, CB & Haung, AC (2005) 'When change becomes excessive', *Research in Organisational Change and Development*, vol. 15, pp. 31–62.

Farazmand, A (2003) 'Chaos and transformation theories: A theoretical analysis with implications for organization theory and public management', *Public Organization Review*, vol. 3, no. 4, p. 339–372.

Fauconnier, G & Turner, M (2002) *The Way We Think: Conceptual Blending and the Mind's Hidden Complexities*. Basic Books, New York.

Fernando, T (2001) 'Institutional individualism and institutional change: The search for a middle way mode of explanation', *Cambridge Journal of Economics*, vol. 25, no. 6, pp. 765–783.

Findhorn-Community (2003) *The Findhorn Garden: Pioneering a New Vision of Humanity and Nature in Cooperation.* Findhorn Press, London.

Fineman, S (1996) 'In search of meaning: Managing for the health of organizations, our communities and the natural world', *Academy of Management Review*, vol. 21, no. 4, p. 1232.

Fisher, D, Rooke, D & Torbert, B (2003) *Personal and Organizational Transformations: Through Action Inquiry*, 4th ed. Edge\Work Press, Boston.

Fisher, D & Torbert, B (1991) 'Transforming managerial practice: Beyond the achiever stage', *Research in Organisational Change and Development*, vol. 5, pp. 143–173.

Flamholtz, E & Randle, Y (1998) *Changing the Game: Organizational Transformations of the First, Second, and Third Kinds.* Oxford University Press, Oxford.

Fletcher, BR (1990), Organization Transformation Theorists and Practitioners, Praeger, New York.

Ford, JD & Backoff, RH (1988) 'Organisational change in and out of dualities and paradox', in *Paradox in Transformation: Toward a Theory of Change in Organisation and Management*, eds. RE Quinn & KS Cameron. Ballinger Publishing, Cambridge, MA, pp. 81–122.

Forster, N (2005) *Maximum Performance: A Practical Guide to Leading and Managing People at Work.* Edward Elgar, Cheltenham, UK.

Freeman, B (2006) 'Substance sells: Aligning corporate reputation and corporate responsibility', *Public Relations Quarterly*, vol. 51, no. 1, p. 12.

French, WL, Bell, C, H. & Zawacki, RA (eds) (2005), Organisation Development and Transformation: Managing Effective Change, 6th Ed. edn, McGraw-Hill, New York.

Frenier, CR (1997) *Business and the Feminine Principle: The Untapped Resource.* Butterworth Heinemann, London.

Fry, LJ & Jon, M (1976) 'The organizational transformation of a federal education program: Reflections on LEEP', *Social Problems*, vol. 24, no. 2, pp. 259–270.

Fry, LW (2005) 'Toward a theory of ethical and spiritual well-being, and corporate social responsibility through spiritual leadership', in *Positive Psychology in Business Ethics and Corporate Responsibility* RA Giacalone, CL Jurkiewiez & C. Dunn (eds.). Information Age Publishing: Charlotte, NC,.

Fry, LW, Vitucci, S & Cedillo, M (2005) 'Spiritual leadership and army transformation: Theory, measurement, and establishing a baseline', *Leadership Quarterly*, vol. 16, no. 5, p. 835.

Fry, LW & Whittington, JL (2005) 'Spiritual leadership as a paradigm for organization transformation and development', in *National Academy of Management Meeting.* Honolulu, HI.

Fuegi, J (1987) *Bertolt Brecht—Chaos According to Plan.* Cambridge University Press, Cambridge.

Galambos, L (2005) 'Recasting the organizational synthesis: Structure and process in the twentieth and twenty-first centuries', *Business History Review*, vol. 79, no. 1, p. 1.

Galtung, J & Inayatullah, S (1997) *Macrohistory and Macrohistorians. Perspectives on Individual, Social, and Civilizational Change.* Praeger, Westport, CT.

Gearing, RE (2004) 'Bracketing in research: A typology', *Qualitative Health Research*, vol. 14, no. 10, pp. 1429–1452.

Gebser, J (1985) *The Ever-Present Origin.* Ohio University Press, Athens.

Geller, ES (1992) 'It takes more than information to save energy', *American Psychologist*, June, pp. 814–815.

Gemmill, G & Smith, C (1985) 'A dissipative structure model of organization transformation', *Human Relations*, vol. 38, no. 8, pp. 751–766.

Gergen, KJ, McNamee, S & Barrett, FJ (2001) 'Toward transformative dialogue', *International Journal of Public Administration*, vol. 24, no. 7/8, p. 679.

Gergen, KJ & Zielke, B (2006) 'Theory in action', *Theory and Psychology*, vol. 16, no. 3, pp. 299–309.

Gersick, CJ (1991) 'Revolutionary change theories: A multilevel exploration of the punctuated equilibrium paradigm', *Academy of Management Review*, vol. 16, no. 1, p. 10.

Ghoshal, S (2005) 'Bad management theories are destroying good management practices', *Academy of Management Learning and Education*, vol. 4, no. 1, pp. 75–91.

Giacalone, RA & Jurkiewica, CL (2003) 'Toward a science of workplace spirituality', in *Handbook of Workplace Spirituality and Organizational Performance*, eds. RA Giacalone & CL Jurkiewica. M. E. Sharp, Armonk, NY, pp. 3–28.

Giddens, A (1984) *The Constitution of Society*. Polity Press, Cambridge.

Giddens, A (1985) *The Constitution of Society*. University of California Press, Berkeley.

Giddens, A (1993) *New Rules of Sociological Method: A Positive Critique of Interpretive Sociologies*, 2nd ed. Stanford University Press, Stanford, CA.

Giddens, A (2000) *Runaway World: How Globalization is Reshaping Our Lives*. Routledge, London.

Giesen, B (1987) 'Beyond reductionism: Four models relating micro and macro levels', in *The Micro-Macro Link*, eds. JC Alexander, B Giesen, R Münch & NJ Smelser. University of California Press, Los Angeles, pp. 337–355.

Gioia, DA (1999) 'Practicability, paradigms, and problems in stakeholder theorizing', *Academy of Management Review*, vol. 24, no. 2, pp. 228–232.

Gioia, DA & Pitre, E (1990) 'Multiparadigm perspectives on theory building', *Academy of Management Review*, vol. 15, no. 4, pp. 584–602.

Gladwin, TN, Kennelly, JJ & Krause, TS (1995) 'Shifting paradigms for sustainable development: Implications for management theory and research', *Academy of Management Review*, vol. 20, no. 4, pp. 874–907.

Glaser, BGHJA (2007) *The Grounded Theory Seminar Reader*. Sociology Press, Mill Valley, CA.

Glass, GV (1976) 'Primary, secondary, and meta-analysis of research', *Educational Researcher*, no. 11, pp. 3–8.

Glass, GV (1977), 'Integrating Findings: The Meta-Analysis of Research', Review of Research in Education, Vol. 5, pp. , vol. 5, pp. 351-379.

Glassman, AM & Cummings, TG (1991) *Cases in Organizational Development*. Irwin, Homewood, IL.

Golembiewski, RT (2004) 'Twenty questions for our future: Challenges facing OD and ODers, or whatever it is labeled', *Organization Development Journal*, vol. 22, no. 2, p. 6.

Goles, T & Hirschheim, R (2000) 'The paradigm is dead, the paradigm is dead . . . long live the paradigm: the legacy of Burrell and Morgan', *Omega*, vol. 28, no. 3, pp. 249–268.

Gottschalg, O & Zollo, M (2007) 'Interest alignment and competitive advantage', *Academy of Management Review*, vol. 32, no. 2, pp. 418–437.

Grandori, A (2001), 'Methodological options for an Integrated perspective on organization', Human Relations, vol. 54, no. 1, pp. 37-47.

Grant, P (1996) 'Supporting transition: How managers can help themselves and others during times of change', *Organizations and People*, vol. 3, no. 1, p.4.

Green, TB & Butkus, RT (1999) *Motivation, Beliefs, and Organizational Transformation*. Quorum Books, Westport, CT.

Greenaway, R (2002) *Experiential Learning Articles and Critiques of David Kolb's Theory*. Available from: http://wilderdom.com (accessed February 10, 2009).

Greenwood, R & Hinings, CR (1988) 'Organizational design types, tracks and the dynamics of strategic change', *Organization Studies*, vol. 9, no. 3, p. 293.

Greenwood, R & Hinings, CR (1993), 'Understanding strategic change: The contribution of archetypes', Academy of Management Journal, vol. 36, no. 5, pp. 1052-1081.

Griffiths, A & Petrick, JA (2001) 'Corporate architectures for sustainability', *International Journal of Operations and Production Management*, vol. 21, no. 12, pp. 1573–1585.

Grubbs, JW (2000), 'Cultural imperialism: A critical theory of interorganizational change', Journal of Organizational Change Management, vol. 13, no. 3, pp. 221-234.

Guba, EG & Lincoln, YS (1998), 'Competing paradigms in qualitative research', in The landscape of qualitative research, eds NK Denzin & YS Lincoln, Sage, London, pp. 195-220.

Habermas, J (1983) 'Interpretive social science vs. hermeneuticism', in *Social Sciences as Moral Inquiry*, eds. N Haan, RN Bellah, P Rabinow & WM Sullivan. Columbia University Press, New York, pp. 251–269.

Habermas, J (1984) *The Theory of Communicative Action*. McCarthy, Boston.

Habermas, J (1995) *Moral Consciousness and Communicative Action*. MIT Press, Cambridge, MA.

Halme, M (2001) 'Learning for sustainable development in tourism networks', *Business Strategy and the Environment*, vol. 10, no. 2, p. 100.

Hamilton, C (2003) *The Growth Fetish*. Allen and Unwin, Sydney.

Hampe, B & Grady, JE (2005) *From Perception to Meaning: Image Schemas in Cognitive Linguistics*. Mouton De Gruyter, Berlin.

Haraway, D (1991) 'Situated knowledges: The science question in feminism and the privilege of partial perspective', in *Simians, Cyborgs and Women: The Reinvention of Nature*. Free Association Books, London, pp. 183–201.

Hart, SL (2005) 'Innovation, creative destruction and sustainability', *Research Technology Management*, vol. 48, no. 5, p. 21.

Hartman, SJ, Yrle, AC, White, MC & Friedman, WH (1998) 'Theory building: Issues and an agenda', *International Journal of Public Administration*, vol. 21, no. 5, pp. 723–755.

Hassard, J & Kelemen, M (2002) 'Production and consumption in organizational knowledge: The case of the paradigms debate', *Organization*, vol. 9, no. 2, pp. 331–355.

Hawken, P, Lovins, A & Lovins, LH (1999) *Natural Capitalism: Creating the Next Industrial Revolution*. Little, Brown and Co., New York.

Hedstrom, P & Swedberg, R (1996) 'Social mechanisms', *Acta Sociologica*, vol. 39, no. 3, pp. 281–308.

Hernes, T & Bakken, T (2003) 'Implications of self-reference: Niklas Luhmann's autopoiesis and organization theory', *Organization Studies*, vol. 24, no. 9, p. 1511.

Hiller, NJ, Day, DV & Vance, RJ (2006) 'Collective enactment of leadership roles and team effectiveness: A field study', *Leadership Quarterly*, vol. 17, no. 4, pp. 387–397.

Hitchcock, DE & Willard, M (2006) *The Business Guide to Sustainability: Practical Strategies and Tools for Organizations*. Earthscan, London.

Hobson, B (2000) 'Agency, identities, and institutions', *Social Politics*, vol. 7, no. 2, p. 238.

Hobson, K (2006) 'Environmental psychology and the geographies of ethical and sustainable consumption: Aligning, triangulating, challenging?' *Area*, vol. 38, no. 3, pp. 292–300.

Hoffman, WM, Frederick, R & Petry, ES (1989) *The Ethics of Organizational Transformation: Mergers, Takeovers, and Corporate Restructuring.* Quorum Books, Westport, CT.

Howard, S (2002) 'A spiritual perspective on learning in the workplace', *Journal of Managerial Psychology*, vol. 17, no. 3, p. 230.

Howley, A, Spatig, L & Howley, C (1999) 'Developmentalism deconstructed', in *Rethinking Intelligence: Confronting Psychological Assumptions about Teaching and Learning*, eds. JL Kincheloe & SR Steinberg. Taylor and Frances/Routledge, Florence, KY, pp. 27–49.

Hurley, JR (1998) 'Agency and communion as related to "Big Five" self-representations and subsequent behavior in small groups', *Journal of Psychology*, vol. 132, no. 3, pp. 337–351.

Inayatullah, S (2005) 'Spirituality as the fourth bottom line?' *Futures*, vol. 37, no. 6, pp. 573–579.

Jackson, N & Carter, P (1993) '"Paradigm wars": A response to Hugh Wilmott', *Organization Studies*, vol. 14, no. 5, pp. 721–725.

Jacques, R (1992), 'Critique and Theory Building: Producing Knowledge "From the Kitchen"', Academy of Management Review, vol. 17, no. 3, pp. 582-606.

Jasperson, J, Carte, TA, Saunders, CS & Butler, BS (2002) 'Power and information technology research: A metatriangulation review', *MIS Quarterly*, vol. 26, no. 4, pp. 397–459.

Jawahar, IM & McLaughlin, GL (2001) 'Toward a descriptive stakeholder theory: An organizational life cycle approach', *Academy of Management Review*, vol. 26, no. 3, p. 397.

Jenkins, JC (1977) 'Radical transformation of organizational goals', *Administrative Science Quarterly*, vol. 22, no. 4, pp. 568–586.

Jones, C (2003) 'Theory after the postmodern condition', *Organization*, vol. 10, no. 3, pp. 503–525.

Jones, C (2005) 'Firm transformation: Advancing a Darwinian perspective', *Management Decision*, vol. 43, no. 1, pp. 13–25.

Jorgensen, B (2004) 'Individual and organisational learning: A model for reform for public organisations', *Foresight: The Journal of Futures Studies, Strategic Thinking and Policy*, vol. 6, no. 2, p. 91.

Joyce, K (2003) 'The power of human relationships', *Organization Development Journal*, vol. 21, no. 2, p. 71.

Juch, B (1983) *Personal Development: Theory and Practice in Management Training.* Wiley, Chichester, NY.

Kaler, J (2003) 'Differentiating stakeholder theories', *Journal of Business Ethics*, vol. 46, no. 1, pp. 71–83.

Kaplan, A (1964) *The Conduct of Inquiry: Methodology for Behavioural Science.* Chandler, New York.

Kark, R (2004) 'The transformational leader: Who is (s)he? A feminist perspective', *Journal of Organizational Change Management*, vol. 17, no. 2, p. 160.

Karlsson, F & Wistrand, K (2006) 'Combining method engineering with activity theory: Theoretical grounding of the method component concept', *European Journal of Information Systems*, vol. 15, no. 1, p. 82.

Kay, JJ, Regier, HA, Boyle, M & Francis, G (1999) 'An ecosystem approach for sustainability: Addressing the challenge of complexity', *Futures*, vol. 31, no. 7, p. 721.

Kets de Vries, MFR & Balazs, K (1998) 'Beyond the quick fix: The psychodynamics of organizational transformation and change', *European Management Journal*, vol. 16, no. 5, p. 611.

Kets de Vries, MFR & Balazs, K (1999) 'Transforming the mind-set of the organization—a clinical perspective', *Administration and Society*, vol. 30, no. 6, pp. 640–675.

Kilburg, RR, Stokes, EJ & Kuruvilla, C (1998) 'Toward a conceptual model of organizational regression', *Consulting Psychology Journal: Practice and Research*, vol. 50, no. 2, pp. 101–119.

Kimerling, J (2001) '"The human face of petroleum": Sustainable development in Amazonia?', *RECIEL*, vol. 10, pp. 65–81.

Kinlaw, DC (1993) *Competitive and Green: Sustainable Performance in the Environmental Age*. Pfeiffer, Amsterdam.

Klein, KJ, Tosi, H & Cannella, AA (1999) 'Multilevel theory building: Benefits, barriers, and new developments', *Academy of Management Review*, vol. 24, no. 2, pp. 243–248.

Knights, D & Kerfoot, D (2004) 'Between representations and subjectivity: Gender binaries and the politics of organizational transformation', *Gender, Work and Organization*, vol. 11, no. 4, p. 430.

Koestler, A (1967) *The Ghost in the Machine*. Arkana, London.

Kolb, DA (1984) *Experiential Learning: Experience as the Source of Learning and Development*. Prentice Hall, Englewood Cliffs, NJ.

Kotter, JP (1995) 'Leading change: Why transformation efforts fail', *Harvard Business Review on Change*. Harvard Business Review, Vol. 73, no. 2, p. 59.

Kotter, JP (2006) 'Transformation: Master three key tasks', *Leadership Excellence*, vol. 23, no. 1, p. 14.

Krarup, K (1979) 'On the sociological significance of N. Elias's sociogenetic modelling approach to societal transformations', *Acta Sociologica*, vol. 22, no. 2, pp. 161–173.

Kreis, S (2008) *The History Guide: Karl Marx, 1818–1883*. Available from: http://www.historyguide.org (accessed January 20, 2009).

Kuepers, W & Weibler, J (2008) 'Emotions in organisation: An integral perspective', *International Journal of Work Organisation and Emotion*, vol. 2, no. 3, pp. 256–287.

Küpers, W & Edwards, MG (2007) 'Integrating plurality: Towards an integral perspective on leadership and organisation', in *Handbook of 21st Century Management*, vol. 2, ed. C Wankel. Sage, London, pp. 311–322.

Lakatos, I (1978) *The Methodology of Scientific Research Programmes: Philosophical Papers Volume 1*. Cambridge University Press, Cambridge.

Lakoff, G & Johnson, M (1999) *Philosophy in the Flesh: The Embodied Mind and its Challenge to Western Thought*. Basic Books, New York.

Landrum, NE & Gardner, CL (2005) 'Using integral theory to effect strategic change', *Journal of Organizational Change Management*, vol. 18, no. 3, pp. 247–258.

Lane, DC & Oliva, R (1998) 'The greater whole: Towards a synthesis of system dynamics and soft systems methodology', *Source: European Journal of Operational Research*, vol. 107, no. 1, pp. 214–236.

Laszlo, E (2003) *The Connectivity Hypothesis: Foundations of an Integral Science of Quantum, Cosmos, Life, and Consciousness*. SUNY Press, Albany, NY.

Laszlo, E & Seidel, P (2006) *Global Survival: The Challenge and its Implications for Thinking and Acting*. Select Books, New York.

Law, J (1999) 'After ANT: Complexity, naming and topology', in *Actor Network Theory and After*, eds. J Law & J Hassard. Basil Blackwell, London, pp. 1–15.

Law, J (2000) 'On the subject of the object: Narrative, technology, and interpellation', *Configurations*, vol. 8, no. 1, pp. 1–29.

Leavitt, HJ (2005) 'Hierarchies, authority, and leadership', *Leader to Leader*, vol. 2005, no. 37, pp. 55–61.

Lee, CC & Grover, V (2000) 'Exploring mediation between environmental and structural attributes: The penetration of communication technologies in manufacturing organizations', *Journal of Management Information Systems*, vol. 16, no. 3, p. 187.

Leigh, DE & Gifford, KD (1999) 'Workplace transformation and worker upskilling: The perspective of individual workers', *Industrial Relations*, vol. 38, no. 2, pp. 174–191.

Lemak, DJ, Henderson, PW & Wenger, MS (2004) 'A new look at organizational transformation using systems theory: An application to federal contractors', *Journal of Business and Management*, vol. 9, no. 4, p. 407.

Leonard, HS & Goff, M (2003) 'Leadership development as an intervention for organizational transformation: A case study', *Consulting Psychology Journal: Practice and Research*, vol. 55, no. 1, pp. 58–67.

Lester, DL, Parnell, JA & Carraher, S (2003), 'Organizational life cycle: A five-stage empirical scale', International Journal of Organizational Analysis, vol. 11, no. 4, pp. 339-54.

Levy, A & Merry, U (1986) *Organizational Transformation: Approaches, Strategies, Theories*. Praeger, New York.

Lewin, K (1952) 'Group decision and social change', in *Readings and Social Psychology*, 3rd ed., eds. EE Maccoby, TM Newcomb & EL Hartley. Henry Holt, New York, pp. 459–473.

Lewis, D (2003) 'NGOs, organizational culture, and institutional sustainability', *Annals of the American Academy of Political and Social Science*, vol. 590, pp. 212–226.

Lewis, MW & Grimes, AJ (1999) 'Metatriangulation: Building theory from multiple paradigms', *Academy of Management Review*, vol. 24, no. 4, pp. 672–690.

Lewis, MW & Kelemen, ML (2002) 'Multiparadigm inquiry: Exploring organizational pluralism and paradox', *Human Relations*, vol. 55, no. 2, pp. 251–275.

Lewis, P (1996) 'Transformational change using stratified systems theory', *International Journal of Public Administration*, vol. 19, no. 6, pp. 801–826.

Lichtenstein, BB (1997) 'Grace, magic and miracles: A "chaotic logic" of organizational transformation', *Journal of Organizational Change Management*, vol. 10, no. 5, p. 393.

Lichtenstein, BB (2000) 'Emergence as a process of self-organizing: New assumptions and insights from the study of non-linear dynamic systems', *Journal of Organizational Change Management*, vol. 13, no. 6, pp. 526–527.

Lincoln, YS & Guba, EG (2000) 'Paradigmatic controversies, contradictions, and emerging confluences', in *Handbook of Qualitative Research*, 2nd ed., eds. NK Denzin & YS Lincoln. Sage, London, pp. 163–188.

Littler, CR, Wiesner, R & Dunford, R (2003) 'The dynamics of delayering: Changing management structures in three countries', *Journal of Management Studies*, vol. 40, no. 2, pp. 225–256.

Lockie, S (2004) 'Collective agency, non-human causality and environmental social movements: A case study of the Australian "landcare movement"', *Journal of Sociology*, vol. 40, no. 1, p. 41.

Loren, G (2005) 'Sustainability; Peter Senge: The dynamics of change and sustainability', *New Zealand Management*, September, pp. 46–50.

Lowe, I (2007) *How Can We Live Together in a Sustainable Way?* Available from: http://www.abc.net.au (accessed February 17, 2009).

Luborsky, M (1994) 'Identification and analysis of themes and patterns', in *Qualitative Methods in Aging Research*, eds. J Gubrium & A Sanakar. Sage, Thousand Oaks, pp. 189–210.

Luhman, N (1990) *Essays on Self-Reference*. Columbia University Press, New York.

Luke, TW (2006) 'The system of sustainable degradation', *Capitalism, Nature, Socialism*, vol. 17, no. 1, p. 99.

Lüscher, LS & Lewis, MW (2008) 'Organisational change and managerial sensemaking: Working through paradox', *Academy of Management Journal*, vol. 51, no. 2, pp. 221–240.

Lynham, SA (2002) 'The general method of theory-building research in applied disciplines', *Advances in Developing Human Resources*, vol. 4, no. 3, pp. 221–241.

Lyotard, J-F (1984) *The Postmodern Condition: A Report on Knowledge*. Manchester University Press, Manchester.

Mainemelis, C, Boyatzis, RE & Kolb, DA (2002) 'Learning styles and adaptive flexibility: Testing experiential learning theory', *Management Learning*, vol. 33, no. 1, pp. 5–33.

Mair, VH (2008) *Danger and Opportunity ≠ Crisis: How a Misunderstanding about Chinese Characters Has Led Many Astray*. Available from: http://www.pinyin.info/chinese/crisis.html (accessed April 20, 2008).

Margolis, SL & Hansen, CD (2002) 'A model for organizational identity: Exploring the path to sustainability during change', *Human Resource Development Review*, vol. 1, no. 3, pp. 277–303.

Mariotti, J (1996) 'Troubled by resistance to change', *Industry Week*, October 7, p. 30.

Marshall, JD & Toffel, MW (2005) 'Framing the elusive concept of sustainability: A sustainability hierarchy', *Environmental Science and Technology*, vol. 39, no. 3, p. 673.

Masood, SA, Dani, SS, Burns, ND & Backhouse, CJ (2006) 'Transformational leadership and organizational culture: The situational strength perspective', *Proceedings of the Institution of Mechanical Engineers*, vol. 220, no. B6, p. 941.

Mathews, J (1996) 'Holonic organisational architectures', *Human Systems Management*, vol. 15, no. 1, p. 27.

Maxwell, TJ (2007) 'Sustainability in paradigms and practices at board level in Anglo American Plc', in *Corporate Governance and Sustainability: Challenges for Theory and Practice*, eds. S Benn & D Dunphy. Routledge, London, pp. 145–164.

McCarthy, B (1987) *The 4mat System: Teaching to Leaning Styles with Right/Left Mode Techniques*. Excel, Inc., Barrington.

McGuire, J, Palus, C & Torbert, B (2007) 'Toward interdependent organizing and researching', in *Handbook of Collaborative Management Research*, eds. A Shani, S Mohrman, W Pasmore, B Stymne & N Adler. Sage, New York, pp. 123–142.

McHugh, M (2001), Managing change: Regenerating business, CIM, London.

McHugh, P, Merli, G & Wheeler, W (1995) *Beyond Business Process Reengineering: Towards the Holonic Enterprise*. John Wiley and Sons, New York.

McKinley, W, Mone, MA & Moon, G (1999), 'Determinants and development of schools in organization theory', The Academy of Management Review, vol. 24, no. 4, pp. 634-650.

McKnight, R (1984) 'Spirituality in the workplace', in *Transforming Work: A Collection of Organizational Transformation Readings*, ed. J Adams. Miles River Press, Alexandria, VA, pp. 139–153.

McLennan, GG (2002) 'Quandaries in meta-theory: against pluralism', *Economy and Society*, vol. 31, no. 3, pp. 483–496.

McNulty, T & Ferlie, E (2004) 'Process transformation: Limitations to radical organizational change within public service organizations', *Organization Studies*, vol. 25, no. 8, pp. 1389–1412.

Mea, WJ, Sims, RR & Veres, JG (2000) 'Efforts in organization transformation: Getting your money's worth', *International Review of Administrative Sciences*, vol. 66, no. 3, pp. 479–493.

Meredith, J (1993), 'Theory building through conceptual methods', International Journal of Operations & Production Management, vol. 13, no. 5, pp. 3-12.

Merton, RK (1957) *Social Theory and Social Structure*. Free Press, Glencoe, IL.

Messinger, SL (1955) 'Organizational transformation: A case study of a declining social movement', *American Sociological Review*, vol. 20, no. 1, pp. 3–10.

Michels, R (1959) *Political Parties*. Dover, New York.

Midgley, G (2003) 'Five sketches of postmodernism: Implications for systems thinking and operational research', *Organizational Transformation and Social Change*, vol. 1, no. 1, pp. 47–62.

Miller, D (1996) 'A preliminary typology of organizational learning: Synthesizing the literature', *Journal of Management*, vol. 22, no. 3, pp. 485–505.

Mimi, B (2006) 'Steam's evolving engine', *Cobblestone*, vol. 27, no. 8, pp. 10–13.

Mingers, J (2004) 'Paradigm wars: Ceasefire announced who will set up the new administration?' *Journal of Information Technology*, vol. 19, no. 3, p. 165.

Mingers, J (2006) *Realising Systems Thinking: Knowledge and Action in Management Science*. Springer, New York.

Mingers, J & Brocklesby, J (1997) 'Multimethodology: Towards a framework for mixing methodologies', *Omega*, vol. 25, no. 5, pp. 489–509.

Mingers, JC (2003) 'Replies to Jackson and Gregory', *Journal of the Operational Research Society*, vol. 54, no. 12, p. 1303.

Mintzberg, H (2006) 'The leadership debate with Henry Mintzberg: Community-ship is the answer', *Financial Times*, October 23.

Mintzberg, H & Westley, F (1992) 'Cycles of organizational change', *Strategic Management Journal*, vol. 13, p. 39.

Molnar, EB & Mulvihill, PR (2003) 'Sustainability-focused organizational learning: Recent experiences and new challenges', *Journal of Environmental Planning and Management*, vol. 46, no. 2, pp. 167–176.

Molz, M (in press) 'Contemporary integral education research: A transnational and transparadigmatic overview', in *Integral Education: Exploring Multiple Perspectives in the Classroom*, eds. S Esbjörn-Hargens, J Reams & O Gunnlaugson. SUNY, Albany, NY.

Molz, M & Hampson, GP (in press) 'Elements of the underacknowledged history of integral education', in *Integral Education: Exploring Multiple Perspectives in the Classroom*, eds. S Esbjörn-Hargens, J Reams & O Gunnlaugson. SUNY, Albany, NY.

Mowen, JC & Voss, KE (2008) 'On building better construct measures: Implications of a general hierarchical model', *Psychology and Marketing*, vol. 25, no. 6, pp. 485–505.

Mudacumura, GM (2006), 'Toward a general theory of sustainability', in Sustainable Development Policy and Administration, eds GM Mudacumura, D Mebratu & MS Haque, Taylor & Francis, Boca Raton, FL, pp. 136-159.

Mumford, A (1992) 'Individual and organizational learning: The pursuit of change', *Management Decision*, vol. 30, no. 6, p. 143.

Murray, P (2002) 'Cycles of organisational learning: A conceptual approach', *Management Decision*, vol. 40, no. 3, p. 239.

Nadler, DA & Tushman, ML (1999) 'The organization of the future: Strategic imperatives and core competencies for the 21st century', *Organizational Dynamics*, vol. 28, no. 1, pp. 45–60.

Nagel, T (1986) *The View from Nowhere*. Oxford University Press, New York.

Nardi, B (1996) *Context and Consciousness: Activity Theory and Human Computer Interaction*. MIT Press, Cambridge, MA.

Nattrass, B & Altomare, M (1999) *The Natural Step for Business; Wealth, Ecology, and the Evolutionary Corporation*. New Society Publishers, Gabriola Island, BC.

Neal, J & Biberman, J (2003) 'Introduction: The leading edge in research on spirituality and organizations', *Journal of Organizational Change Management*, vol. 16, no. 4, p. 363.

Neal, JA, Lichtenstein, BMB & Banner, D (1999), 'Spiritual perspectives on individual, organizational and societal transformation', Journal of Organizational Change Management, vol. 12, no. 3, p. 175.

Nelson, L & Burns, FL (1984), 'High-performance programming: A framework for transforming organisations', in Transforming Work: A Collection of Organizational Transformation Readings, ed. J Adams, Miles River Press, Alexandria, VA., pp. 226-242.

Newhouse, DR & Chapman, ID (1996) 'Organizational transformation: A case study of two aboriginal organizations', *Human Relations*, vol. 49, no. 7, p. 995.

Newman, KL (1998a) 'Leading radical change in transition economies', *Leadership and Organization Development Journal*, vol. 19, no. 6, p. 309.

Newman, KL (1998b) *Managing Radical Organizational Change*. Sage, London.

Newman, KL (1999) 'Radial organizational change: The role of starting conditions, competion, and leaders', *Organization Development Journal*, vol. 17, no. 4, pp. 9–28.

Newman, KL (2000) 'Organizational transformation during institutional upheaval', *Academy of Management Review*, vol. 25, no. 3, pp. 602–619.

Newman, P & Rowe, M (2003) *Hope for the Future: A Vision for Quality-of-Life in Western Australia*. Western Australian Government, Perth.

Nicoll, D (1984) 'Grace beyond the rules', in *Transforming Work: A Collection of Organizational Transformation Readings*, ed. JD Adams. Miles River Press, Alexandria, VA, pp. 4–16.

Nooteboom, S (2006) *Adaptive Networks: The Governance for Sustainable Development*. Eburon Academic Publishers, Delft.

Nutt, PC (2003) 'Implications for organisational change in the structure process duality', *Research in Organisational Change and Development*, vol. 14, pp. 147–193.

Nutt, PC & Backoff, RW (1997a) 'Facilitating transformational change', *Journal of Applied Behavioral Science*, vol. 33, no. 4, p. 490.

Nutt, PC & Backoff, RW (1997b) 'Organizational transformation', *Journal of Management Inquiry*, vol. 6, no. 3, pp. 235–254.

O'Reilly, CA & Tushman, ML (2004) 'The ambidextrous organization', *Harvard Business Review*, vol. 82, no. 4, pp. 74–81.

Old, DR (1995) 'Consulting for real transformation, sustainability, and organic form', *Journal of Organizational Change Management*, vol. 8, no. 3, p. 6.

Ollman, B (2003) *Dance of the Dialectic: Steps in Marx's Method*. University of Illinois Press, Urbana.

Overton, WF (2007) 'A coherent metatheory for dynamic systems: Relational organicism-contextualism', *Human Development*, vol. 50, no. 2/3, pp. 154–159.

Owen, H (1987), Spirit: Transformation and Development in organizations, Abbott Publishing, Potomac, Md.

Owen, H (2000) *The Power of Spirit: How Organizations Transform*. Berrett-Koehler, San Francisco.

Paolucci, P (2000) 'Questions of method: Fundamental problems reading dialectical methodologies', *Critical Sociology*, vol. 26, no. 3, pp. 301–328.

Paolucci, P (2003) 'The scientific method and the dialectical method', *Historical Materialism*, vol. 11, no. 1, pp. 75–106.

Parameshwar, S (2005) 'Spiritual leadership through ego-transcendence: Exceptional responses to challenging circumstances', *Leadership Quarterly*, vol. 16, no. 5, pp. 689–722.

Parker, B & Caine, D (1996) 'Holonic modelling: Human resource planning and the two faces of Janus', *International Journal of Manpower*, vol. 17, no. 8, p. 30.

Paterson, BL, Thorne, SE, Canam, C & Jillings, C (2001) *Meta-Study of Qualitative Health Research: A Practical Guide to Meta-Analysis and Meta-Synthesis*. Sage Publications, Thousand Oaks, CA.

Patton, MQ (1990) *Qualitative Evaluation and Research Methods*. Sage Publications, London.

Paul, K & Zimbler, A (1989) 'Cashbuild of South Africa: Company response to Black employee demands', *International Journal of Value-Based Management*, vol. 2, no. 2, pp. 1–15.

Pava, ML (2004) 'Re-imagining a working definition of spirituality: A review of how the way we talk can change the way we work: Seven languages for transformation', *Business and Society Review*, vol. 109, no. 1, pp. 115–125.

Payne, SL (2000) 'Challenges for research ethics and moral knowledge construction in the applied social sciences', *Journal of Business Ethics*, vol. 26, no. 4, pp. 307–318.

Pennington, M (2006) 'Sustainable development and British land use planning: A Hayekian perspective', *Town Planning Review*, vol. 77, no. 1, p. 75.

Pettigrew, AM (1987) 'Context and action in the transformation of the firm', *Journal of Management Studies*, vol. 24, no. 6, pp. 649–670.

Pettigrew, AM, Woodman, RW & Cameron, KS (2001) 'Studying organizational change and development: Challenges for future research', *Academy of Management Journal*, vol. 44, no. 4, pp. 697–713.

Pfeffer, J (2005) 'Why do bad management theories persist? A comment on Ghoshal', *Academy of Management Learning and Education*, vol. 4, no. 1, pp. 96–100.

Pfeffer, J & Fong, CT (2005) 'Building organization theory from first principles: The self-enhancement motive and understanding power and influence', *Organization Science*, vol. 16, no. 4, pp. 372–390.

Philip, G & McKeown, I (2004) 'Business transformation and organizational culture: The role of competency, IS and TQM', *European Management Journal*, vol. 22, no. 6, p. 624.

Placet, M, Anderson, R & Fowler, KM (2005) 'Strategies for sustainability', *Research Technology Management*, vol. 48, no. 5, p. 32.

Polanyi, M (1962) *Personal Knowledge: Toward a Post-Critical Philosophy*. University of Chicago Press, Chicago.

Poole, PP (1998) 'Words and deeds of organizational change', *Journal of Managerial Issues*, vol. 10, no. 1, pp. 45–59.

Popper, K (1970) 'Normal science and its dangers', in *Criticism and the Growth of Knowledge*, eds. I Lakatos & A Musgrave. Cambridge University Press, Cambridge, pp. 51–58.

Porras, JI (1987) *Stream Analysis: A Powerful New Way to Diagnose and Manage Change*. Addison-Wesley, Reading, MA.

Porras, JI & Silvers, RC (1991) 'Organization development and transformation', *Annual Review of Psychology*, vol. 42, pp. 51–78.

Preston, CJ (2005) 'Pluralism and naturalism: Why the proliferation of theories is good for the mind', *Philosophical Psychology*, vol. 18, no. 6, p. 715.

Quinn, RE & Cameron, KS (1988) 'Paradox and transformation: A framework for viewing organisation and management', in *Paradox and Transformation: Toward a Theory of Change in Organization and Management*, eds. RE Quinn & KS Cameron. Ballinger, Cambridge, MA, pp. 289–308.

Reed, M (1997) 'In praise of duality and dualism: Rethinking agency and structure in organizational analysis', *Organization Studies*, vol. 18, pp. 21–42.

Reicher, S, Haslam, SA & Hopkins, N (2005) 'Social identity and the dynamics of leadership: Leaders and followers as collaborative agents in the transformation of social reality', *Leadership Quarterly*, vol. 16, no. 4, pp. 547–568.

Reidy, C (2005) *The Eye of the Storm: An Integral Perspective on Sustainable Development and Climate Change Response*. University of Technology, Sydney.

Reynolds, B (2006) *Where's Wilber At?: Ken Wilber's Integral Vision in the New Millennium*. Paragon, St. Paul, MN.

Richardson, B (1996) 'Modern management's role in the demise of sustainable society', *Journal of Contingencies and Crisis Management*, vol. 4, no. 1, pp. 20–31.

Ritzer, G (1988) 'Sociological metatheory: A defense of a subfield by a delineation of its parameters', *Sociological Theory*, vol. 6, no. 2, pp. 187–200.

Ritzer, G (1990) 'Metatheorizing in sociology', *Sociological Forum*, vol. 5, no. 1, pp. 2–15.

Ritzer, G (1991a) *Metatheorizing in Sociology*. Lexington, Toronto.

Ritzer, G (1991b) 'The recent history and the emerging reality of American sociological theory: A metatheoretical interpretation', *Sociological Forum*, vol. 6, no. 2, pp. 269–277.

Ritzer, G (1991c) 'Reflections on the rise of metatheorizing in sociology', *Sociological Perspectives*, vol. 34, no. 3, pp. 237–248.

Ritzer, G (2001) *Explorations in Social Theory: From Metatheorizing to Rationalisation*. Sage, London.

Ritzer, G (2006) *Blackwell Encyclopedia of Sociology*. Wiley, New York.

Ritzer, G & Gindoff, P (1992) 'Methodological relationism: Lessons for and from social psychology', *Social Psychology Quarterly*, vol. 55, no. 2, p. 128.

Ritzer, G, Zhao, S & Murphy, J (2001), 'Metatheorizing in Sociology', in Handbook of Sociological Theory, ed. JH Turner, Springer New York, pp. 113-131.

Robertson, BJ (2006), 'Holacracy: A complete system for agile organisational governance and steering.', Agile Project Management, vol. 7, no. 7, pp. 1-21.

Romanelli, E (1991) 'The evolution of new organizational forms', *Annual Review of Sociology*, vol. 17, no. 1, pp. 87–103.

Romme, AGL & Witteloostuijn, A (1999) 'Circular organizing and triple loop learning', *Journal of Organizational Change Management*, vol. 12, no. 5, pp. 439–454.

Rooke, D & Torbert, WR (1998) 'Organizational transformation as a function of CEO's developmental stage', *Organization Development Journal*, vol. 16, no. 1, pp. 11–28.

Rooke, D & Torbert, WR (2005) 'Seven transformations of leadership', *Reflections*, vol. 6, no. 2/3, p. 35.

Rosch, E (2002) 'Lewin's field theory as situated action in organizational change', *Organization Development Journal*, vol. 20, no. 2, pp. 8–14.

Rosendaal, BR (2006) 'Learning cycles in knowledge-intensive organisations: An exploratory study of the nature and dimensions of knowledge development in four departments', *Knowledge Management Research and Practice*, vol. 4, no. 4, pp. 261–274.

Ryan, GW & Bernard, HR (2003) 'Techniques to identify themes', *Field Methods*, vol. 15, no. 1, pp. 85–109.

Sachs, JD (2006) 'Is sustainable development feasible?', in *State of the Earth Conference*. Earth Institute, Columbia University. Available from: http://www.earthinstitute.columbia.edu (accessed April 16, 2009).

Sammut-Bonnici, T & Wensley, R (2002) 'Darwinism, probability and complexity: Market-based organizational transformation and change explained through the theories of evolution', *International Journal of Management Reviews*, vol. 4, no. 3, pp. 291–315.

Sandelowski, M (2006) '"Meta-Jeopardy": The crisis of representation in qualitative metasynthesis', *Nursing Outlook*, vol. 54, no. 1, pp. 10–16.

Santos, FM & Eisenhardt, KM (2005) 'Organizational boundaries and theories of organization', *Organization Science*, vol. 16, no. 5, pp. 491–508.

Sarros, JC, Tanewski, GA, Winter, RP, Santora, JC & Densten, IL (2002) 'Work alienation and organizational leadership', *British Journal of Management*, vol. 13, no. 4, pp. 285–304.

Saunders, CS, Carte, TA, Jasperson, J & Butler, BS (2003) 'Lessons learned from the trenches of metatriangulation research', *Communications of AIS*, vol. 2003, no. 11, pp. 245–269.

Saxe, JG (1873) *The Poems of John Godfrey Saxe*. James R. Osgood and Company, Boston.

Schillo, M, Zinnikus, I & Fischer, K (2003) *Towards a Theory of Flexible Holons: Modelling Institutions for Making Multi-Agent Systems Robust*. Available from: http://www.virtosphere.de/schillo/research/publications.html (accessed May 28, 2008).

Schultz, M & Hatch, MJ (1996) 'Living with multiple paradigms: The case of paradigm interplay in organizational culture studies', *Academy of Management Review*, vol. 21, no. 2, p. 529.

Schumacher, EF (1977) *A Guide for the Perplexed*. Jonathon Cape, London.

Schwandt, DR & Marquardt, MJ (1999) *Organisational Learning: From First-Class Theories to Global Best Practice*. St. Lucie Press, Boca Raton, FL.

Schwing, R (2002) 'A mental model proposed to address sustainability and terrorism issues', *Risk Analysis: An International Journal*, vol. 22, no. 3, pp. 415–420.

Scott, A (2001) 'BASF aligns R&D with sustainable development', *Chemical Week*, vol. 163–164, no. 12, p. 39.

Seidl, D (2005) *Organisational Identity and Self-Transformation: An Autopoeitic Perspective*. Ashgate, Burlington, VT.

Sendjaya, S & Sarros, JC (2002) 'Servant leadership: It's origin, development, and application in organizations', *Journal of Leadership and Organizational Studies*, vol. 9, no. 2, p. 57.

Senge, PM (2003) 'Taking personal change seriously: The impact of organizational learning on management practice', *Academy of Management Executive*, vol. 17, no. 2, p. 47.

Senge, PM, Lichtenstein, BB, Kaeufer, K, Bradbury, H & Carroll, JS (2007) 'Collaborating for systemic change', *MIT Sloan Management Review*, vol. 48, no. 2, pp. 44–53.

Shakun, MF (1999) 'Consciousness, spirituality and right decision/negotiation in purposeful complex adaptive systems', *Group Decision and Negotiation*, vol. 8, no. 1, p. 1.

Shweder, RA (2001) 'A polytheistic conception of the sciences and the virtues of deep variety', *Annals of New York Academy of Sciences*, vol. 935, pp. 217–232.

Siebenhüner, B & Arnold, M (2007) 'Organizational learning to manage sustainable development', *Business Strategy and the Environment*, vol. 16, no. 5, pp. 339–353.

Simpson, S & Cacioppe, R (2001) 'Unwritten ground rules: Transforming organization culture to achieve key business objectives and outstanding customer service', *Leadership and Organization Development Journal*, vol. 22, no. 7/8, p. 394.

Simsek, H & Louis, KS (1994) 'Organizational change as paradigm shift', *Journal of Higher Education*, vol. 65, no. 6, pp. 670–695.

Singh, J (1995) 'Integration of matter and spirit towards the philosophy of the codevelopment', in *Holistic Approach to Sustainable Development*, ed. P Singh. M.D. Publications, New Delhi, pp. 21–27.

Sirgy, MJ (1988) 'Strategies for developing general systems theories', *Behavioral Science*, vol. 33, no. 1, pp. 25–37.

Skibbins, GJ (1974), Organizational Evolution: A Program for Managing Radical Change, AMACOM, New York.ocpol, T (1987) 'The dead end of metatheory', *Contemporary Sociology*, vol. 16, no. 1, pp. 10–12.

Smith, G (2001) 'Group development: A review of the literature and a commentary on future research directions', *Group Facilitation*, vol. 3, pp. 14–45.

Sonntag, V (2000) 'Sustainability—in light of competitiveness', *Ecological Economics*, vol. 34, no. 1, pp. 101–113.

Sorensen, E & Torfing, J (2005) 'The democratic anchorage of governance networks', *Scandinavian Political Studies*, vol. 28, no. 3, pp. 195–218.

Sorge, A & van Witteloostuijn, A (2004) 'The (non)sense of organizational change: An essay about universal management: Hypes, sick consultancy metaphors, and healthy organization theories', *Organization Studies*, vol. 25, no. 7, pp. 1205–1231.

Sorokin, P (1958) 'Integralism is my philosophy', in *This is My Philosophy: Twenty of the World's Outstanding Thinkers Reveal the Deepest Meanings They Have Found in Life*, ed. W Burnett. Ruskin House, London, p. 185.

Spears, LC (ed.) (1998) *Insights on Leadership: Service, Stewardship, Spirit and Servant-Leadership*. John Wiley, New York.

Spears, LC & Lawrence, M (eds.) (2001) *Focus on Leadership: Servant-Leadership for the 21st Century*, 3rd ed. Wiley, New York.

Spitaletta, J (2003) 'The transformation battlefield', *Industrial Engineer*, vol. 35, no. 1, p. 38.

Spittles, B (2004) '"To be or not to be": Deconstructing indigenous sustainability', *Social Alternatives*, vol. 23, no. 2, pp. 59–64.

Starik, M & Rands, GP (1995) 'Weaving an integrated web: Multilevel and multisystem perspectives of ecologically sustainable organizations', *Academy of Management Review*, vol. 20, no. 4, p. 908.

Steingard, D (2005) 'The spiritually whole-system classroom: A transformational application of spirituality', *World Futures: The Journal of General Evolution*, vol. 61, no. 1/2, pp. 228–246.

Steurer, R, Langer, ME, Konrad, A & Martinuzzi, A (2005) 'Corporations, stakeholders and sustainable development I: A theoretical exploration of business–society relations', *Journal of Business Ethics*, vol. 61, no. 3, p. 263.

Stewart, D (2001), 'Reinterpreting the Learning Organisation', The Learning Organization, vol. 8, no. 3/4, pp. 141-151.

Stowell, FA (1997) *Systems for Sustainability: People, Organizations, and Environments*. Plenum Press, New York.

Stroeh, U & Jaatinen, M (2001) 'New approaches to communication management for transformation and change in organisations', *Journal of Communication Management*, vol. 6, no. 2, pp. 148–165.

Sun, H & Venuvinod, PK (2001) 'The human side of holonic manufacturing systems', *Technovation*, vol. 21, no. 6, p. 353.

Sutherland, JW (1975) *Systems, Administration and Architecture*. Van Nostrand, New York.

Swanson, RA (2000) 'Theory and other irrelevant maters', *Human Resources Development International*, vol. 3, no. 3, pp. 273–278.

Szmatka, J & Lovaglia, MJ (1996) 'The significance of method', *Sociological Perspectives*, vol. 39, no. 3, pp. 393–415.

Takla, TN & Pape, W (1985) 'The force imagery in Durkheim: The integration of theory, metatheory, and method', *Sociological Theory*, vol. 3, no. 1, pp. 74–88.

Taylor, J & Every, E (2000) *The Emergent Organisation: Communication as its Site and Surface*. Lawrence Erlbaum Associates, Mahwah, NJ.

Terenzi, G (2005) 'Metasystem transitions in human organizations: A route towards global sustainability', *Journal of Organisational Transformation and Social Change*, vol. 2, no. 3, pp. 213–235.

Thomas, H & Pruett, M (1993) 'Introduction to the special issue: Perspectives on theory building in strategic management', *Journal of Management Studies*, vol. 30, no. 1, pp. 3–10.

Thorne, S, Jensen, L, Kearney, MH, Noblit, G & Sandelowski, M (2004) 'Qualitative metasynthesis: Reflections on methodological orientation and ideological agenda', *Qualitative Health Research*, vol. 14, no. 10, p. 1342.

Thrane, S & Hald, KS (2006) 'The emergence of boundaries and accounting in supply fields: The dynamics of integration and fragmentation', *Management Accounting Research*, vol. 17, no. 3, pp. 288–314.

Tilbury, D (2004) 'Rising to the challenge: Education for sustainability in Australia', *Australian Journal for Environmental Education*, vol. 20, no. 2, pp. 103–114.

Torbert, WR (1976) *Creating a Community of Inquiry: Conflict, Collaboration, Transformation*. Wiley, London.

Torbert, WR (1989) 'Managerial learning and organizational learning: A potentially powerful redundancy', *Managerial Learning*, vol. 25, no. 1, pp. 57–70.

Torbert, WR (1991) *The Power of Balance: Transforming Self, Society, and Scientific Inquiry*. Sage, Newbury Park.

Torbert, WR (1999) 'The distinctive questions developmental action inquiry asks', *Management Learning*, vol. 30, no. 2, pp. 189–206.

Torbert, WR (2000) 'Transforming social science: Integrating quantitative, qualitative and action research', in *Transforming Social Inquiry, Transforming Social Action: New Paradigms for Crossing the Theory/Practice Divide in Universities and Communities*, eds. FT Sherman & WR Torbert. Kluwer, Boston, pp. 66–91.

Torbert, WR & Associates (2004) *Action Inquiry: The Secret of Timely and Transforming Leadership*. Berrett-Koehler, San Francisco.

Torraco, RJ (2002) 'Research methods for theory building in applied disciplines: A comparative analysis', *Advances in Developing Human Resources*, vol. 4, no. 3, pp. 355–376.

Tosey, P & Robinson, G (2002) 'When change is no longer enough: What do we mean by "transformation" in organizational change work?', *TQM Magazine*, vol. 14, no. 2, p. 100.

Tsai, M-T & Lee, K-W (2006) 'A study of knowledge internalization: From the perspective of learning cycle theory', *Journal of Knowledge Management*, vol. 10, no. 3, pp. 57–71.

Tsoukas, H & Knudsen, C (2003a) 'Introduction: The need for meta-theoretical reflection in organization theory', in *The Oxford Handbook of Organization Theory: Meta-Theoretical Perspectives*, eds. H Tsoukas & C Knudsen. Oxford University Press, Oxford, pp. 1–38.

Tsoukas, H & Knudsen, C (eds.) (2003b) *The Oxford Handbook of Organization Theory: Meta-Theoretical Perspectives*. Oxford University Press, Oxford.

Tudge, C (1995) *The Day Before Yesterday*. Cape, London.

Tushman, ML & O Reilly, CA (1996), 'Ambidextrous organizations: Managing evolutionary and revolutionary change', California Management Review, vol. 38, no. 4, p. 8.

Van de Ven, AH (1999) 'The buzzing, blooming, confusing world of organization and management theory: A view from Lake Wobegon University', *Journal of Management Inquiry*, vol. 8, no. 2, p. 118.

Van de Ven, AH (2007) *Engaged Scholarship: A Guide for Organizational and Social Research*. Oxford University Press, Oxford.

Van de Ven, AH & Poole, MS (1988) 'Paradoxical requirements for a theory of organisational change', in *Paradox in Transformation: Toward a Theory of Change in Organisation and Management*, eds. RE Quinn & KS Cameron. Ballinger Publishing, Cambridge, MA, pp. 19–63.

Van de Ven, AH & Poole, MS (1995) 'Explaining development and change in organizations', *Academy of Management Review*, vol. 20, no. 3, p. 510.

van Eijnatten, FM & Putnik, GD (2004) 'Chaos, complexity, learning, and the learning organization: Towards a chaordic enterprise', *Learning Organization*, vol. 11, no. 6, p. 418.

van Eijnatten, FM & van Galen, M (2002) 'Chaos, dialogue and the dolphin's strategy', *Journal of Organizational Change Management*, vol. 15, no. 4, p. 391.

van Gigch, JP & Le Moigne, JL (1989) 'A paradigmatic approach to the discipline of information systems', *Behavioral Science*, vol. 34, no. 2, pp. 128–147.

van Marrewijk, M (2003) 'European corporate sustainability framework for managing complexity and corporate transformation', *International Journal of Business Performance Management*, vol. 5, no. 2/3, p. 213.

van Marrewijk, M & Becker, HM (2004) 'The hidden hand of cultural governance: The transformation process of Humanitas, a community-driven organization providing cure, care, housing and well-being to elderly people', *Journal of Business Ethics*, vol. 55, no. 2, p. 205.

van Marrewijk, M & Hardjono, TW (2003) 'European corporate sustainability framework for managing complexity and corporate transformation', *Journal of Business Ethics*, vol. 5, no. 2,3, pp. 121–132.

van Marrewijk, M & Werre, M (2003) 'Multiple levels of corporate sustainability', *Journal of Business Ethics*, vol. 44, no. 2/3, pp. 107–119.

Van Valen, L (1972) 'Laws in biology and history: Structural similarities of academic disciplines', *New Literary History*, vol. 3, no. 2, pp. 409–419.

Volckmann, R (2005) 'Assessing executive leadership: An integral approach', *Journal of Organizational Change Management*, vol. 18, no. 3, pp. 289–302.

von Eemeren, FH (2003) *Anyone Who Has a View: Theoretical Contributions to the Study of Argumentation*. Kluwer Academic, Dordrecht.

Vygotsky, LS (1982) *Collected Works, Vol. I: Problems in the Theory and History of Psychology*. Izdatel'stvo Pedagogika, Moscow.

Wacker, JG (1998) 'A definition of theory: Research guidelines for different theory-building research methods in operations management', *Journal of Operations Management*, vol. 16, no. 4, p. 361.

Wacker, JG (2004), 'A theory of formal conceptual definitions: Developing theory-building measurement instruments', Journal of Operations Management, vol. 22, no. 6, p. 629.

Wagner, DG & Berger, J (1985) 'Do sociological theories grow?' *American Journal of Sociology*, vol. 90, no. 4, pp. 697–728.

Waldersee, R (1997), 'Becoming a learning organization: The transformation of the workforce', Journal of Mangement Development, vol. 16, no. 4, pp. 262-274.

Walkerdine, V (1993) 'Beyond developmentalism?', *Theory Psychology*, vol. 3, no. 4, pp. 451–469.

Wall, AB (2003) *Mapping Shifts in Consciousness: Using a Constructive Developmental Perspective to Explore Key Variables in Organizational Transformation, 3114995*. Union Institute and University: Cincinnati, Ohio.

Watson, TJ (2006) 'Review essay. The organization and disorganization of organization studies', *Journal of Management Studies*, vol. 43, no. 2, pp. 367–382.

Weaver, GR & Gioia, DA (1994) 'Paradigms lost: Incommensurability vs. structurationist inquiry', *Organization Studies*, vol. 15, no. 4, pp. 565–590.

Weber, KM (2003) 'Transforming large socio-technical systems towards sustainability: On the role of users and future visions for the uptake of city logistics and combined heat and power generation', *Innovation: The European Journal of Social Sciences*, vol. 16, no. 2, pp. 155–175.

Weick, KE (1989) 'Theory construction as disciplined imagination', *Academy of Management Review*, vol. 14, no. 4, p. 516.

Weick, KE (2000) 'Emergent change as a universal in organizations', in *Breaking the Code of Change*, eds. M Beer & N Nohria. Harvard Business School Press, Boston, pp. 223–241.

Weick, KE & Quinn, RE (1999) 'Organizational change and development', *Annual Review of Psychology*, vol. 50, p. 361.

Weinstein, D & Weinstein, MA (1991) 'The postmodern discourse of metatheory', in *Metatheorizing*, ed. G Ritzer. Sage, Newbury Park, pp. 135–150.

Welsh, MA & Murray, DL (2003) 'The ecollaborative: Teaching sustainability through critical pedagogy', *Journal of Management Education*, vol. 27, no. 2, p. 220.

Wertsch, JV, Del Rio, P & Alvarez, A (1995) 'Sociocultural studies: History, action and mediation', in *Sociocultural Studies of Mind*, eds. JV Wertsch, P Del Rio & A Alvarez. Cambridge University Press, Cambridge, pp. 1–36.

West, MA, Markiewicz, L & Trimpop, RM (2004) 'Building team-based working: A practical guide to organizational transformation', *European Psychologist*, vol. 9, no. 4, pp. 285–286.

White, H (1973) *Metahistory: The Historical Imagination in Nineteenth-Century Europe*. Johns Hopkins University Press, Baltimore.

Wikipedia (2009) *Metanarrative*. Available from: http://en.wikipedia.org/wiki/Grand_narrative (accessed April 16, 2009).

Wilber, K (1980) *The Atman Project: A Transpersonal View of Human Development*. Quest, Wheaton, IL.

Wilber, K (1990) *Eye to Eye: The Quest for the New Paradigm*, 3rd ed. Shambhala, Boston.

Wilber, K (1998) *The Marriage of Sense and Soul: Integrating Science and Religion*. Hill of Content, Melbourne.

Wilber, K (1999a) *The Collected Works of Ken Wilber, Vol. 2*. Shambhala, Boston.

Wilber, K (1999b) *The Collected Works of Ken Wilber, Vol. 3*. Shambhala, Boston.

Wilber, K (1999c) *Collected Works, Volumes I–IV*. Shambhala, Boston.

Wilber, K (1999d) *Integral Psychology: Consciousness, Spirit, Psychology, Therapy*. Shambhala, Boston.

Wilber, K (1999e) *One Taste: The Journals of Ken Wilber*. Shambhala, Boston.

Wilber, K (2000a) *The Collected Works of Ken Wilber, Vol. 8*. Shambhala, Boston.

Wilber, K (2000b) *Collected Works, Volumes V–VIII*. Shambhala, Boston.

Wilber, K (2000c) *Integral Psychology: Consciousness, Spirit, Psychology, Therapy*. Shambhala, Boston.

Wilber, K (2001) *Sex, Ecology, Spirituality: The Spirit of Evolution*, 2nd ed. Shambhala, Boston.

Wilber, K (2003a) *Excerpt A from the Kosmos Trilogy, Vol. 2: An Integral Age at the Leading Edge*. Available from: http://wilber.shambhala.com (accessed April 16, 2009).

Wilber, K (2003b) *Excerpt B from the Kosmos Trilogy, Vol. 2: The Many Ways We Touch—Three Principles Helpful for Any Integrative Approach*. Available from: http://wilber.shambhala.com (accessed April 16, 2009).

Wilber, K *Excerpt D from the Kosmos Trilogy, Vol. 2: The Look of a Feeling: The Importance of Post/Structuralism*. Available from: http://wilber.shambhala.com (accessed April 16, 2009).

Wilber, K (2005a) 'Introduction to integral theory and practice: IOS basic and the AQAL map', in *Knowledge Base of Futures Studies Volumes Three: Directions and Outlooks*, ed. RA Slaughter. Foresight International, Brisbane.

Wilber, K (2005b) *Introduction to Integral Theory and Practice: IOS Basic and the AQAL Map*. Foresight International, Brisbane.

Wilber, K (2005c) *On Critics, Integral Institute, My Recent Writing, and Other Matters of Little Consequence: A Shambhala Interview with Ken Wilber.* Available from: www.wilber.shambhala.com (accessed April 16, 2009).

Wilber, K (2006) *Integral Spirituality*. Shambhala, Boston.

Wilber, K & Zimmerman, M 2005, Clearing the Fog: A Conversation between Ken Wilber and Michael Zimmerman., vol. 2005, Tulane University.

Wilber, K, Patten, T, Leonard, A & Morelli, M (2008) *Integral Life Practice*. Integral Books, Boston.

Wilson, EO (1998) *Consilience: The Unity of Knowledge*, 1st ed. Knopf, New York.

Winter, G (2006) *Multilevel Governance of Global Environmental Change: Perspectives from Science, Sociology and the Law.* Cambridge University Press, Cambridge.

Wischnevsky, JD & Damanpour, F (2004) 'Punctuated equilibrium model of organizational transformation: Sources and consequences in the banking industry', *Research in Organizational Change and Development*, vol. 15, pp. 207–239.

Wood, JR (1975) 'Legitimate control and organizational transcendence', *Social Forces*, vol. 65, pp. 199–211.

Yammarino, FJ & Dansereau, F (2008) 'Multi-level nature of, and multi-level approaches to, leadership', *Leadership Quarterly*, vol. 19, no. 2, pp. 135–141.

Young, R (1997) 'Comparative methodology and postmodern relativism', *International Review of Education*, vol. 43, no. 5/6, pp. 497–505.

Zajac, EJ, Kraatz, MS & Bresser, RKF (2000) 'Modeling the dynamics of strategic fit: A normative approach to strategic change', *Strategic Management Journal*, vol. 21, no. 4, p. 429.

Zhao, S (1991), 'Metatheory, Metamethod, Meta-Data-Analysis: What, Why, and How?', Sociological Perspectives, vol. 34, no. 3, pp. 377-390.Zhao, S (2001) 'Metatheorizing in sociology', in *Handbook of Social Theory*, eds. G Ritzer & B Smart. Sage, London, pp. 386–394.

Zsolnai, L (2006) 'Extended stakeholder theory', *Society and Business Review*, vol. 1, no. 1, pp. 37–44.

Zwirn, G (2007) 'Methodological individualism or methodological atomism: The case of Friedrich Hayek', *History of Political Economy*, vol. 39, no. 1, p. 47.

Author Index

Subject Index